ELV S

in

VEGAS

How the King Reinvented
the Las Vegas Show

RICHARD ZOGLIN

SIMON & SCHUSTER

New York   London   Toronto   Sydney   New Delhi

Simon & Schuster
1230 Avenue of the Americas
New York, NY 10020

First Simon & Schuster hardcover edition July 2019

SIMON & SCHUSTER and colophon are
registered trademarks of Simon & Schuster, Inc.

For information about special discounts for bulk purchases, please contact
Simon & Schuster Special Sales at 1-866-506-1949 or business@simonandschuster.com.

The Simon & Schuster Speakers Bureau can bring authors to your live event.
For more information or to book an event, contact the
Simon & Schuster Speakers Bureau at 1-866-248-3049 or
visit our website at www.simonspeakers.com.

Interior design by Ruth Lee-Mui

Manufactured in the United States of America

1   3   5   7   9   10   8   6   4   2

Library of Congress Control Number: 2018057437

ISBN 978-1-5011-5119-4
ISBN 978-1-5011-5121-7 (ebook)

CONTENTS

One

VEGAS MEETS ELVIS

In a town addicted to building things, blowing them up, and then building them all over again, the New Frontier Hotel in 1956 was a fine example of Las Vegas progress. It was originally built in 1942 and called the Last Frontier, the second resort to open on what would become known as the Las Vegas Strip. Like its predecessor, El Rancho Vegas, the Last Frontier was a luxury resort in old Western garb— "The Early West in Modern Splendor," as its promotional slogan put it. Rifles and stuffed animal heads decorated the hotel lobby; wagon-wheel chandeliers hung on chains from the timber ceilings; cow horns were mounted above the beds in the guest rooms. There was even an ersatz Western village next door, filled with frontier artifacts and populated by life-size papier-mâché characters like Rabbit Sam and Sheriff Bill McGee.

But as ever more modern and luxurious hotels opened along the

Strip, the Last Frontier decided it was time for an update, and in early 1955 the hotel closed down, gave itself a makeover, and reopened as the New Frontier. Gone were the stuffed animal heads and wagon-wheel chandeliers. Instead, visitors were greeted by a sleek new brick-and-glass façade, with a long canopy in front and a 126-foot-high steel-frame tower that bathed the hotel in colored lights at night. Inside, the old Western-themed showroom was transformed into the spiffy new thousand-seat Venus Room, with five tiered rows of booths and an expansive stage, "with sides running to such length that the whole thing looks like a gigantic cinemascope screen," in the words of one awed reporter.

The hotel's grand reopening in April 1955 was something of a disaster. Mario Lanza, the internationally renowned opera singer and movie star, was booked as the opening headliner, but he suffered a meltdown before the show—an attack of stage fright compounded by drinking—and never set foot onstage. After an hour's delay, the hotel announced that Lanza had laryngitis, and Jimmy Durante appeared as a last-minute replacement. (Too last-minute for *Las Vegas Sun* columnist Ralph Pearl, who filed his review early to make his deadline and raved about Lanza's phantom performance. "Seldom in the history of this town," he wrote, "has a star done a greater show or received a greater standing ovation.")

One year later the New Frontier played host to the Las Vegas debut of another, very different performer. He was nervous, too, but he *did* show up—though many in the audience were probably mystified as to what he was doing there. On April 23, 1956, Elvis Presley came to town.

The twenty-one-year-old rockabilly sensation from Memphis was in the midst of his phenomenal breakthrough year. Elvis Aron Presley was born on January 8, 1935, in Tupelo, Mississippi (in later years he

began using the more common spelling of his middle name, Aaron),
the son of a doting mother and a sporadically employed father who
once served jail time for check fraud. The family moved to Memphis
when Elvis was thirteen. In high school he was a greasy-haired, flashy-
dressing misfit, who played the guitar and entertained in school talent
shows. He began hanging out at Sam Phillips's Sun Records studio,
making a few country and gospel recordings. When one of them, a
rocking version of Arthur Crudup's old blues song "That's All Right,
Mama," caught on with country-music stations in the South, Phillips signed him to a recording contract. Soon Elvis was touring with
the *Louisiana Hayride* and creating a frenzy among teenage audiences
across the South. He was mainly a regional phenomenon until December 1955, when RCA Records bought out his Sun contract and
launched a major campaign to sell America on this white country boy
who sounded black, drove teenage girls wild, and was pioneering a new
kind of music—a revved-up mix of country and rhythm and blues that
people were starting to call rock 'n' roll.

He recorded his first RCA single, "Heartbreak Hotel," in January.
By April he had the No. 1 record in America; his gyrating TV appearances, on Tommy Dorsey's variety show and *The Milton Berle Show*,
were the talk of the country; and Paramount Pictures had signed him
to a movie contract. Still to come was *The Ed Sullivan Show* (where
he was shown, notoriously, only from the waist up), a string of chart-
topping hits like "Don't Be Cruel," "Blue Suede Shoes," and "All Shook
Up," and a virtual revolution in popular music and American culture.

But first, Elvis played Vegas.

The idea was his manager Colonel Tom Parker's, and not a very
good one. Elvis's frenetic rock 'n' roll performances, which were causing such a sensation in the rest of the country, were hardly geared for a
crowd of middle-aged Vegas showgoers. Yet there he was at the New

Frontier, touted as "The Atomic-Powered Singer" (in a town where people could watch real atomic tests taking place in the Nevada desert nearby), the "extra added attraction" on a bill headed by Freddy Martin's orchestra and comedian Shecky Greene. Elvis got paid $15,000 for the two-week gig, and the Colonel asked for it in cash. "No check is any good," he said. "They're testing an atom bomb out there in the desert. What if someone pushed the wrong button?"

The audience at the New Frontier must have thought someone *had* pushed the wrong button. Freddy Martin, whose "sweet music" orchestra was known for its pop versions of classics like Tchaikovsky's Concerto in B-flat, opened the show with several of his instrumental hits and a medley of songs from the musical *Oklahoma!* Next came Shecky Greene, a Chicago-born comedian just gaining notoriety for his raucous Vegas lounge act; *Variety* called him "easily the talking point of this show."

Elvis was the closing act. Backed by his three-piece rhythm group—guitarist Scotty Moore, bassist Bill Black, and drummer D. J. Fontana—Elvis performed four songs and was onstage for just twelve minutes. The response was polite at best. One high roller sitting at ringside, according to a witness, got up midway through the show, cried, "What is all this yelling and noise?," and fled to the casino. The critics weren't much kinder. "Elvis Presley, coming in on a wing of advance hoopla, doesn't hit the mark here," wrote Bill Willard in *Variety*. "The loud braying of the tunes which rocketed him to the big time is wearing, and the applause comes back edged with a polite sound. For the teenagers, he's a whiz; for the average Vegas spender, a fizz." *Newsweek* said the young rock 'n' roller was "like a jug of corn liquor at a champagne party." For Elvis and his backup group, accustomed to the pandemonium they were causing in concerts across the country, the response was sobering. "For the first time in months we could hear ourselves when we played out of tune," said Bill Black. "They weren't my kind of audience," Elvis would say later. "It was strictly an adult audience. The first night especially I was absolutely scared stiff."

Shecky Greene got friendly with Elvis during the run and could see that the kid was out of his element—unable to relate to the audience and lacking the stage experience to win them over. He didn't even dress right. "He came out in a dirty baseball jacket, just shit," Greene recalled. "I went to Parker and I said, you can't let him come out on the stage like that." The Colonel apparently took Greene's advice; for the rest of the engagement, Elvis and his band wore neat sport jackets, slacks, and bow ties. But after the first night, they no longer closed the show. Shecky Greene did.

By happy chance, a recording of Elvis's 1956 Vegas show exists—taped by an audience member on the last night of the two-week engagement. Freddy Martin makes a polite, if rather patronizing, introduction, noting that it's Elvis's last performance: "We hate to see him go; he's a fine young lad and a fine talent." Elvis opens his set with "Heartbreak Hotel"—slower and bluesier than the recorded version, with Elvis playfully changing the lyric to "Heartburn Motel" in the last verse. His patter with the audience is disarmingly modest; Elvis is acutely aware that he's a fish out of water. "We've got a few little songs we'd like to do for you," he says at the outset, "in our style of singing—if you want to call it singing." He alludes to the difficulties he's been having in the engagement: "It's really been a pleasure being in Las Vegas. We had a pretty hard time—uh, a pretty *good* time. . . ." He makes a few awkward, country-boy jokes, asking the orchestra at one point if they know his next song, "Get out of the Stables, Grandma, You're Too Old to Be Horsin' Around." After three more numbers—"Long Tall Sally," "Blue Suede Shoes," and "Money Honey"—it's over.

Elvis's only chance to connect with his real audience came on a special Saturday matinee, scheduled by the hotel expressly for the teen-agers who weren't allowed into the casino for the evening shows. For a $1 admission (the proceeds donated to a local Little League baseball program), the kids got a free soft drink and a chance to shower Elvis with the kind of screaming adulation he was getting almost everywhere but in Las Vegas.

"The carnage was terrific," reported Bob Johnson in the *Memphis Press-Scimitar*. "They pushed and shoved to get into the one-thousand-seat room and several hundred thwarted youngsters buzzed like angry hornets outside. After the show, bedlam! A laughing, shouting, idola-trous mob swarmed him; he fled to the insufficient sanctuary of his suite. The door wouldn't hold them out. They got his shirt, shredded it. A triumphant girl seized a button, clutched it as though it were a diamond. A squadron of police had to be called in to clear the area."

A few of the old-timers in Vegas tried to get hip to the new music phenom. "This cat, Presley, is neat, well gassed and has the heart," wrote Ed Jameson in a tongue-in-cheek column for the *Las Vegas Sun* entitled "A Cat Talks Back." "His vocal is real and he has yet to go for an open field. He is hep to the motion of sound with a retort that is tremen-dous. These squares who like to detract their imagined misvalues can only size a note creeping upstairs after dark. This cat can throw 'em downstairs or even out the window. He has it."

Though it was a tough engagement for him, Elvis enjoyed Las Vegas. He didn't gamble much, but he checked out other entertainers in town (among them Johnny Ray, the Four Aces, and Liberace), went to the movies, and rode the bumper cars at the Last Frontier Village next door. He kept company with Judy Spreckels, a sugarcane heiress from Los Angeles, and Vampira, the campy TV horror-show host who was appearing in Liberace's show at the Riviera. An Elvis fan from Al-buquerque, Nancy Kozikowski, was on a vacation in Las Vegas with her parents and ran into Elvis several times during her stay—in the hotel lobby, at the restaurant, and one afternoon when he was wandering alone at the Last Frontier Village. "He recognized me and was very nice," she recalled. "We took pictures in the twenty-five-cent picture booth together and alone. We also made a very funny talking record together. . . . Elvis was very nice, very gentle, a perfect gentleman."

Elvis's first visit to Las Vegas had one unexpected by-product. Among the lounge acts Elvis went to see was Freddie Bell and the Bellboys, a sextet from Philadelphia that did a kind of slicked-up, finger-snapping, nightclub-friendly version of early rock 'n' roll. (The group had a bit role in the movie *Rock Around the Clock*, which had just opened in theaters.) One of the highlights of their show was an uptempo version of "Hound Dog," a blues number that had been a hit in 1953 for Willie Mae ("Big Mama") Thornton. Elvis was so taken with Bell's performance that he began doing the song in his own act and recorded it later that summer. "Hound Dog" became Elvis's fastest-selling record yet, and his signature hit.

His 1956 Las Vegas engagement is regarded by most Elvis chroniclers as a rare misstep in a year of meteoric success, otherwise orchestrated to perfection by Colonel Parker, the onetime carny promoter and manager of country star Eddy Arnold, who became Elvis's manager and career guru early that year. The Colonel would later defend the booking, saying it gave Elvis a chance to reach a new audience and pointing out that the New Frontier couldn't have been too disappointed, since the hotel asked him back for a return engagement. Shecky Greene—who thought Elvis was a "wonderful kid," but turned down an offer from Colonel Parker to tour with Elvis as his opening act, finding the prospect faintly absurd—never quite understood what all the fuss was about. One day he ran into Bing Crosby, who was in Vegas during Elvis's engagement. "What is the thing about this kid?"

Shecky asked the elder statesman of American pop singing. "He's a nice kid, but ..."

"Shecky," Bing replied, "he'll be the biggest star in show business."

"Man, I really like Vegas," Elvis told a reporter when he got home to Memphis. "I'm going back there the first chance I get." And he did. He returned to Las Vegas later that year, in November, just before flying to New York for the premiere of his first movie, *Love Me Tender*. He stayed again at the New Frontier and saw a few shows, including Liberace's at the Riviera; the popular Vegas headliner introduced Elvis in the audience and later posed for some publicity photos with him. And for the next thirteen years—with an enforced break for his two-year hitch in the Army—Vegas became Elvis's favorite getaway and playground. He would typically go there to unwind after his movie shoots were finished. He was there in the summer of 1963 filming *Viva Las Vegas*, probably the most famous of all Vegas movies. He got married there in 1967, to Priscilla Beaulieu, the daughter of a US Air Force officer whom he had met while stationed in Germany. And in July 1969, after nearly a decade away from the stage, he would make his long-awaited return to live performing in Las Vegas, at the newly opened International Hotel.

Elvis's comeback show was a landmark event, both for Elvis and for Las Vegas. For Elvis it was a big gamble, a last-ditch attempt to revitalize a career that had fallen into disrepair—treading water in a sea of bad movies, records that no longer made the charts, and a decade of increasing irrelevance in the fast-changing world of rock 'n' roll. For Las Vegas, it was a transformational moment: the biggest show (Elvis was backed by a six-piece rhythm band, two vocal groups, and a forty-plus-piece orchestra), in the biggest venue (the International's two-thousand-seat showroom was double the size of any other room in Vegas), heralded by the biggest publicity campaign (Colonel Parker's handiwork, naturally) that Vegas had ever seen.

And it was a monumental success. A record-breaking 101,000 people saw Elvis during the engagement—two shows a night, seven nights a week, for four solid weeks, every show sold out. The reviews, from the trade press to some of the nation's top rock critics, were nearly all ecstatic. *Rolling Stone* pronounced Elvis "supernatural, his own resurrection." The show not only revived Elvis's career, but it changed the face of Las Vegas entertainment.

The years in between Elvis Presley's two Las Vegas appearances—up-and-coming rock 'n' roller in 1956, reborn superstar in 1969—spanned the golden age of Vegas entertainment. They were the heyday years of the classic Vegas show, an era of high-rolling glamour, all-night excitement, and a convergence of show-business talent—stars from Hollywood, television, Broadway, nightclubs, burlesque, Paris music halls—that fully justified the title this self-promoting city loved to bestow upon itself: the entertainment capital of the world.

Vegas entertainment was born in the 1940s, when the few hotels that had popped up along US Route 91, the highway leading south from downtown Las Vegas toward Los Angeles—soon to be known as the Strip—discovered that star entertainers were the key to attracting customers to their lucrative casinos. It came of age in the 1950s, as the hotels multiplied and the city became a gathering place for the biggest names in show business. By 1960 it was entering its glorious maturity. The city's first great building boom was over, the Strip now lined with nearly a dozen resort hotels, all competing for top entertainment. Nonstop air travel from the East Coast, inaugurated in 1960, was making Las Vegas more accessible for visitors from across the country. (And

Havana, once a rival destination for high-rolling gamblers, was now off-limits, following Cuban dictator Fidel Castro's takeover in 1959.) Big-city nightclubs were on the wane, hurt by changing tastes in music and growing competition from television. Yet television was actually helping Vegas—providing a fresh pool of stars to fill the showrooms, home-screen favorites who were instantly recognizable to folks from the Midwest who never went to nightclubs.

The event that really ignited Vegas' 1960s golden age, however, was the famous Rat Pack shows in January and February of 1960. Frank Sinatra, a top draw in Vegas since the early fifties, was booked to appear at the Sands Hotel during the filming of *Ocean's 11*, a caper film about a band of former Army buddies who plot a Las Vegas casino heist on New Year's Eve. At night, after the day's shooting was over, he would be joined onstage by four of his costars—Dean Martin, Sammy Davis Jr., Peter Lawford, and Joey Bishop—for a freewheeling session of songs, jokes, drinking, and ad-libbed antics. Their four-week run at the Sands' Copa Room was a sensation: the hottest ticket in Vegas history, a magnet for celebrities (among them the handsome Massachusetts senator running for president, John F. Kennedy), and a stroke of promotional genius. Over the next few years, separately and together, the Rat Pack ruled Las Vegas and came to embody the swinging, boozing, broad-chasing image of Vegas cool.

The bounty of top entertainers who could be found on the Las Vegas Strip on almost any given week in the 1960s would be hard to imagine today. A visitor on the last week of June in 1964, just to pick a typical example, could have seen George Burns headlining at the Riviera Hotel, joined by Hollywood glamour girl Jane Russell; movie song-and-dance man Donald O'Connor at the Sahara; television favorite Red Skelton at the Sands; jazz great Ella Fitzgerald at the Flamingo (with Jewish-dialect comedian Myron Cohen as her opening act); and legendary French entertainer Maurice Chevalier making a rare US appearance at the Desert Inn. And that was just in the main showrooms; among the acts filling the smaller, open-all-night lounges were jazz singer Sarah Vaughan, insult comic Don Rickles, Bob Hope's longtime sidekick Jerry Colonna, and Tommy Dorsey's orchestra featuring a new boy singer named Frank Sinatra Jr. All that plus three lavish, French-accented production shows—the *Folies Bergere*, *Lido de Paris*, and *Casino de Paris*—and a full-scale Broadway musical, *High Button Shoes*.

Nearly every major nightclub performer in America turned up on a Vegas stage at one time or another during the 1960s. Show-business legends like Marlene Dietrich and Ethel Merman. Broadway stars like Carol Channing and Anthony Newley. Virtually all the great pop singers of the era, from Judy Garland to Harry Belafonte, Nat King Cole to Barbra Streisand. Most of the top comedians—not just Vegas regulars like Don Rickles, Shecky Greene, and Buddy Hackett, but the new wave of more cerebral satirists, like Bob Newhart, Shelley Berman, and Woody Allen. Baseball stars like Maury Wills and Denny McLain would hang out in Vegas, and sometimes even entertain. Muhammad Ali defended his heavyweight boxing title against Floyd Patterson in Las Vegas in 1965. Evel Knievel staged one of his most famous daredevil stunts there, an attempted motorcycle leap over the Caesars Palace fountains on New Year's Eve, 1967. Evel crashed, but Vegas soared.

Vegas' population in 1960 was just fifty-nine thousand (plus an average twenty thousand visitors a day), and in many ways it was still a small town. The entertainers would hang out together and go to one another's shows; if one star got sick and had to cancel a performance, another was usually there to fill in at the last minute. Sammy Davis Jr. would host all-night parties for the showgirls, dancers, and other performers in town, often capped off by a breakfast of Chinese food in the

Garden Room at the Sands. Singer Buddy Greco was leaving a party late one night when he heard a local DJ's voice on the radio: "Buddy Greco, if you're hearing this, get home, your wife is looking for you."

"The town was so much fun," said Norm Johnson, a former newspaper reporter who came to Vegas in 1965 and did publicity for Robert Goulet and other Vegas entertainers. "It was friendly, looser. Everybody knew everybody. Nobody had an entourage. The stars hung out after the show. Cyd Charisse and Tony Martin would be dealing cards in the casino. Pearl Bailey would kick off her shoes onstage at the Flamingo. It was glorious."

Flush with profits from the casinos, the Vegas hotels could pay their stars more than anywhere else in the country. And treat them like royalty: lavish suites or bungalows for their stay, spreads of food and drink in the dressing rooms, liberal credit at the casinos. "You told 'em what you wanted for dinner, it was waiting when you came off after the first show," recalled Pete Barbutti, a trumpet-playing comedian who moved to Vegas in 1960 and entertained there for years. "There was always a setup in your dressing room with all your booze, hors d'oeuvres. Anybody you wanted to get comped got comped. Needed a car to drive, had a car. There was nothing like it in the world."

Vegas in the sixties was an exciting last hurrah for the fading world of swanky, big-city nightclubs. The stars wore tuxedos onstage, and the audience dressed up too—the men in jackets and ties, the women in their fanciest outfits. Gorgeous, feathered showgirls adorned the stage in almost every show—and stayed around afterward to decorate the casinos and attract the big gamblers. The mob-connected tough guys who were often on hand added a frisson of danger. The town buzzed. "Vegas was kind of an adult Magic Kingdom," wrote Paul Anka in his autobiography, *My Way*. "It was another world, a dream world, the Sh-Boom Sh-Boom Room where everything is mellow and cool, where life could be a dream sweetheart. The soft pink glow from the little lamp on your table, hot chicks, champagne on ice. Torch-song paradise. It's my version of the American Dream."

Yet Vegas entertainment never got much respect. Even in its 1960s heyday it was all too often patronized, made fun of, dismissed as schlocky, mass-audience kitsch—almost the definition of bad taste. Vegas in the 1960s was where every showroom singer seemed to have a syrupy rendition of "The Impossible Dream" or "What the World Needs Now Is Love (Sweet Love)." Where cuff-linked comedians told stale gambling jokes and complained about their nagging wives. Where Eddie Fisher would open his show from the back of the showroom, sashaying down the aisle singing "Let Me Entertain You." Where Liberace, the all-time champ of Vegas glitz and schmaltz, would send middle-aged matrons into ecstasy by parading around in red-white-and-blue hot pants, or being lowered onto the stage by wire from the rafters, the Peter Pan of camp overkill.

Every hip magazine writer took a shot at the place. "It's syrup city, soppy city, woozy, sentimental city," wrote Ron Rosenbaum in *Esquire*. "People go there for nostalgia: to help them make it through the night, to cry a tear for the good times they've lost." Hunter Thompson didn't have much time for showgoing in *Fear and Loathing in Las Vegas*, but he was predictably appalled when he saw Debbie Reynolds at the Desert Inn—"yukking across the stage in a silver Afro wig . . . to the tune of Sergeant Pepper, from the golden trumpet of Harry James." ("Jesus, creeping shit!" cried his attorney-companion. "We've wandered into a time capsule!") Among the burnt-out cases that John Gregory Dunne encounters in his semiautobiographical novel *Vegas: A Memoir of a Dark Season* is a desperate stand-up comic named Jackie Kasey (modeled on a real stand-up comic, Sammy Shore, who opened for Elvis), who has worked his way up from dives in Peoria to the showrooms in

Vegas, only to realize that "his act was not working and there was still no one who knew his name."

"Dante did not write in the age of malls," wrote the journalist and Dean Martin biographer Nick Tosches, "but he would have recognized Las Vegas, in any age, for what it is: a religion, a disease, a nightmare, a paradise for the misbegotten. It is a place where fat old ladies in wheel-chairs, like wretched, disfigured supplicants at Lourdes, roll and heave in ghastly faith toward cold, gleaming maws of slot machines. A place where Jerry Lewis maketh the heart merry with the guffaw of the abyss, where Barbra Streisand lendeth wings to the soul with the unctuous simulacrum of pay-as-you-go sincerity."

And that doesn't even count Wayne Newton, "Mr. Las Vegas," a homegrown product who started out as a teenage singer in the down-town Fremont Hotel and grew up to become the longest-running headliner in Vegas history. His phenomenal success in Las Vegas was as much of a mystery to outsiders as it was an inspiration to the fans who flocked to his over-the-top shows, which often ran past two hours and featured everything from Wayne singing "God Bless America" accompanied by a patriotic slide show, to his soupy version of "Mac-Arthur Park," complete with a cake being drenched in a fake rainstorm. "The biggest no-talent dork to simultaneously be the biggest thing in contempo-squaresville make-believe," wrote the rock critic Richard Meltzer—and who had the nerve to argue?

Yet there was something irresistible, even essential, about Vegas en-tertainment in its glory years. Listen to any of the "Live from Vegas" al-bums from the 1960s and you can hear some of the greatest pop singers of the century—Frank Sinatra, Nat King Cole, Tony Bennett, Bobby Darin—at their very best, backed by sumptuous, swinging orchestras and energized by live, appreciative audiences. Watch any of the flam-boyantly over-the-top musical numbers on the annual Grammy Awards telecast, and you can see Vegas glitz and bombast updated for the hip-hop era. Even when it's used as a pejorative ("He's so Vegas"), the Las Vegas esthetic has become ingrained in American culture, its influence seen in everything from Broadway megamusicals to Super Bowl half-time shows. No one with a love of all-out, all-American showmanship can hate it. No one who appreciates the craft of putting together an hour's worth of music and patter for an audience of cocktail-sipping nightclub patrons can dismiss it. No one who wants to understand the enduring appeal of American popular entertainment can ignore it.

What was Vegas entertainment? First of all it was big: big voices, big productions, big emotions. Vegas shows were brash, upbeat, and high-energy—particularly in the freewheeling (and for many years free-of-charge) lounges, where constant action, ad-libbing, and audience participation were part of the package. *Tumult* was the word used to describe high-voltage acts like Louis Prima and Keely Smith—the raspy-voiced bandleader and his deadpan vocalist wife, who rocked the Sahara lounge in the late fifties, probably the most influential of all Vegas lounge acts.

The comedians were fast, loud, and in-your-face. The singers tugged at the heartstrings and cuddled up to the audience—but were careful not to put a damper on the heady, high-spirited atmosphere. Vic Damone, the Sinatra-influenced singer who performed in Las Vegas and nightclubs across the country throughout the 1950s and '60s, discovered that he had to cut down on the love songs for the Vegas crowd. "You gotta do a lot of up things," he said. "Nothing that's maudlin or a downer. Because it's a party. When people go to Vegas, they want to have a good time."

Despite the slick presentation and packaged emotions, Vegas shows had an appealing intimacy and informality. In between numbers, the singers would talk to the audience—about the hotel, the gambling, the desert heat, all the experiences they were sharing in this exotic re-sort town. The stars would talk about one another too: introducing fellow performers in the audience, sometimes even bringing them up onstage. It's no accident that impressions were a big part of so many Vegas acts (Sammy Davis Jr., Debbie Reynolds, Donald O'Connor, Bobby Darin—even José Feliciano, for gosh sakes, did impressions). It was a way of making the audience feel clued in, with it, part of the showbiz crowd too.

Vegas entertainment was comforting and familiar—never edgy or disruptive. "There was no experimenting," said Dennis Klein, a TV comedy writer (*Mary Hartman, Mary Hartman*; *The Larry Sanders Show*) who began his career writing jokes for Vegas comics such as Jack Carter and Pat Henry. "Vegas is about smoothing out the rough edges, doing only what you think the audience wants or expects." Yet Vegas entertainment also had a transgressive side, pushing the boundaries of what was acceptable in the broader, mass-audience culture. Comedians like Buddy Hackett and Don Rickles used words and racial epithets you could never hear on television. Nudity made its first appearance on a mainstream Las Vegas stage in 1957, when the Dunes Hotel in-troduced a new edition of *Minsky's Follies* featuring a chorus line of topless showgirls. The *Lido de Paris*, *Folies Bergere*, and other pro-duction shows followed, making bare-breasted showgirls a Las Vegas staple. It was "naughty" entertainment for sheltered Middle America, helping to loosen the puritanical standards of the Eisenhower-era fif-ties and opening the door to the more audacious taboo-breaking of the late sixties.

By that time, however, Vegas was struggling to keep pace. The ar-rival of the Beatles, the rise of the counterculture, the era of sex, drugs, and rock 'n' roll, all combined to make Vegas in the late sixties look dated and square, your parents' entertainment. Vegas singers might cover a Beatles song or two, but they stuck mainly to the pop standards from Tin Pan Alley and Broadway. None of the major rock groups or solo stars of the era—the Rolling Stones or the Doors, Bob Dylan or Janis Joplin—wanted anything to do with Las Vegas. Hip young comics like George Carlin and Richard Pryor took a stab at Vegas early in their careers, but either got drummed out of town or left in frustration. At the beginning of the 1960s, Sinatra and the Rat Pack were the coolest guys in show business. By the end of the decade they were looking stale and worn, like a cigarette-stained shag rug from last night's party.

Vegas itself was changing as well. In 1967 Howard Hughes began buying up hotels on the Strip, replacing the old mob bosses and initiating a new, more cost-conscious corporate era. Caesars Palace opened in 1966, the first of the "themed" hotels that would ultimately remake the Strip and transform Las Vegas into a more family-friendly tourist destination. Even Sinatra, the town's most celebrated star, was losing his luster—as his mob ties drew unflattering scrutiny, his longtime relationship with the Sands Hotel came to an abrupt end, and his cultural preeminence was threatened by a new generation of singers who wrote their own songs, styled themselves as anti-establishment rebels, and were idols of a younger audience who had no interest in Las Vegas.

So, in a town that got blindsided by the rock revolution, it was only fitting that Vegas would turn to the original rock 'n' roller, Elvis Presley, as the agent of its reinvention. With his spectacular 1969 comeback show at the International Hotel, Elvis supplanted Sinatra as Vegas' signature star and most bankable attraction. He would return to the hotel—later the Las Vegas Hilton—every six months for the next seven years, and each of his sellout engagements was a bonanza for the city, bringing in visitors from around the world and giving a boost to business all over town.

Las Vegas was also a witness to Elvis's sad, oft-chronicled decline:

the ballooning weight, the mounting drug use, the gradual deterioration of a star who grew increasingly bored and isolated in the Hilton's thirtieth-floor penthouse suite—a prisoner of the town as well as its savior. His shows grew more bombastic, his performances more lazy and undisciplined. Even before his death in Memphis from a drug overdose in August 1977, Elvis had become a parody of himself. "For many," wrote Dylan Jones in *Elvis Has Left the Building*, "Vegas Elvis was already Dead Elvis."

Yet, in that 1969 comeback show and for at least a year or two after it, Elvis was at his peak as a stage performer: trim and still impossibly handsome, his voice richer and more expressive than ever, his onstage charisma undimmed by age and the years of absence. He was no longer the transgressive young rock 'n' roller of the 1950s. But he reinvented himself, expanded his range, and deepened his artistry in a way that few other entertainers have.

Elvis's comeback show at the International Hotel had a huge impact on Las Vegas. It raised the stakes, both in terms of money (his $125,000-a-week salary was a record at the time, soon to be surpassed) as well as production scale and promotional hype. He showed that Vegas audiences could be receptive to a broader range of music than the city was usually accustomed to—not just rock (at least in limited, nonthreatening doses), but also country, rhythm and blues, and even gospel. Most crucially, he created the model for a different kind of Vegas show: no longer an intimate nightclub encounter for an audience of a few hundred, but a big-star extravaganza, playing to thousands. He paved the way for the lavish shows of stars like Cher and Dolly Parton—and, much later, Céline Dion, Elton John, and a new generation of pop stars enlisted for Vegas "residencies."

Elvis, moreover, attracted a new kind of audience to Las Vegas. His fans were not the high rollers and sophisticated nightclub patrons who came to see Sinatra or Dean Martin. They were middle-class folks on a budget, thirtyish housewives who had screamed for Elvis when they were teenagers, families from the heartland who made Elvis the center-piece of their once-a-year vacation splurge. It was the same audience that would later flock to Vegas for the extravagantly staged magic shows of Siegfried and Roy, the acrobatic spectacles of Cirque du Soleil, and the theme-park hotels re-creating the canals of Venice, the pyramids of Egypt, and the streets of Paris. In a sense, Elvis sounded the starting gun for all the changes that would transform Vegas over the next couple of decades, from a gambling-and-nightclub town for adults into a vaca-tion destination for the whole family.

Elvis, of course, never really left the building. Decades after his death, the city's most famous star still looms over Las Vegas—in the Elvis impersonators and Elvis wedding chapels still sprinkled around the city, in the Elvis tribute shows and Elvis festivals that keep his mem-ory and music alive. And why not? It was a fruitful relationship for both. Las Vegas saved Elvis, at least for a little while. And Elvis showed Vegas its future.

HOW VEGAS HAPPENED

The Las Vegas Valley, with its abundant freshwater springs, was a convenient way station for travelers on the road to California in the nineteenth century. The Mormons briefly established a missionary outpost there in the 1850s. But permanent settlers in the area were rare until 1905, when the town of Las Vegas was officially incorporated, designated as a major division point on the newly completed railroad line connecting Salt Lake City and Los Angeles.

The town grew slowly over the next couple of decades. With a dearth of local industry but a steady stream of railroad passengers using the town as a stopover, Las Vegas early on marketed itself to tourists, who were drawn to its downtown hotels, bustling saloons, and houses of prostitution. Then, in 1931, two events helped set the stage for Las Vegas' modern development. In March, Governor Fred B. Balzar signed a bill making Nevada the first state in the nation to allow legalized gambling. And a month later, on April 20, construction began on Boulder—later known as Hoover—Dam. This mammoth public works project, approved by Congress in 1928 to harness water from the nearby Colorado River, brought thousands of construction workers to the area. Most were housed in a new community, Boulder City, built expressly for the workers. But nearby Las Vegas, with its casinos and wide-open downtown, gave them a place to relax, let off steam, and spend their money.

The first establishment to bring topflight entertainment to Las Vegas was the Meadows Club, a hotel and casino opened in 1931 on the highway connecting Las Vegas and Boulder City by a couple of bootleggers from Los Angeles, Frank and Louis Cornero. Hoping to lure big spenders from LA, they hired a former Broadway producer named Jack Laughlin to book entertainment for the club. Opening night was a gala black-tie affair that drew a crowd of five thousand and featured music by Jack Liddell and his band, the Meadow Larks. Among the nightclub acts that played the Meadows Club over the next few months were the singing Gumm Sisters—featuring nine-year-old Frances, later known as Judy Garland.

But when a fire destroyed much of the hotel just a few months after opening, the Corneros sold out, and the Meadows closed down within a year. Las Vegas, meanwhile, looked for other ways of luring visitors to the thriving town. In 1935 it hosted the first Helldorado Days, an annual festival and parade celebrating the town's Western heritage. Hollywood celebrities also discovered Las Vegas; some, like silent film star Clara Bow and her husband, Rex Bell, bought houses there. Another big draw was Nevada's liberalized divorce laws (also instituted in 1931), which required only six weeks of residency to obtain a divorce decree. When Ria Gable spent a six-week vacation in Las Vegas in 1939 to secure a divorce from her husband, Clark (who was having an affair with film star Carole Lombard), Vegas reaped even more publicity and Hollywood cachet.

Then, in 1940, a San Diego hotel man and former big-band musician named Thomas Hull decided that Las Vegas needed a first-class resort hotel. Rather than build it in the busy downtown, however, Hull had the novel idea of situating it just outside the city limits (thus avoiding city taxes), on thirty-three acres of land on US Route 91, the highway leading to Los Angeles. He called the place El Rancho Vegas, after a chain of El Rancho hotels he operated in other cities. The rambling, dude-ranch-like complex had sixty-three bungalow-style rooms, along with a casino, swimming pool, riding stables, and, towering above the hotel, a windmill with neon-lit blades, which served as a beacon for travelers approaching the desert town from the southwest.

El Rancho Vegas promised not only luxury accommodations, but also top entertainment. Its grand opening, on April 3, 1941, featured former vaudeville star Frank Fay and Garwood Van's orchestra. Among the acts that followed in the next few months were comedienne Fifi D'Orsay, singer Martha Demeter, and the comedy-dance team of Burton and Kaye—not major stars, but first-class nightclub entertainment was now coming to Las Vegas regularly.

El Rancho had managerial problems, and Hull sold out after a year. But the hotel was enough of a success to quickly attract a competitor. In October 1942, Texas movie-theater magnate R. E. Griffith opened another hotel on Route 91, a mile south of El Rancho, which he called the Last Frontier. Determined to outdo El Rancho in both entertainment and luxury accommodations, Griffith hired Maxine Lewis, a singer from Los Angeles, to book acts for the hotel's six-hundred-seat Ramona Room. She used her Hollywood connections (and a hefty talent budget) to bring in such well-known entertainers as comedian Bert

Wheeler and country singer Jimmy Wakely. But her biggest coup came in January of 1944, when Lewis hired an old friend from vaudeville for a two-week engagement, at the then-lofty salary of $5,000 a week: Sophie Tucker.

Tucker, the brassy, zaftig "Last of the Red-Hot Mamas," was an internationally known vaudevillian who remained a popular figure in nightclubs and on radio through the 1930s and '40s. The biggest star yet to appear on a Las Vegas stage, she was greeted with much hoopla: escorted from the train station to the hotel on a hook-and-ladder fire truck, her opening night hailed with sirens and sky-sweeping search-lights. In terms of world-class entertainment, it was Las Vegas' coming-out party.

With World War II came a temporary halt in hotel construction—though not in Las Vegas' rapid growth. A giant magnesium plant was built nearby, in the newly created town of Henderson, to manufacture the metal alloy needed for planes, bombs, and other war matériel. An Air Force flight-training facility was opened just north of the city, on what later became Nellis Air Force Base. The defense workers and military men who poured into the area provided yet more customers for the town's busy clubs and casinos. The now-completed Hoover Dam—no longer a job creator, but by this time a big tourist attraction—drew even more visitors to the area. By the end of the war, Las Vegas was ready for its next big leap forward. And a new group of investors were there to cash in: the mob.

According to (somewhat romanticized) Vegas legend, it was all Bugsy Siegel's idea. The New York hoodlum—born Benjamin Siegel, one of the most ruthless members of New York's organized-crime syndicate—had moved to Los Angeles in the 1930s to oversee the mob's West Coast operations. There he became a gregarious, sharp-dressing, if borderline psychotic, fixture on the Hollywood scene. But in 1941 his sights turned toward Las Vegas, when he was sent there by Meyer Lansky to get mob control over the local race-betting operations. Seeing the possibilities in the booming gambling town, Siegel (or by some accounts it was Lansky) came up with the idea of opening a mob-controlled luxury resort there. Thus was born the famous Flamingo.

Actually, it was already being built—by Billy Wilkerson, an LA nightclub owner and founder of the *Hollywood Reporter*. In 1945 he had begun construction of a luxury hotel on a parcel of land farther south on Route 91 than either El Rancho or the Last Frontier. But he ran out of money and went for help to his friend Siegel, who convinced his mob partners to invest $1 million in the hotel. In short order, Siegel took over the project and began spending wildly. He paid premium prices on the black market for scarce wartime materials, added needless frills like a separate sewer line for each room, and paid thousands of dollars in overtime in an effort to get the place ready by Christmas of 1946.

The Flamingo just about made it: though only partially completed, it opened on December 26, 1946. The new hotel marked a departure for Las Vegas in a number of ways. Instead of the Old West decor of El Rancho and the Last Frontier, the Flamingo had an LA-inspired Sunbelt-modern design—sleek lines, pastel colors, a glass façade, and a signature flamingo sitting atop its tall entry sign. Inside, too, the Flamingo broke with tradition, establishing the design strategy for virtually every Vegas hotel-casino to come. Unlike El Rancho, where the casino was almost hidden away behind the restaurant, the Flamingo made the casino the hub of the action, forcing everyone who entered or left the hotel to pass through it. The casino had no windows or clocks: a sunless, timeless netherworld where the gambling, booze, and good times could continue nonstop.

Determined to make the Flamingo the prime Vegas destination for big spenders from Los Angeles, Siegel brought in a first-class array of talent for opening night: Jimmy Durante, the big-schnozzed veteran of Broadway, movies, and nightclubs, along with emcee George Jessel, singer Rose Marie, and Xavier Cugat's orchestra. Despite a rainstorm that grounded some of the celebrities who planned to fly in from Los Angeles, the opening was a glittery, star-studded affair. "The town has been converted to an opulent playground," AP's Bob Thomas reported.

But after the splashy opening, traffic at the half-finished hotel dropped off, and Siegel closed the place after just four weeks so construction could be completed. "The third day all the stars went back, and we were working to nine or ten people in the dining room," Rose Marie recalled. The Flamingo reopened in March, the most luxurious hotel with the biggest stars in Las Vegas. But Siegel's overspending had ballooned the total cost to around $6 million (from an initial projection of $1.5 million), and the bosses back East were not happy. They suspected that Siegel was pocketing some of the money and that his girlfriend, Virginia Hill, was spiriting it out of the country to Swiss bank accounts. True or not, Siegel's tenure as a Vegas entrepreneur would come to an abrupt halt. On June 20, 1947, just six months after his dream project opened, Siegel was shot to death in Virginia Hill's Beverly Hills bungalow. One bullet knocked his eye clean out of the socket.

The Flamingo carried on under the new, more efficient mob management of Gus Greenbaum and Dave Berman, and for the rest of the 1940s it set the pace for Vegas glamour and big-name entertainment. Siegel had hired Maxine Lewis away from the Last Frontier as entertainment director, and she opened the checkbook for such major stars as the Andrews Sisters, Abbott and Costello, Lena Horne, Frankie Laine, and (in 1948, when they were the hottest nightclub act in the country) the comedy team of Dean Martin and Jerry Lewis.

The Flamingo's older rivals on the Strip had to ratchet up their own entertainment to compete. El Rancho booked top acts like the

Ritz Brothers and saloon comic Joe E. Lewis, who remained a fixture at the hotel throughout the 1950s. The Last Frontier, meanwhile, introduced a flamboyant, wavy-haired pianist who would become one of Vegas' most popular stars, then going by the name of Walter Liberace.

Even as big-name entertainers began coming to Las Vegas, the city retained much of its frontier, small-town vibe. Fremont Street downtown had an old-time, honky-tonk charm. The few hotels along Route 91 were still lonely outposts separated by expanses of desert. Locals and tourists alike flocked to the cheap, all-you-can-eat "chuckwagon" buffets. "The fun of Las Vegas then was its smallness, its rustic, Old West quality," said singer Mel Tormé, who first appeared at El Rancho Vegas in 1946. "In those days, I got the feeling that people might have had in old Virginia City, or Tombstone, Arizona. I wouldn't have been a bit surprised to see guys walking down the street with six-guns strapped to their hips."

But the Old West town was growing rapidly. In 1948 a fourth hotel opened on what would soon become known as the Strip—the Thunderbird, with a Native American theme and headliners like Nat King Cole and Ella Fitzgerald. Then, in 1950, came the biggest, most elegant Vegas resort yet: Wilbur Clark's Desert Inn.

Clark, a former bellhop, craps dealer, and bar owner from San Diego, started building the hotel in 1946, on a parcel of land he had bought across the street from the Last Frontier. But like the Flamingo's Billy Wilkerson, he ran short of money, had to stop construction, and only finished it with backing from a group of Cleveland investors headed by racketeer Moe Dalitz. Clark remained the hotel's ubiquitous front man (it would always be known as Wilbur Clark's Desert Inn), a popular civic leader and public-relations spokesman for the city—"one of the greatest handshakers in all of Las Vegas," as columnist Ralph Pearl put it. The Desert Inn was another modern pleasure palace, with Bermuda-pink buildings, curved swimming pool, and a glass-enclosed third-floor bar with a panoramic view of the desert. The hotel's opening in April 1950 (with Edgar Bergen and Charlie McCarthy as headliners in the showroom, the largest in Vegas) was the splashiest, most widely covered event yet in Las Vegas' short history—"probably the turning point in the nationwide acceptance of Las Vegas as the entertainment as well as the gambling center of the country," noted longtime Vegas columnist Bill Willard.

National attention was also being focused on the men behind the scenes. For organized crime, the Las Vegas casinos were a golden opportunity: an ideal place to launder money and skim off some of the casino profits (tax-free) for themselves in the process. The mob presence was an open secret in Las Vegas, benignly accepted by the entertainers and the locals alike. "The boys," after all, invested big money in Las Vegas, brought in top entertainment, and were careful to keep the most unsavory stuff out of town. "The rule was, in fact, that nobody gets killed in Vegas," said Susan Berman, daughter of the Flamingo's manager Dave Berman.

The mob's involvement in Vegas made national headlines in November 1950, when Tennessee senator Estes Kefauver brought his traveling hearings on organized crime to the city. (Wilbur Clark was among those who testified; he denied knowing anything about the criminal background of the Desert Inn investors.) But the hearings had little immediate effect. Not until several years later, in 1955, did Nevada finally establish a Gaming Control Board, to approve new licenses for casinos, and a few years after that a "Black Book" of undesirables who were banned from any casino in the state. In fact, Kefauver's investigation may actually have helped spur Vegas' growth: by highlighting mob involvement in illegal gambling operations around the country, it led to a crackdown on unlawful betting elsewhere, which made Las Vegas more attractive as a relative safe zone.

Las Vegas' rapid growth as an entertainment center reached a critical mass late in 1952, with the opening of two more Strip hotels, boasting perhaps the savviest entertainment operations yet. In October, Los Angeles jeweler Milton Prell, with the help of Phoenix builder and part owner Del Webb, opened a new hotel on the site of the old Club Bingo, which they named the Sahara. Two months later came yet another desert-themed hotel, the Sands, owned by Texas oilman Jake Friedman, with backing from an array of mob-connected figures from back East and run by one of the nation's top nightclub men, Jack Entratter.

Entratter, a charismatic, six-foot-two-inch impresario who had been manager of New York's renowned Copacabana, brought an infusion of New York glamour and sophistication to Las Vegas. The Sands opened in December 1952 with a four-day orgy of festivities—"a hunk of promotion surpassing the palmy days of P. T. Barnum," *Variety* reported—with nightclub star Danny Thomas as the opening headliner. When Thomas had to bow out one night with voice problems, his replacements were Jimmy Durante, Frankie Laine, Jane Powell, and the Ritz Brothers. Entratter brought in key staffers from the Copa (including a crackerjack PR man named Al Freeman) and signed up many of the stars he had established relationships with back in New York, among them Frank Sinatra, Dean Martin, and Jerry Lewis. In short order the Sands became the premier entertainment venue on the Vegas Strip. "Jack Entratter is responsible for the transformation of Las Vegas from a little desert village to a town boiling over with glamour," wrote journalist John Gunther.

To compete with the Sands for talent, the Sahara had to be more creative. Entratter and others had snapped up many of the biggest nightclub stars, so entertainment director Stan Irwin hired a top booker, Bill Miller—a onetime vaudeville hoofer and owner of the famed Riviera nightclub in Fort Lee, New Jersey—to go after new attractions, many of them Hollywood stars who had never done a nightclub act before. Ray Bolger, the Broadway and Hollywood song-and-dance man (the Scarecrow in *The Wizard of Oz*), was the opening headliner. Mae West, the sixty-one-year-old former Hollywood sex queen, came out of retirement for a Sahara show, surrounded by a chorus line of male bodybuilders. In perhaps its biggest coup, the Sahara convinced film legend Marlene Dietrich to make her nightclub debut at the hotel, for a record $30,000 a week. ("It's worth any price, if it's a first," Bill Miller liked to say.) She caused quite a stir with her revealing gown, a skintight black net affair that appeared to be transparent above the waist. Show business's first "topless grandmother" got a standing ovation.

By 1953 Vegas was riding high. The city's population had grown to forty-three thousand, up from just eighty-four hundred in 1940. Eight million tourists were visiting annually. Seven resort hotels now lined the Strip, with several more in the planning stages. Top entertainers were tripping over one another in the showrooms. "Las Vegas, as now constituted, is the No. 1 cafe town in America, which means the world," *Variety* editor Abel Green wrote. "No resort, spa, or capital has as much big-league, top-name talent concentrated in one spot as this gambling Gehenna."

Las Vegas had come up with an ingenious, almost-foolproof business plan. The hotels needed big stars to attract visitors to their money-making casinos. And they could pay those stars top salaries by using the profits from the moneymaking casinos. By the mid-fifties Vegas hotels were routinely shelling out $25,000 a week for the biggest stars—and charging patrons next to nothing to see them. (Most Vegas showrooms had no cover charge in the 1950s, and in many cases not even a minimum on food and drink.) No ordinary nightclub in New York or Miami or Chicago could compete with that.

Concerns about the escalating salaries for top stars were raised almost from the start. As early as 1950 the casino bosses talked about banding together to centralize booking in an effort to eliminate bidding wars. But this prompted a backlash from the performers and their agents, who threatened to boycott Las Vegas altogether if the hotel owners colluded to hold down salaries. Another worry was that the gold rush for star headliners would soon deplete the pool of talent. "Failure of the entertainment industry to develop new names will eventually affect the growth of Las Vegas, according to local bonifaces," *Variety* reported in December 1952. "At this point the hotel owners believe that the insufficient supply of top talent for all the inns will cause a diminishing of interest in the hotels."

But Vegas proved amazingly resourceful in finding new talent to keep the showrooms filled. TV comedians like Red Buttons and Phil Silvers were lured out to Vegas during the summer breaks of their popular shows. Hollywood stars on the downswing of their movie fame— Betty Hutton, Esther Williams, Ginger Rogers, Van Johnson—found new life (and a fat payday) as Vegas performers. For virtually every top nightclub singer in the country—Nat King Cole, Dinah Shore, Rosemary Clooney, Vic Damone—Vegas was an essential stop.

The scramble for new acts led to some strange bookings. In 1954 a down-on-his-luck movie actor named Ronald Reagan debuted his own nightclub show at the Last Frontier Hotel. "We put him with a musical group called the Continentals," recalled George Schlatter, the future *Laugh-In* producer, who was then booking talent for the Last Frontier. "The act was terrible." The Sands brought in the formidable Broadway diva Tallulah Bankhead for a much-publicized Vegas show in 1953. She croaked out a few songs ("I'll Be Seeing You," "Bye Bye

Blackbird"), made some jokes about Vegas casinos, and did a dramatic reading of a Dorothy Parker story about a woman waiting in vain for a phone call from her lover. "The artistry of her delivery carried it unfailingly, and brought her a near ovation from the capacity crowd," raved *Variety*. "Why do we do it?" Bankhead said in an interview with *Time*. "Dahling, for the loot, of course."

Perhaps the unlikeliest Vegas headliner of the fifties was British playwright, songwriter, and raconteur Noël Coward. He had urged Dietrich not to demean herself with a Vegas show, but nonetheless agreed to appear at the Desert Inn for three weeks in June 1955, serving up witty songs and patter to an audience filled with celebrity friends like Frank Sinatra, Humphrey Bogart, Judy Garland, and Cole Porter. "This is a fabulous, extraordinary madhouse," Coward wrote in his published diaries. "I have made one of the most sensational successes of my career and to pretend that I am not absolutely delighted would be idiotic."

By the mid-1950s, the popular image of Vegas—gambling capital, celebrity playground, mob hangout, entertainment Valhalla—was firmly fixed in the national consciousness. Hollywood stars came there to get married: Arlene Dahl and Fernando Lamas, Rita Hayworth and Dick Haymes, Joan Crawford and Pepsi Cola chairman Alfred N. Steele. Vegas became a popular location for Hollywood musicals and crime dramas—*Las Vegas Story* (with Jane Russell and Victor Mature) in 1952, *Meet Me in Las Vegas* (with Dan Dailey and Cyd Charisse) in 1956. Ed Sullivan and other TV hosts brought their variety shows out to Las Vegas, where big-name guest stars were always plentiful. The bright-light city seemed a perfect symbol of postwar optimism, prosperity, and progress. Even the most ominous force of the age, the atomic bomb, couldn't darken the mood. When atomic testing began in the Nevada desert in 1951, Vegas turned it into just another tourist attraction: the hotels organized rooftop viewing parties and packed "atomic box lunches" for guests who wanted to make an outing of it. The radiation fears would come later; for now Vegas radiated only glamour, excitement, and good times.

The shows themselves, for the most part, adhered to the standard nightclub format of the era: an opening production number, usually featuring a chorus line of scantily clad showgirls; an opening act (often a comedian if the main act was a singer, or vice versa); followed by the headliner. Two performances a night (dinner show at 8:00 p.m., late show at midnight), with engagements typically lasting for two weeks— until the Sands' Entratter came up with the idea of extending the runs to four weeks, to reduce the number of acts that needed to be booked. In return for their tops-in-the-business salaries, the performers had to abide by just one rule: keep the show to a strict time limit, usually an hour or less, to make sure patrons weren't away from the casino for too long.

For keeping people in the casino was the key to Vegas' whole business model. That led to one of Las Vegas' great innovations of the 1950s: the lounge show.

In addition to the main showroom, most of the hotels also had bar-lounge areas inside or adjacent to the casino, with a small stage where music groups often played. In the early days, this was simply background music for the casino action. Then some hotel operators hit on the notion of turning the lounge entertainment into an attraction itself—a way to keep the party going (and customers in the casino) all through the night.

The first Vegas act to really exploit the possibilities of the lounge was the Mary Kaye Trio, a vocal group made up of singer-guitarist Mary Kaye Kaaihue and her brother Norman (children of a Hawaiian-born vaudeville entertainer who called himself Johnny Ukulele), along with comedian-accompanist Frank Ross. They were working nightclubs in the Midwest and West and had just finished a popular engagement in the main room at the Last Frontier in 1953 when the hotel offered to extend their run by moving them over to the hotel's Gay Nineties lounge.

At the time, entertainment in the lounge could not include singing or talking, only music; otherwise, the casino would incur a 20 percent entertainment tax. To get around that, the Last Frontier curtained off the lounge, separating it from the casino, so that Mary Kaye and her group could do their full act. Even then, the trio got complaints that their singing was too loud. "[Hotel boss] Jake Kosloff wanted them to stop singing, to avoid distracting the gamblers," recalled George Schlatter, who booked the trio into the hotel. "I convinced him to let them do one song every fifteen minutes. Then I told them to make it a medley— he'll never know." The audiences were soon clamoring for more. "They came on after midnight, invited all the chorus girls to come see them," said Schlatter. "By the third night the place was packed. That was the first real lounge act."

The Mary Kaye Trio was a close-harmony group with a bright, upbeat, early-fifties pop sound (*Time* compared them to "the Andrews Sisters doing a Pepsodent commercial"). But what made the act click was the third member of the trio—Frank Ross, who played the accordion, harmonized in the vocals, and added freewheeling comedy. He would improvise bits, do parody versions of their songs, ad-lib with the audience. "Frank Ross stirred the pot. He made it a party," said Lorraine Hunt-Bono, who grew up in Las Vegas, worked as a lounge singer for years, and later became lieutenant governor of Nevada. "Frank would see some goofy-lookin' guy at the bar, and he'd go, 'Hey, do you want me to make a drink for you?' And Frank jumps down behind the bar, and he gets a big mixing glass, and he puts in this and that, and pretty soon the whole thing is fuming, smoking. And this cowboy would drink it, and the audience would just go crazy."

"Mary Kaye was incredible," said comedian Pete Barbutti, who appeared in Vegas lounges throughout the sixties. "She played the guitar like a guy—just monster. Ella Fitzgerald, Sarah Vaughan, they would all go to see Mary Kaye. And Frank Ross was the first comic I ever saw to actually work a Vegas lounge the way it was worked for forty or fifty years. The bartender would walk by and he would do a routine with the bartender, or somebody would sit down up front, a real tall guy, and he would become part of the next routine. To this day, I think they were the strongest act I've ever seen."

The Mary Kaye Trio introduced the elements that would define Vegas lounge entertainment for decades: improvisation, music mixed with comedy, and interaction with the audience. "You could shout out requests," wrote *Las Vegas Review-Journal* entertainment reporter Mike Weatherford in *Cult Vegas*. "You could joke with the act. It was the place with no wall between performer and audience, no pretense and seemingly no script." Said Sonny King, a singer who started out as a sidekick to Jimmy Durante and later became one of Vegas' most popular lounge acts, "The lounges were freedom."

That often meant freedom to experiment musically. While singers in the main room stuck primarily to pop standards, Vegas lounge groups were dabbling in the newfangled sounds of rock 'n' roll. One of them was Freddie Bell and the Bellboys, the bopping sextet that introduced Elvis to "Hound Dog" in 1956. Perhaps even more important in the development of rock 'n' roll were the Treniers, a black group that delivered a rollicking mix of rhythm and blues and swing, and (with songs like "It Rocks! It Rolls! It Swings!" in 1952) was one of the first to actually popularize the term *rock 'n' roll*.

The group was started by Claude and Cliff Trenier, identical twin brothers from Alabama, and eventually grew to eight or nine members, most of them part of the extended family. The Treniers had a playful, rambunctious act, with lots of synchronized choreography and comical stage business. One of their props, for example, was a giant wooden straight razor, which they would wield menacingly at any member of the group who fouled up. They had a novelty number called "The Suitcase Song," full of lewd double entendres ("I saw her snatch . . . her suitcase from the window"). Once, in the middle of a set, Cliff looked up at the keno board, saw that his numbers had come up, and raced out of the lounge to collect his winnings. "It was like a three-ring circus. You didn't know who to watch," recalled Skip Trenier, a nephew who joined the group in the late fifties. "Everybody loved the Treniers," said Joe Darro, a longtime Vegas musician. "They had energy, they were funny, great music. If you were in a bad mood, you went to see the Treniers. When you came out, man, you felt terrific."

Black entertainers like the Treniers, however, were not treated so well offstage. Throughout the 1940s and '50s, Las Vegas was one of the most segregated cities outside the South—the Mississippi of the West, some called it—with blacks forbidden to work in the Strip hotels, except as menial busboys, maids, and dishwashers. African American performers could not stay in the hotels where they entertained, eat in the restaurants, or gamble in the casinos. Even big stars, like Sammy Davis Jr., were forced to stay in run-down rooming houses and motels on the predominantly black west side and had to enter and leave the hotels through the kitchen entrances. "The other acts could move around the hotel, go out and gamble, or sit in the lounge and have a drink," Sammy wrote in his 1965 autobiography, Yes I Can, "but we had to leave through the kitchen, with the garbage, like thieves in the night."

This was a concession to the high-rolling Southerners, who were a big segment of Vegas' clientele in the early days. "There was a color line in Vegas," said Stan Irwin, of the Sahara Hotel. "Headlining black performers could not stay or eat at the hotel. At that time, many of the money people that came in were Southern, Texas, and [the hotel owners] catered to their people's whims, regardless of what their own standards were. At the Sahara in those days, we had a luxurious trailer placed outside in our parking lot, which had an immediate entrance to the back stage of the Casbar Theater. For many major artists, I'm sorry to say, their dressing room and their living quarters, for the time they were there, was that trailer. At night they still had to go to the west side. Being a New Yorker and not understanding this, I tried to compensate, but you feel like an idiot."

Most black entertainers gritted their teeth and tolerated the indignities; a few rebelled. When Josephine Baker, the expatriate American chanteuse living in Paris, appeared at the Last Frontier during a US tour in 1952, she had a clause written into her contract ensuring that black people would be allowed to attend the show—making her probably the first Vegas entertainer ever to perform before an integrated audience. When Harry Belafonte made his Las Vegas debut at the Thunderbird Hotel in 1952, he was shocked to discover that he was expected to stay across town, at a fleabag motel in a room that smelled of dog urine. "What's wrong with it?" the proprietor asked. "It was good enough for Pearl Bailey's dog—it's good enough for you." After one night there, Belafonte recalled in his autobiography, he phoned a mob-connected friend and got the Thunderbird to relent and give him a room. The next day, he celebrated by taking a dip in the pool, to gasps from some white guests—and requests for autographs.

The racial barriers were challenged again in 1955 with the opening of the city's first integrated hotel—the Moulin Rouge, located on the largely black west side. Aiming to rival the big hotels on the Strip in both luxury and entertainment, the Moulin Rouge hired former heavyweight champ Joe Louis as host and jazzman Benny Carter's orchestra as the house band. It opened in March 1955 with much fanfare and over the next few months drew big crowds from both sides of the tracks, including many Strip patrons who would rush across town to catch the last show at 2:15 a.m. "We were the only ones in town doing a late show," recalled Anna Bailey, who danced in the chorus line. "All of the Strip would empty out and come over to the Moulin Rouge. You've never seen so many stars—Tallulah Bankhead and Belafonte and Sammy Davis, all of them would hang out there."

But the Moulin Rouge soon ran into trouble. Two nights after the opening, Wardell Gray, the highly regarded tenor sax player in Benny Carter's orchestra, left after the second set and never came back. His body was later found dumped in a weed field, with a broken neck. (The murder, which was suspected of being drug-related, was never solved.) Six months later, the Moulin Rouge abruptly closed, under mysterious circumstances. Some claimed financial mismanagement; others contended that the hotel owners on the Strip, upset at the business they were losing to the new club, made sure the Moulin Rouge didn't stay open for long. In Vegas, anything was possible.

Along with stars, Vegas in the 1950s offered splash—and plenty of skin.

With the competition for big-name talent at a fever pitch, Vegas entertainment directors were constantly on the lookout for alternatives to what *Variety* called the "tyranny of names"—that is, entertainment that didn't depend on high-salaried stars. Broadway shows were one potential solution, and a few hit musicals, like *Guys and Dolls* and *Pajama Game*, made their way to Vegas showrooms in the 1950s. But for a long-term answer to the shortage of big stars, Vegas soon turned not to Broadway, but to Paris.

The French music-hall revue was born, by most accounts, in 1887 at the Folies-Bergère theater in Paris. The theater had opened in 1869, and for the first several years offered mainly concerts, operettas, and pantomime. But in 1887 it introduced a new show called *Place aux Jeunes*, which featured, for the first time, a chorus line of beautiful, ornately costumed dancing girls, along with a potpourri of acrobats, jugglers, singers, comedians, and other variety acts. The show was a spectacular success, and it made the Folies-Bergère the most popular music hall in Paris. Nudity began to appear on the Folies stage a few years later, and by the 1920s, Folies shows were famous for their chorus lines of topless dancers, in their feathered costumes and elaborate head-dresses, as well as for some of the most celebrated stage entertainers of the era, such as Maurice Chevalier, Josephine Baker, and the popular French singer Mistinguett.

In the years just after World War II, the Folies had a popular new rival in Paris: a club on the Champs-Élysées called Le Lido, best known for its chorus line of Bluebell Girls. Where the Folies dancers were pe-tite, the Bluebells were tall and statuesque (a minimum of five feet nine inches), all handpicked and trained by a former Folies-Bergère dancer from Liverpool named Margaret Kelly, known as Madame Bluebell. The Lido shows had an especially international flavor. Most of the Bluebell Girls came from Britain or other English-speaking countries such as South Africa. There were lots of highly visual, circus-style acts, designed to appeal to an audience of non-French-speaking tourists. And its shows were staged by, of all things, an American: a St. Louis–born choreographer named Donn Arden, who had established a rela-tionship with the Lido while doing shows for US troops in Europe during World War II.

In 1958, Desert Inn owner Moe Dalitz was getting ready to open a new hotel in Las Vegas, the Stardust. With eleven hundred rooms, it was the largest hotel yet in Vegas, a bland, barrackslike structure that aimed more for mass than class: a big casino for low rollers, rather than a small casino for high rollers. The Desert Inn's entertainment director, Frank Sennes, was put in charge of booking acts for the new hotel—a tall order, given that most of the top stars had already been snapped up by other hotels. So Sennes came up with the bright idea of getting Donn Arden, who had been staging dance numbers for the Desert Inn since the early fifties, to bring over his Lido show from Paris to the Stardust.

It would be the most elaborate production Las Vegas had ever seen. Arden fashioned a new show out of numbers from past Lido productions, along with new elements created especially for Vegas. Rehearsals were held in Paris, using the French costumes and sets and a troupe of more than fifty, including twelve Bluebell Girls. Back in Vegas, the Stardust's seven-hundred-seat showroom was redesigned, expanded, and outfitted with three hydraulic lifts, and the orchestra was moved off to the side to open up more space for the mammoth show.

The *Lido de Paris* opened at the Stardust on July 1, 1958, with a splash, literally. For the opening number, a curtain of showgirls lined the revolving stage, while others descended from the ceiling and dove into an eleven-by-thirty-foot swimming pool. One eye-popping number was set in ancient Rome, with a giant mirror reflecting the aquatic maneuvers for the audience. Another was a re-creation of Maxim's in turn-of-the-century Paris. A giant ice rink rose to stage level for a skating display by Olympic figure skater Jacqueline du Bief. Interspersed with the production numbers was a parade of variety acts, including a magician, a pair of singing acrobats, and a juggler who kept bowls and plates spinning simultaneously on poles.

What got most of the attention, however, were the topless Bluebell Girls. *Las Vegas Review-Journal* columnist Les Devor described what was at the time a startling sight: "From the ceiling descend platforms, each with a bare-bosomed beauty, standing cool as you please, and before the surprise has caused nearsighted gentlemen to repair their thoughtlessness by putting on glasses, the girls are whisked upward into the rafters. . . . Being bashful by disposition tends to inhibit anything but professional analysis of the plenteous expanse of anatomies presented."

Nudity was not entirely new to the Las Vegas stage. Strippers had long been part of the burlesque shows downtown, and one of the most famous strippers, Lili St. Cyr—known for her onstage bubble baths— was still appearing regularly at El Rancho Vegas, often paired with comedian Joe E. Lewis. In January 1957, the Dunes Hotel, in a last-ditch effort to turn around its struggling fortunes, brought in a new edition of *Minsky's Follies*, Harold Minsky's racy burlesque shows that had gotten drummed out of New York City during the reformist administration of Mayor Fiorello La Guardia. *Minsky's Goes to Paris*, the new Dunes show, featured topless showgirls for the first time ever on a mainstream Vegas stage. The show was a smash hit and almost single-handedly saved the hotel.

Minsky's Goes to Paris, however, was in the lowbrow burlesque tradition—where bump-and-grind strippers were frankly meant to be titillating and intended for a mostly male audience. The *Lido de Paris* was a classy show, aimed at a general audience, and its great triumph was to make its nudity look tasteful and artistic. "Even with bare-breasted beauts all over the place, even dripping from ceiling wells, there is nothing overly sexy in the production numbers," *Variety* said. "It's done with refinement and an accent on art." Even gossip columnist Hedda Hopper, certainly no libertine, called the show "the most spectacular I've ever seen, and it's all in perfect taste."

The *Lido* was originally booked for six months, but with business booming the run was extended to a year, and it sparked a rush by other producers to jump on the topless bandwagon. A few weeks after the *Lido* opened, producer Barry Ashton added six topless girls to the chorus line of his floor show at El Rancho Vegas, and he promised more to come. "Bare chests are the coming thing here—it's what the public wants and we're giving it to them," Ashton told reporters. "It will soon be nothing to see a nude girl on the Strip. All the showgirls along the Strip are going to be replaced by nudes."

The prediction titillated some, threw the fear of God into others. Bishop Robert J. Dwyer of the Reno diocese of the Catholic Church sent a letter to pastors in the state, urging all Catholics to boycott the nude shows. Other religious leaders chimed in, hinting that the campaign against nudity might be a wedge to ridding the state of its other vices—namely, gambling and quickie divorces. "It is time that the people of Nevada protected themselves and their homes against those whose only concern is to turn a profit, at the cost of untold hurt to the citizenry," said the Reverend Walter Bishop of Las Vegas' First Baptist Church. "Whence are our liberal laws leading? Will legalized prostitution and the sale of narcotics be advocated next?"

Religious leaders were not the only ones with qualms about the great uncovering. Many of the hotel bosses also assailed the nudity trend. A split emerged, between the hotels on the east side of the Strip (the Sands, Riviera, Desert Inn, and other old-line Vegas resorts that had a lock on most of the major stars), and the newer upstarts on the west side (the Dunes, Stardust, and—the one old-timer—El Rancho Vegas) that were looking for new ways to compete. Jack Entratter of the Sands led the opposition, in what *Variety* inevitably dubbed the Battle of the Bosoms. "The spread of nude shows along the Strip is the worst thing that could happen to Las Vegas," said Entratter. "It could destroy six years of work, expensive campaigns, and sincere efforts to make Las

Vegas the top entertainment resort in the world." Monte Proser, the former New York theater producer now overseeing entertainment at the Tropicana, warned, "Nudes are bad for this town. Family groups who might be planning to come here may think all shows come under that category."

Beldon Katleman, owner of El Rancho Vegas, caved quickly to the pressure, removing his nude showgirls and vowing that henceforth all women on his stage would be covered up. "Please accept my reassurance," Katleman wrote in a telegram to the state's clergymen, "that it was at no time the intention of El Rancho Vegas to offend the public conscience or moral standard with our show presentations." But the Dunes and the Stardust, counting their hefty box-office receipts, refused to buckle. The Dunes opened a new edition of its *Minsky's* show and even added five more nude showgirls to the six original ones. "We certainly do not mean to offend anyone, and we don't want anyone who might be offended to attend our show," said Major A. Riddle, the Dunes' president. "We clearly advertise that the show is for adults only." The Stardust vowed that the *Lido* would continue unchanged, pointing out that the show was doing excellent business and that audience members were writing to praise its "good taste."

Before long, Vegas set its sights on the French revue that had started it all at the Folies-Bergère. Lou Walters, the New York nightclub impresario known for his lavish floor shows at the Latin Quarter and other nightclubs (and father of TV newscaster Barbara Walters), had earlier tried to bring the *Folies Bergere* to the New Frontier Hotel, but the deal fell through when the hotel ran into financial trouble. Then Walters was hired to help turn around another struggling Vegas hotel, the Tropicana, and he looked once again to Paris, making a deal to bring the *Folies Bergere* to Las Vegas for the first time.

Billed as "The Show That Made Paris Famous," the *Folies Bergere* opened at the Tropicana on Christmas Eve, 1959. Another sumptuous production, it had a cast of eighty, including fourteen topless "mannequins," dozens of other dancing girls—performing, among other things, their trademark, high-kicking cancan number—and an assortment of variety acts, from Georges Lafaye's marionettes to the singing Kim Sisters. The *Folies Bergere* was more traditional than the *Lido*: no high-tech stage machinery or levitating ice rinks, just an illuminated runway encircling the orchestra pit, to show off the girls in their sequins, furs, and feathered bustles, backpacks, and headdresses—all designed in Paris by Folies artistic director Michel Gyarmathy. "The Lou Walters show, which begins in a furious swirl and builds to a literal maelstrom of petticoats and pulchritude, may be around for as long as dice role in this neon jungle," raved Cecil Smith in the *Los Angeles Times*. It was frothy, French, and fabulous.

The *Lido* and *Folies Bergere* created the model for the splashy, slightly racy production show that would be a staple of the Las Vegas Strip for decades. They didn't emphasize or promote their nudity, always presenting their shows as artistic, sophisticated Continental entertainment. But once the topless Rubicon had been crossed, nudie shows were soon popping up all over Vegas—in lounges and as opening numbers in the main showrooms, with tacky, punning titles like "Naughty 'n' Ice," "Good Nudes of '61," "Around the World in Sexty Minutes," and "Panties Inferno." (The last, too silly even for Vegas, was soon changed to "Oriental Inferno.") Sometimes the hotels had the girls cover up for the dinner show, when kids might be in the audience, and uncover at midnight. (In truth, they were never entirely nude: G-strings always hid the private parts, and pasties sometimes covered the nipples—though less in the interest of modesty than esthetic uniformity.) Some Vegas stars, like Marlene Dietrich, objected to the topless fad, pointing out that their own sex appeal depended on suggestion, not explicit skin. Carol Channing canceled an engagement at the Tropicana because she didn't want to follow the *Folies Bergere*. "Nothing kills laughs like nudity," she said. But everyone now seemed to have skin in the game: nudity was in Vegas to stay.

Even as the production shows thrived, however, the stars continued to reign. The Vegas headliner show was not a new form of entertainment, but a fresh iteration of an old one: a nightclub show with more splash, more action, more fun. The tony nightclubs that flourished in major cities during the 1940s and '50s—the Copa and the Latin Quarter in New York, the Chez Paree in Chicago, Ciro's in Los Angeles—catered to a sophisticated, well-mannered, big-city audience. Vegas drew a broader, more middle-class crowd—most of them people on vacation, dazzled by the casino action and showbiz electricity, eager to be entertained.

Seeing big stars they knew from movies and television—Frank Sinatra, Milton Berle, Martin and Lewis—was part of the thrill. But Vegas also created its own stars. Two enormously popular acts from the 1950s seemed to embody much of what made Vegas entertainment special. They weren't invented in Las Vegas, but they honed their unique acts there, and they could not have flourished anywhere else. Even their nicknames seemed to encapsulate the Vegas style and spirit. One was a lounge act so manic and uninhibited that it became known simply as the Wildest. The other was a one-of-a-kind performer who had the temerity to call himself Mr. Showmanship. They were Vegas' two great creations of the 1950s.

Louis Prima was born in New Orleans in 1910, the son of Italian immigrants. He learned to play the trumpet at age fourteen and by his twenties was leading a Dixieland group in New York City jazz clubs. Through the 1930s and early '40s Prima worked with various small groups and big bands in both New York and Los Angeles, had a few hit recordings, and wrote "Sing, Sing, Sing," the signature number for Benny Goodman's orchestra. But by the late forties, as the big bands were breaking up, Prima's career was suffering. Even when he added a new singer—a girl from Norfolk, Virginia, named Dorothy Smith, whom he met on the road and married in 1953—the gigs were harder to come by. Growing desperate, Prima called up his friend Bill Miller—the former owner of the Riviera club in New Jersey, who was now booking acts for the Sahara in Las Vegas—and pleaded for a job.

Miller told him the showroom was booked solid, but offered Prima and Smith (now calling herself Keely—her last name at birth, before her mother's divorce) two weeks in the hotel's lounge. It was something of a comedown for the pair; they had played the main room at El Rancho Vegas two years before. But they needed the work, so they made the cross-country drive from New York to Las Vegas, opening in the 150-seat Casbar Lounge on November 24, 1954. Smith was five months pregnant, and Prima almost backed out of the whole gig when he found out no blacks were allowed in the audience. (An Italian American jazzman with a distinctively raspy voice, Prima was sometimes mistaken by listeners for black.) But they were an immediate hit—"absolutely the hottest combo to hit this town yet," said the *Las Vegas Sun*—and before the end of their run, Miller offered to extend them in the lounge indefinitely.

Nobody else was like them. Prima was a swinging trumpet player, an inventive jazz singer, and a natural comedian. He gave songs like "That Old Black Magic" and "Just a Gigolo" a raucous, improvisational energy—bouncing around onstage, playing with the lyrics, making fun of the song even as he put his own, inimitable stamp on it. Soon he added a saxophonist from New Orleans, Sam Butera, who gave the act another jolt. Butera, the most animated sax man in the business, would bob up and down wildly as he played, while drummer Bobby Morris—whom Prima convinced to leave his jazz quartet at the Black Magic club and join the group—drove everything forward with a supercharged, four-four "shuffle beat" that many considered an early influence on rock 'n' roll. "The sound, the feel, the excitement, the intensity of the group, was beyond belief," Morris recalled. "Buddy Rich once said to me, 'Nobody could work that hard and live.'"

What really made the act unique, however, was the interplay between Louis and Keely. She would typically stand impassively, waiting for her turn to sing, while Prima bounced and brayed, taunted and teased her, like a hyperactive kid trying to crack up his straitlaced sister. When she finally took the microphone, her voice was as pure and unfussy—no showy flourishes or vibrato—as Prima's was raw and untamed. The obvious sexual heat between them added spice to the combination: it was the lady and the tiger, Tracy and Hepburn (or Sonny and Cher, whose act a few years later bore a lot of similarities). A match made in lounge-show heaven.

Prima and Smith did five shows a night at the Sahara, from midnight until dawn, six nights a week, at least thirty weeks a year for the next five years. They were the hottest lounge show in town. The Casbar Lounge (a tiny space, with the bar in between the audience and the stage) was enlarged to accommodate the crowds, which were sometimes lined up ten deep in the casino to get in. They were dubbed the wildest show in Vegas, soon shortened to simply the Wildest. They rocked the place with a "wild, relentless, driving beat that punched through the lounge's smoke and chatter and left crowds in awe," wrote jazz critic Scott Shea. Said Bobby Morris, "It was havoc. Absolute havoc."

Their success in Las Vegas reignited Prima and Smith's career. They

recorded hit albums for Capitol Records, were frequent guests on Ed
Sullivan's and Dinah Shore's variety shows, and starred in two movies
together. In 1960 they graduated from the Sahara lounge to the main
showroom at the Desert Inn, where some of the intimate lounge-show
magic was lost, but they still drew sellout crowds. Only their divorce in
1961 ended their remarkable Vegas run together—a galvanizing blend
of music and mayhem, the greatest lounge act in Las Vegas history.

Five months after Prima and Smith began cooking in the Sahara
lounge, a new hotel opened down the street. The $8.5 million Riviera
was perhaps the most elegant resort yet on the Las Vegas Strip: nine
stories tall (the Strip's first high-rise), with plush European decor and
a state-of-the-art showroom big enough to accommodate Broadway
musicals. For its grand opening in April 1955, the hotel also set a new
salary record for Las Vegas, paying $50,000 a week to an entertainer
who was already a Vegas favorite: Liberace.

He was born Wladziu (Americanized to Walter) Liberace in West
Allis, Wisconsin, just outside Milwaukee, on May 16, 1919. A child
prodigy at the piano, he began playing professionally soon after high
school—both classical concerts (performing a Liszt concerto with the
Chicago symphony at age twenty) and popular tunes with dance bands
and at cocktail lounges in the area. Gradually he developed a nightclub act that combined the two: mixing Beethoven and boogie-woogie,
turning "Home on the Range" into a Strauss waltz, or doing "Mairzy
Doats," a popular nonsense song at the time, in the classical style of
Bach, Brahms, and Chopin. The act was catching on in clubs across the
Northeast and Midwest when Maxine Lewis booked him for an engagement at the Last Frontier in November 1944. After a smash opening night, she doubled his salary and made him a regular at the hotel,
where he would appear twenty-five times over the next ten years.

Liberace soon dropped his first name and developed a flamboyant, tongue-in-cheek stage persona. He dressed in gaudy dinner jackets and always had a candelabra (a prop he picked up from the 1945 Chopin biopic, *A Song to Remember*) sitting atop his grand piano. He flaunted a showy, romantic, highly visual keyboard style—embellishing every piece with extravagant runs and exaggerated wrist bounces. He could turn "Chopsticks" into a concerto, slide effortlessly from Grieg to Gershwin. "I longed to please the man on the street," he said, "the people who had relatively little appreciation of music."

In the early 1950s Liberace became a nationwide sensation: recording hit albums, playing sold-out concerts, and starring in a popular syndicated TV series. His dimpled smile, silky voice, and over-the-top outfits (campy before people knew what camp was; gay before gay was allowed to be spoken) made him a matinee idol for millions of middle-aged women—a surrogate son, nonthreatening boyfriend, and endlessly charming tea companion, all wrapped up in one tuxedo.

By the time the Riviera lured him away from the New Frontier, he was pushing that image to the hilt. For his April 1955 opening, Liberace came out in a white silk lamé tuxedo, designed for him by Christian Dior. Midway through the act, he changed into another, even flashier outfit, a dinner jacket decorated with what was advertised as more than a million sequins. Along with piano selections ranging from "Clair de Lune" to "Beer Barrel Polka," there were three choreographed production numbers, including a dream sequence featuring an eight-year-old dancer playing Liberace as a child. The show ran an exorbitant hour and forty minutes, and for an encore Liberace made yet another costume change, coming out in an ornate, beaded black satin jacket. "Go ahead and laugh," he told the crowd. "You paid for it."

Like each splashy new hotel that opened in Vegas during the 1950s, Liberace had to keep topping himself. In later years the outfits would grow more outrageous (a calf-length ermine coat trimmed in diamonds), the stage gimmicks more outré (wiring himself with twin-kling lights, or being driven onstage in a Rolls-Royce), but always with a knowing wink to the audience. "Finally it was impossible to make fun of Liberace, because he was having too much fun making fun of him-self," wrote *Time*'s Richard Corliss. "He was in on the joke; he may have created it. In doing so he exploited the showbiz principle that nothing succeeds like shameless excess."

Liberace liked to tell the story of an epiphany he had early in his ca-reer, at a concert in La Crosse, Wisconsin. At the end of a classical-music program, which drew polite applause, an audience member shouted out a request for him to play "Three Little Fishies." Liberace took the popu-lar novelty song and performed it in the style of Bach. The audience loved it. "They relaxed and enjoyed themselves and . . . they smiled," he recalled in his autobiography. "That was the big thing, for me. They smiled a way they hadn't for the straight classical repertoire, no matter how well I performed." Liberace kept going for those smiles. The crit-ics often scorned his ostentatious piano technique and *Reader's Digest* treatment of the classics. But for his exuberant showmanship, his self-mocking good humor, his democratic embrace of both "high" and "low" music, and above all the sheer joy he so obviously took in performing, Liberace was the ideal Vegas entertainer. He made people happy.

In April 1956, a year after his Riviera opening, Liberace was back in Las Vegas for a second appearance at the hotel. By chance, it coincided with Elvis Presley's own bumpy debut in Las Vegas, at Liberace's old stomp-ing ground, the rechristened New Frontier Hotel.

Backstage one night at the Riviera, Liberace had a visit from Elvis's manager, Colonel Tom Parker. The colonel told him that "my boy" was having some problems across the street, and he wondered if Liberace might be able to help. "He admires you so much," said Parker. "If I could bring him over for a picture, he'd really appreciate it." Liberace obliged, posing for some publicity shots and offering a little advice. He told Elvis that his act needed more glitz.

It was the start of a long, improbable friendship between the two performers. When Elvis was back in Vegas for a couple of days in November 1956, he came to see Liberace's new show at the Riviera. Afterward, the two posed for some famous newsreel footage—Elvis donning Lee's gold lamé jacket while playing the piano, Liberace hamming it up while he strums Elvis's guitar. Liberace's style and showmanship had a clear impact on the young rock 'n' roller. The following spring, when Elvis began a ten-day tour of the Midwest and Northeast, he was wearing a new outfit: a $2,500 gold-leaf suit, modeled on the one Liberace had worn in Las Vegas.

They stayed in touch over the years. For each of Liberace's Vegas openings, Elvis would send him a bouquet of flowers in the shape of a guitar. In later years they had homes just blocks apart in Palm Springs, and Liberace would sometimes invite Elvis and his entourage over for dinner. Elvis even bought Liberace's dune buggy, decorated with a candelabra on each side. "Elvis never forgot that Liberace was very supportive when he first got to Las Vegas," said Jerry Schilling, a friend from Memphis who worked for Elvis off and on through the 1960s and '70s. "Elvis would talk about it afterwards: 'You know, he made me feel comfortable.' He never forgot stuff like that."

Elvis and Liberace had another unusual connection. Elvis Aron Presley was famously one of twins; his brother, Jesse Garon, died at birth. This haunted Elvis throughout his life. He often visited Jesse's grave, and his mother, Gladys, would tell him, "When one twin died, the one that lived got all the strength of both." Liberace, startlingly,

also had a twin who died at birth. And when Walter, the surviving
brother, emerged from the womb, he was wrapped in birth mem-
brane, or a caul—regarded in some cultures as a sign of wondrous
things to come.

It's not clear whether the two knew of the matching circumstances
of their birth, or ever spoke about it. But for these two self-created,
almost mystically inspired performers—two of the great originals of
twentieth-century American entertainment—the coincidence is hard
to dismiss.

Elvis was entranced by Las Vegas. He loved the hotels, the shows,
the round-the-clock activity. "When you grew up in Memphis, they
closed in those days pretty early; we were the only people up late at
night," said Jerry Schilling. "You go to Vegas and at three o'clock in the
morning it's like noon. Elvis liked the lights." He came back to Vegas
for a ten-day vacation in October 1957, traveling by train from Memphis with several of his friends and staying at the Sahara Hotel, where
Colonel Parker had become friends with owner Milton Prell. Elvis saw
shows and had his pick of women, among them a red-haired stripper named Tempest Storm. When a picture of the two of them in her
dressing room got out to the press, Colonel Parker blew his top. He
didn't want his boy contributing to the negative image of rock 'n' roll
by "dating a stripper." "I didn't date her," Elvis replied. "I just spent the
night with her."

Elvis's regular visits to Vegas were forced to stop in March 1958,
when he was drafted into the US Army—the start of a two-year
tour of duty that brought teenage girls to tears and Elvis's career to
a screeching halt. Las Vegas, in the meantime, was suffering through
some growing pains. New hotels continued to open: the Dunes (with
its smiling, thirty-foot-high sultan greeting visitors out front) and the
Royal Nevada in 1955; the downtown Fremont in 1956; the luxurious

Tropicana, at the south end of the Strip, in 1957; and the space-age Stardust in 1958, boasting the city's gaudiest sign—216 feet long, with 7,100 feet of neon tubing and 11,000 lightbulbs. But as the nation struggled through recessionary times in the late fifties, Las Vegas' rapid growth hit a speed bump. The Royal Nevada closed down, and several hotels, including the Riviera and Tropicana, ran into financial trouble. The press, which had covered Vegas' progress so enthusiastically, began to ask whether the boom times were over.

By 1960, Vegas was in a period of consolidation. The city's initial construction boom was over; though several hotels expanded and a new convention center was completed in 1959, no new hotels would open on the Strip until 1966. Yet Las Vegas had secured its grip on the American imagination, and its place at the very center of the entertainment world. "This desert never-never land, more than ever, is a standing movie set of almost unbelievable make-believe," wrote *Variety*'s Abel Green in January 1960. "Complete abandon and dedication to entertainment exists as in no other geographical center of the world. The Riviera, Florida, and assorted spas or fun-and-sun-worshipping spots have their seasons. Las Vegas seemingly has none."

Even more remarkable, the party was just getting started.

Three

THE COOL GUYS

Jack Entratter, the top man at the Sands Hotel, was having trouble making a left turn. He was coming out of the Sands driveway and trying to head south on the Las Vegas Strip, but the traffic wouldn't let him. It was the early days of Vegas, when the few hotels lining the Strip were still separated by expanses of desert, and no one wanted to slow down traffic with anything as mundane as a stoplight. But for the impresario of the classiest, starriest hotel in Las Vegas, the man sometimes called the Ziegfeld of the Desert, it seemed unjust.

"You're the big man on campus," said his girlfriend, an LA actress and model named Corinne Cole, who was sitting in the passenger seat next to him. "Why don't you just tell the city hall you need a light there?" Sure enough, the next time she and Entratter were negotiating the same intersection, a traffic light had suddenly appeared.

Jack Entratter had clout. A beefy six-footer with prematurely gray hair and what Corinne called "electric Paul Newman—blue eyes," he was a commanding figure, a former street kid who wore custom-made suits and traveled in rarefied circles. "I used to call him crudely refined," said Corinne, who later married and divorced him, twice. The waters parted when Entratter walked into a room; the Sands shook when he got angry. "He had a physical presence that was just extraordinary— as strong a presence as any of the major stars I've met over the years," said Kevin Thomas, former film critic for the *Los Angeles Times* and a frequent Vegas visitor in those years. "An overwhelming presence. Yet he was soft-spoken and direct. You knew you were in the presence of a very powerful man."

He was born Nathan Entratter in Brooklyn, the youngest of eight children of Austrian Jewish parents. A bout of osteomyelitis as a child left him with a bad foot and a permanent limp. (The doctors said he would be crippled for life, but little Nate walked home from the hospital.) At eighteen he went to Miami, where he worked as a reservations clerk at the French Casino, then returned to New York and got a job as host at the famed Stork Club. In 1940 he moved to the Copacabana, the tony nightclub on East Sixtieth Street, where he eventually became a co-owner and head of entertainment. Under his guidance, the Copa became the most famous, star-studded nightclub in America.

In 1952 the Copa's mob-connected owners (chief among them New York crime boss Frank Costello) were preparing to open a new outpost in Las Vegas, the Sands Hotel, and Entratter, then thirty-eight, was the man they sent to run the place. In Las Vegas, Entratter drew on all the relationships he had established at the Copa to assemble a lineup of stars unrivaled by any other hotel on the strip—including Dean Martin and Jerry Lewis (together, when they were the top comedy team in America; separately, after they split up), Frank Sinatra,

Danny Thomas, Nat King Cole, and Lena Horne. He added a chorus line of statuesque Copa Girls, handpicked by Entratter and billed as the most beautiful showgirls in Vegas. Among the big-name acts he brought to Las Vegas during his first year at the Sands were Edith Piaf, Tallulah Bankhead, and a double bill of opera star Robert Merrill and jazz great Louis Armstrong.

The Sands was the jewel of the Strip, with its sleek, Sunbelt-modern design, fifty-six-foot-high entry sign (the tallest on the Strip), and sprawling grounds where golf carts shuttled between the guest buildings named for famous racetracks. Entertainment was presented in the Copa Room, an intimate venue that seated just under four hundred, at tables arrayed in a semicircle around a shallow thrust stage. Guests entered just off the casino, through two curtains (to block out all the light from the casino), and were greeted by a tuxedoed maître d', who needed to be tipped if you wanted a good table. Entratter had his own table, just to the right of the entrance, at the very back so he could survey the whole scene.

A gregarious host, he treated his stars like family and fostered great loyalty in return. "Jack Entratter was the Genghis Khan of Las Vegas," said Jerry Lewis. When Martin and Lewis, one of the first acts Entratter booked at the Sands, were hit up by the IRS for $400,000 in back taxes, "Jack put it on the table, four hundred grand, cash, and said, 'Now get busy doing your fucking show.' He was tough. Put him in a business meeting and he'll eat your lunch and dinner. But he was a great friend." When Frank Sinatra altered the lyrics to "I Love Paris" for his Sands shows, it became a different kind of love song:

I love Vegas.
Why, oh why, do I love Vegas?
Because Entratter's here.

"I cater to the overprivileged," Entratter liked to say. Yet he always kept two pockets full of money, according to Corinne, one for himself and one for any Sands employee who might need help with a debt or a doctor's bill. He helped found the first synagogue in Las Vegas and raised money for local schools and hospitals. But his chief project was building the Sands into the premier entertainment venue in Las Vegas. Al Freeman, the savvy publicist Entratter had brought with him from the Copa in New York, came up with newsreel-ready publicity stunts like putting a floating crap table in the Sands swimming pool. Each Sands anniversary in December was a gala event, with the return of the hotel's opening-night headliner, Danny Thomas, and a barrage of Freeman-supplied statistics. (On December 15, 1955, its third anniversary, the hotel had been in operation for 95 million seconds; hosted 7.4 million visitors; spent $1.63 million on entertainment; and was preparing a birthday cake made with the "five millionth egg purchased by the hotel since it opened.")

Entratter's greatest promotional coup, however, came in January 1960, when not one or two but five major stars—Frank Sinatra, Dean Martin, Sammy Davis Jr., Peter Lawford, and Joey Bishop—took the stage of the Copa Room for a show that broke all the records and all the rules. It was the ultimate in Vegas glamour and star power, and it launched the city's most glamorous, star-packed decade. It was dubbed the Summit—a reference to the Cold War summit meeting soon to be held between President Eisenhower and Soviet premier Khrushchev. The two world leaders were even sent invitations to the show. They didn't come, but it seemed everyone else did. In the era of *Sputnik*, U-2 flights, and the space race, the Rat Pack launched Vegas into orbit.

Frank Sinatra owed a lot to both Las Vegas and Jack Entratter. The singer, born on December 12, 1915, in a working-class Italian American neighborhood in Hoboken, New Jersey, had burst onto the music scene in the early forties, as the swoon-inducing vocalist for Tommy Dorsey's big band. Striking out on his own in 1942, he was soon America's top recording artist (replacing Bing Crosby in *Downbeat's* poll as the nation's most popular singer in 1943); an idol of teenage bobby-soxers, who mobbed his shows with a fervor never before seen in American show business; a star on radio and in such MGM musicals as *Anchors Aweigh* and *On the Town*. By the end of the 1940s, however, his career was in a slump: his records no longer selling, his movie career at a dead end, his personal life a mess (he divorced his first wife, Nancy, amid a stormy affair with screen beauty Ava Gardner, whom he married in 1951 and separated from two years later), his public temper tantrums and rumored links to mob figures making him one of the most controversial stars in Hollywood.

Las Vegas helped keep his career afloat. He made his Vegas debut in September 1951 at the Desert Inn (where he discovered a lounge pianist named Bill Miller, who became his longtime accompanist) and appeared there again the following July. But when Jack Entratter came out from New York to run the Sands, Sinatra had a new friend in town. Entratter had been one of Sinatra's champions at the Copa, giving him much-needed bookings even in the depths of his career doldrums, and the Sands' boss offered Sinatra the spot as headliner for the hotel's opening night on December 15, 1952.

Sinatra demurred, saying he didn't want to work during the holidays. But he made his Sands debut the next year, in October 1953. He drew capacity crowds, but only mixed reviews—a reflection of the bumpy career transition he was going through. "As he meanders down memory lane, Sinatra slams the door on his former worshipers to please an older and less exuberant set of applauders," noted *Variety*, which praised the "unmistakeable mark of quality," but faulted his "tendencies to insert dubious gags or parody lines in great established melodies, ennui, and mechanically phrased offerings of humility." Hank Greenspun, editor of the *Las Vegas Sun*, raved about him in a front-page column—"Oooooh, Frankie, you almost gave me goosebumps last night"—suggesting that Sinatra was back "almost to the point 10 years ago when the world loved you." A separate review inside the paper, however, griped about Sinatra's abrasive behavior onstage, calling him "arrogant, ill-tempered, and downright insulting."

But Sinatra's debut at the Sands coincided with one of the great career turnarounds in show-business history. Just two months before, Columbia Pictures had released *From Here to Eternity*, an adaptation of James Jones's World War II–era bestseller, with Sinatra in the key supporting role of Private Maggio. The performance would win him an Academy Award the following spring and rejuvenate his movie career. In 1953 Sinatra also signed with a new record label, Capitol, and began a career-transforming collaboration with arranger Nelson Riddle. Their first album together, *Songs for Young Lovers*, released in January 1954, introduced a new Sinatra—his voice fuller and more expressive, his orchestrations more swinging, his emotional investment in the lyrics of America's great popular songwriters unmatched by any other singer of his generation. "The new Sinatra was not the gentle boy balladeer of the forties," wrote critic John Lahr. "Fragility had gone from his voice, to be replaced by a virile adult's sense of happiness and hurt. . . . Sinatra's sound had acquired the edge that comes with suffering: something gallant, raffish, and knowing."

Sinatra became closely linked with Las Vegas. Though he appeared only sporadically at the Sands during the mid-1950s, busy with movies and recording work, he was a great booster for the city, and the Sands became his home away from home. He acquired a 2 percent ownership stake in the hotel (increased to 9 percent in 1961) and was there often, taking up residence in a three-bedroom suite in the Aqueduct building. "I've been trying for more than a year to get a foothold in Las Vegas, because I believe it has a great future," he told reporters. "I want to be a part of that future." He helped open the Dunes Hotel in 1955, riding into the newly built casino on a camel. He starred as Joe E. Lewis—the veteran Vegas comic who survived a brutal throat-slashing by Al Capone's thugs while performing in Chicago nightclubs during the 1920s—in the 1957 biopic *The Joker Is Wild* and attended the film's gala premiere in Las Vegas in August. (When Lewis himself took the stage at El Rancho Vegas and tried to coax Frank out of the audience to sing, Sinatra grabbed his date, Lauren Bacall, and walked out. His deal with Entratter prohibited him from singing anywhere in Vegas but the Sands.)

Sinatra brought something else to Las Vegas: an aura of New York glamour and sophistication, new to a town still emerging from its raffish frontier days. Lorraine Hunt-Bono, who came to Vegas as a child with her family in 1943, recalled the impact Sinatra had on a teenage girl seeing him for the first time in the early 1950s: "The thing that amazed me was the way he was dressed. Because he wasn't a cowboy; he didn't have cowboy boots on, as so many of the guys did here. All of a sudden I see this fantastic black tuxedo. And I looked out as a young girl and I'm just staring at his shoes, black patent leather shoes. And I'm going, 'Wow, this is so cool.' Sinatra brought New York, that class, to Vegas. And everybody followed."

But it was Sinatra's singing—his impeccable voice, his cool stage presence, his masterly way with lyrics—that made him the model for so many of his contemporaries. "Frank was the king, the one who really taught us all," said Vic Damone, another Italian American singer from back East, who actually made his Vegas debut before Sinatra, at the

Flamingo in 1949. "When I was a kid, I used to listen to him. And what I found was that his interpretation of the lyrics was so good—he lived it when he sang it. He told a great story. I recognized that when I was fifteen, sixteen years old. And I used to copy him." Even many of the younger rock 'n' roll singers who came to Vegas in the early sixties, like Paul Anka and Bobby Darin, saw Sinatra as an aspirational role model. "He was the number one guy," said Anka. "He ruined it for anybody that wanted to get up in front of an orchestra."

Sinatra's great musical achievement of the 1950s rests mainly in the albums he recorded for Capitol (mostly with Riddle), in which he presented his definitive, deeply felt interpretations of the Great American Songbook. Only when Sinatra started his own record label, Reprise, in 1961, did he get around to recording any of his live performances. In November 1961 he brought in a crew for the first time to record five nights of shows at the Sands, for an album that was never released (Sinatra shelved it when he got distracted by plans for a 1962 world tour). But as reconstructed for a later box set—*Sinatra: Vegas*, released in 2006—it offers a vivid sampling of Sinatra's power as a Vegas performer in his classic period.

Accompanied by the Sands house orchestra conducted by Antonio Morelli (with help from two Sinatra regulars, pianist Bill Miller and guitarist Al Viola), Sinatra is in superb voice, energized by the live crowd, and totally at ease in his home venue. He's a hurtling locomotive on up-tempo numbers like "The One I Love Belongs to Somebody Else" (with a great Sy Oliver arrangement), yet he caresses ballads like "Without a Song" and "The Second Time Around" with the kind of sensitivity and tonal nuance that one doesn't usually associate with Vegas bravado. He slows down Cole Porter's "Just One of Those Things" and turns it into a brooding torch song and delivers a parody version of "River, Stay Away from My Door," with special lyrics by Sammy Cahn that pay tribute, once again, to Sinatra's patron at the Sands: "Entratter, stay away from my door!"

Sinatra's patter in between songs is relatively restrained, especially compared with that on some of his later Vegas albums. Drinking, as usual, is topic A: "Fell off the wagon with a boom-bang last night. I woke up this morning and my hair hurt." He tinkers with some of the lyrics—doing a mocking Italian accent at the end of "You Make Me Feel So Young," for example, or embellishing the bridge of "The Lady Is a Tramp" with his ring-a-ding-ding flourishes:

> She loves the free, fine, cool, wild, cuckoo wind in her hair,
> Life without care . . .

Sinatra could go overboard with this sort of thing in later years, especially when he was performing live. But here it is just enough—a dash of spontaneity for a vocal performance that's as focused and technically fine as anything in his studio albums.

Sinatra was a familiar sight in Las Vegas during these years, even when he wasn't performing—often in the audience for other Vegas shows, holding court in all-night drinking sessions with an assortment of friends, fellow performers, and hangers-on. "He'd always be there," said lounge singer Freddie Bell. "You'd never know when you were gonna see Frank. It was a close-knit group in those days. Fly in and fly out, you know? You gotta understand, he partied pretty heavy in those days." "Frank enjoyed a good time," said actress and sometime girlfriend Angie Dickinson. "After his shows we would hang out with him and whoever was around in those days. You convened around him, and the table would grow before the night was over, since Frank would always invite people to come and sit at his table." And from that Vegas revelry came something called the Rat Pack.

It was, more correctly, the second Rat Pack. The nickname was first applied to a band of hard-drinking Hollywood friends who coalesced around Humphrey Bogart in the mid-1950s—a group that included Sinatra, Judy Garland, David Niven, the agent Swifty Lazar, and songwriter Jimmy Van Heusen. Lauren Bacall, Bogart's young wife, supposedly coined the term one night in Las Vegas, when she walked in on the group as they were sitting around a showroom table, looking the worse for an evening's wear. "You look like a goddamn rat pack," she cracked. As a lark, they embraced the name and turned the group into a tongue-in-cheek club—electing officers, creating a coat of arms, voting on new members.

The Bogart Rat Pack came to an end with Bogart's death from throat cancer in 1957. But Sinatra soon became the center of another circle of hard-partying showbiz friends. Some date its origins to August 1958, when Sinatra, Dean Martin, and Shirley MacLaine bonded while on location in southern Indiana shooting the movie *Some Came Running*. The Sinatra-Martin bromance went public when the pair came to see Judy Garland's show at the Sands in October 1958. When Garland—the former MGM star (and onetime Sinatra girlfriend) who was battling alcohol, drug, and weight problems—seemed to falter during her performance, Martin and Sinatra began catcalling from the audience. Garland played along, bringing them up onstage to chastise them like unruly schoolboys, and the resulting interplay was "a comedy routine that was out of this world," said Louella Parsons. The following January, Sinatra and Martin traded guest appearances in each other's shows at the Sands—Dean filling in for Frank at the last minute when he had to cancel a performance because of voice problems, Frank returning the favor a couple weeks later, joining Dean onstage for his own Sands opening night.

Martin—born Dino Crocetti in Steubenville, Ohio, on June 7, 1917—had much in common with Sinatra. Both came from working-class Italian American families; both were high school dropouts; and both were well acquainted with neighborhood characters of ill repute. (Steubenville at the time of Dino's youth was a notorious center of illegal gambling and prostitution.) Dino began singing with local bands in Ohio, then moved to New York City and was gaining attention as a nightclub singer when he teamed up with a brash young comic ten years his junior, born Joseph Levitch and now calling himself Jerry Lewis. They made their debut together at Atlantic City's 500 Club in July 1946, improvising a unique musical-comedy act—Dean playing the cool, crooning straight man, while Jerry, dressed as a busboy, kept interrupting him and causing general mayhem. Martin and Lewis's madcap stage antics caught on quickly, and they were soon the hottest nightclub act in America, the stars of hit movies, and top-rated hosts of TV's *Colgate Comedy Hour*.

Sinatra was initially unimpressed with the singing half of Martin and Lewis. "The dago's lousy, but the little Jew is great," he reportedly said when he first saw the team in 1948. But they got to know each other as fellow Capitol recording artists and members of Jack Entratter's stable of entertainers at the Sands. After his breakup with Lewis in 1956, Martin made his solo debut at the Sands in 1957 and was signed by Entratter to a five-year contract. (Like Sinatra, Martin also got a small piece of the hotel.) He developed a drunk stage persona that became one of the most recognizable acts in Vegas. "And now, direct from the bar," went the announcer's typical introduction, as Martin staggered onstage with a cocktail glass in hand (usually filled with apple juice) and delivered woozy comedy patter in between laid-back performances of his hit songs, like "Memories Are Made of This" and "Volare." Sinatra admired Martin's ease onstage, his matinee-idol good looks, and his defiantly blasé attitude—such a contrast with Sinatra's intense, high-strung personality. "Sinatra was enthralled by Dean," wrote Martin biographer Nick Tosches. "In his eyes he saw the man he himself wanted to be."

With Sammy Davis Jr., it was pretty much the opposite. Born in Harlem in December 1925, he was a decade younger than Sinatra, and a child of show business unlike either Frank or Dean. His parents were vaudeville performers, and Sammy was a childhood dancing prodigy, starring in a movie musical short, *Rufus Jones for President*, when he was just seven. Soon he was appearing with his father and veteran vaudeville hoofer Will Mastin as part of the Will Mastin Trio, a song-and-dance act that played the nightclub circuit in the forties and fifties. Sammy loyally remained part of the group (billed as the Will Mastin Trio Starring Sammy Davis Jr.) even as he became one of the most prominent black stars of the 1950s. He had hit records ("Hey There" from *Pajama Game* put him on the charts in 1954), starred in the 1956 Broadway musical *Mr. Wonderful*, and played Sportin' Life in the 1959 film version of *Porgy and Bess*. On a nightclub stage he was a versatile, inexhaustible performer: he danced, sang, told jokes, did impressions, even played the drums. If you asked a veteran of the golden age to name the best all-around entertainer ever to play Las Vegas, chances are the answer would be Sammy Davis Jr.

But he was also a needy, driven performer, and he felt indebted to Frank Sinatra. Frank had given the Will Mastin Trio a big break in 1947 by requesting them as his opening act at New York's Capitol Theater. When Sammy lost an eye in a serious car accident, on a drive from Las Vegas to LA in 1954, Sinatra spent days at his hospital bedside, let him recuperate at Frank's home in Palm Springs, and even invited him to his mother's house in Hoboken the following Christmas. A longtime opponent of race discrimination, Sinatra was a champion of Sammy's in the days when segregation still ruled Las Vegas, insisting that he be allowed to stay, dine, and gamble at the Sands when he appeared there. Sammy and the Will Mastin Trio had already broken that color barrier in 1954, when the Last Frontier dropped its all-white policy and allowed them to stay at the hotel during their engagement. Still, Frank's support meant a lot to Sammy.

Yet he also knew the perils of getting on Sinatra's bad side. In 1957, during a radio interview in Chicago, Sammy let his mouth run on when asked about Sinatra: "Talent is not an excuse for bad manners. It does not give you the right to step on people and treat them rotten. This is what he does occasionally." Worse, when asked whether he considered himself "bigger than Frank" as a singing star, Sammy replied, "Oh yeah." Sinatra refused to talk to him for months and even had him written out of the movie *Never So Few*—in a part Sinatra had had written expressly for Sammy. "That was it for Sammy," said Peter Lawford. "For the next two months Sammy was on his knees begging for Frank's forgiveness, but Frank wouldn't speak to him."

Peter Lawford knew well what a Sinatra freeze-out could mean. The British actor (born out of wedlock in 1923 to a couple of lesser members of the English aristocracy) came to Hollywood in 1942, while still in his teens. He got to know Sinatra at MGM, where Lawford was a pleasant if unexceptional supporting player in such films as *Easter Parade* and (with Sinatra) *It Happened in Brooklyn*. But the two had a falling-out in 1953, when a gossip columnist reported seeing Lawford having a drink with Ava Gardner, the wife from whom Sinatra had just separated. The jealous Sinatra didn't speak to Lawford for five years. Only after Peter married Patricia Kennedy, and her older brother Jack was making noises about running for president, did Sinatra see the advantage of reestablishing friendly relations.

Dean, Sammy, and Peter were fully credentialed members of Sinatra's inner circle by late 1958, when the press began to take notice. *Life*
magazine devoted a feature story to the group in December, dubbing
them the Clan and providing a helpful guide for readers, listing the
group's chief members (including a few peripheral figures, like Eddie
Fisher and Tony Curtis), explaining their nonconformist ethos ("a public and aggressive indifference, not only to what the customers expect
of their movie stars but also to what Hollywood expects of its own citi-
zens"), and even supplying a glossary of their private slang: *Charlie* was
the name they affectionately called one another; women were *broads*;
a good show a *gasser*; *clyde*, a catchall noun to replace almost anything
they pleased. They were the embodiment of Hollywood cool—what
passed for hipsters at the end of the button-down 1950s and the dawn
of the New Frontier.

It was Lawford who was responsible for their defining group ad-
venture. In 1955 he ran into a Hollywood assistant director named
Gilbert Kay, who was peddling a script about a band of former Army
buddies who plot a heist of five Las Vegas casinos on New Year's Eve.
Kay wanted to direct the film himself, but when he couldn't make a
deal after a couple of years, he sold the script outright to Lawford. He
took it to Sinatra, who "flipped" for the idea, envisioning it as a vehicle
for himself and as many of his Hollywood friends as he could jam into
the cast. Warner Bros. agreed to back the picture, which would be produced by Sinatra's own Dorchester Productions and directed by Hollywood veteran Lewis Milestone (*All Quiet on the Western Front*). After
multiple script revisions by a battalion of screenwriters, filming was set
to begin in Las Vegas in January 1960.

Sinatra was booked for a four-week engagement at the Sands at
the same time, and he suggested combining the two events—bringing
some of his *Ocean's 11* costars to join him onstage each night after the

day's shooting was finished. Someone, most likely Al Freeman, came up with the idea of calling it the Summit, and the publicity drumbeat began. "Producer Jack Entratter comes up with the show of the year, or for that matter, of the century," announced Les Devor in the *Las Vegas Review-Journal* on January 8, "when he presents IN ONE BIG SHOW AT THE SAME TIME—FRANK SINATRA, DEAN MARTIN, SAMMY DAVIS JR. AND PETER LAWFORD."

Joey Bishop appears to have been a late addition. Born in the Bronx and raised in Philadelphia, another high school dropout (five Rat Packers and not a single high school diploma among them), he had been working as a stand-up comedian for more than a decade. In Chicago, his hangdog, deadpan style got him dubbed the Frown Prince of Comedy. He opened for Sinatra at the Copa in New York, played Las Vegas a few times, and was a frequent guest on *The Ed Sullivan Show* and other TV variety programs. According to Corinne Entratter, Bishop talked his way into the Rat Pack show when he found himself on a flight from New York to Las Vegas with Jack Entratter, buttonholed the Sands boss, and pleaded for the job. Entratter felt the act needed an emcee of sorts, and Sinatra was a fan, so Bishop was added to the cast. By the January 20 opening, the Sands was touting all five stars—though not necessarily all of them all the time: "Which star shines tonight?" read the ads. "It's a guessing game, and you'll be the winner of the show-of-shows any night."

The opening night was a winner all the way around. Lucille Ball, Cyd Charisse, Dinah Shore, Sammy Cahn, Zsa Zsa Gabor, Peter Lorre, and world heavyweight champion Ingemar Johansson were among the many celebrities in the audience. Sinatra opened the show, with a twenty-minute set that included "Pennies from Heaven," "The Road to Mandalay," and "What Is This Thing Called Love?" "That was a great opening act," quipped Bishop, who came out next to oversee the roundelay of singing, dancing, drinking, wisecracking, and general anarchy that followed. Sammy did a few numbers, and Lawford joined him for a soft-shoe routine to "Shall We Dance," in which Sammy did most of the work. "What a great team," Sinatra cracked. "One dances, the other applauds." Martin handled the anchor leg, wedging a few songs in between the heckling and other stage antics around him. The show ran for two hours and closed with the whole crew together on-stage, with the Copa Girls and Entratter himself joining in.

"Mr. Entratter, sir, you have a 'gasser' on your hands," wrote Les Devor in the *Review-Journal*, leading the parade of rave reviews. "The only possible topper to this show is booking of the Civil War and its original cast, and we hear you're working on that." Raved Hedda Hopper, "I flew to Las Vegas for what Frank Sinatra called his summit meeting. It sure was, plus New Year's Eve and Christmas. If Ike has anything like that in Russia, we won't have to fear their missiles." The *Los Angeles Times* called it "an entertainment ball which will be very difficult to match in the future anywhere."

Twice a night for four weeks, the Rat Pack would reassemble on the Copa Room stage after their day's filming was done. (Shooting days were rarely taxing, usually requiring only one or two of the stars on set for a few hours in the afternoon.) Every show was sold-out (cover charge: $5.95, which included dinner), and in the first week alone the Sands reportedly had to turn away eighteen thousand requests for room reservations. Seemingly every celebrity in Hollywood turned up in the audience sooner or later; some, like Red Skelton, Bob Hope, and Milton Berle, got up onstage to join in the act. "This is an evening I will never forget," said Berle. "Because I remembered every joke."

The myth of the Rat Pack shows has somewhat eclipsed what actually took place onstage—which, judging by the spotty film excerpts available, was a scrappy and self-indulgent affair. Booze was the bonding agent: a drink cart would be wheeled out early in the show and tended to assiduously by the stars for the rest of the evening. "When you're drinkin' / When you're drinkin' / The show looks good to you," sang Martin—and apparently it did, at least to them. But the frat-boy antics and wisecracks, both planned and unplanned, were pretty crude. In one bit, Bishop and Lawford parade across the stage in front of Sinatra with their pants off—followed by Sammy, waving a scarf and asking in a fey, lisping voice, "I beg your pardon, did you see two fellas go by here?" They interrupt one another's numbers and goose each other's asses. One night a giant birthday cake was brought out for pianist Bill Miller's birthday, and the show devolved into an all-out food fight.

Bishop did most of the writing, and certain bits and lines would be repeated nightly. "Any *old* business?" Joey would interject at random moments, poking fun at the group's clubby reputation. Or he'd needle Sinatra: "Why don't you tell us about the *good* the Mafia does?" (Not a bad line, considering Frank's sensitivity about the subject. "Joey was a ballsy guy," said Henry Silva, an *Ocean's 11* cast member. "Frank loved anybody who had balls.") They called Sinatra the Leader, or the Pope, and their fealty to him became a running gag. When Sammy sings "The Lady Is a Tramp," Sinatra takes mock-offense, and Martin chastises Sam, "You know you shouldn't sing the leader's song, boy!" Later, when Sinatra does an impression of James Cagney, Sammy gets offended in return; impressions are *his* turf.

The racial and ethnic wisecracks are nearly constant, and hard to stomach today. "I tell you, the dagos are taking over the world," Sinatra says on introducing Martin, the other Italian singer. One night the gang comes out dressed in hokey Indian headdresses, holding tomahawks and talking like Tonto. (Dean: "Me no take single drink all year. Just doubles.") The dismissive, *Mad Men*–era treatment of women is also painfully retrograde. Martin trots out lewd song parodies, like "You

made me love you / You woke me up to do it." One night Sinatra spies
a female violinist in the all-male orchestra and exclaims, "Hey, look at
that—there's a broad in the band!" On his way offstage, Martin casually
swipes his hand across her cheek.

Sammy, a black man and recent convert to Judaism, comes in for
most of the ribbing. Frank and Dean—and Sammy too—lapse frequently into minstrel-like *Amos 'n' Andy* dialect. At one point Sinatra grabs a white tablecloth, puts it over his head, and announces, "All
right, folks, the meeting is on Friday afternoon." Sammy responds to
these antics with hysterical laughter, and occasionally a lame comeback.
When Peter wants to join Sammy in a dance number, Sammy bristles,
"If I were you, I wouldn't want to dance with one of the great Jewish
Mao-Mao dancers of our time." In one oft-repeated gag, Sammy leaps
into Dean's arms, and Dean, carrying him like a child out of a burn-
ing building, announces, "I want to thank the NAACP for this award."
(Bishop, who wrote the line, originally wanted it to be the B'nai B'rith,
but Dean had too much trouble pronouncing the name.)

Sammy's collusion in all this tomfoolery gives the group some
cover, but doesn't make the racial banter any less disquieting. The Rat
Pack members, most of them political liberals, thought of themselves
as above prejudice; they were thumbing their nose at societal taboos,
satirizing racial stereotypes by making fun of them. But at a time when
Lenny Bruce and other stand-up comedians were challenging those
taboos with much more pointed satire, the Rat Pack's juvenile japery
seemed more like an outlet for the locker-room banter of four privileged white guys—and one complicit black one.

Not everyone in Las Vegas was taken with the Rat Pack shows. "I
hated the idea that people got so crazy about this piece of shit act," said
Shecky Greene, probably the leading lounge comic in Vegas at the time.
"I mean, it was nothing. It was grammar-school kids having a good

time." Jerry Lewis called up Martin, his former partner, and complained that the Rat Pack were basically recycling old Martin and Lewis bits. "They were doing our act," said Lewis, reminiscing many years later. "I told Dean, 'You want me to come over? Glad to come over and help you out.' Dean said, 'No, everything is working great, leave it alone.' So I left it alone." Lewis's take on the Rat Pack's achievement: "They showed up, is what they did."

But showing up was enough. For all the juvenile, politically incorrect horseplay, audiences got to see three of Las Vegas' greatest entertainers—Sinatra, Martin, and Davis—onstage together at their performing peak. (Bishop's role was simply to manage the chaos, and Lawford seemed there mainly for the booze.) They gave audiences an insider's peek at how Hollywood stars acted in real life, when they let their hair down. "For the first time on such a visible platform," wrote Shawn Levy in *Rat Pack Confidential*, "American entertainers acknowledged their adultness. They smoked, drank, caroused, talked of their sex lives, their ex-wives, their politics; they used jazzy slang. . . . They made fun of their own professions; they carried on as if they were alone and the audience had paid to see what they were really like." This was liberating for audiences emerging from the 1950s world of Emily Post and Dale Carnegie—but not so threatening as to bother them when they returned home to their jobs, kids, and PTA meetings.

The Rat Pack, moreover, became closely identified with the coming generational change in American politics. John F. Kennedy, the charismatic young senator from Massachusetts, made a stop in Las Vegas in the midst of his campaign for the 1960 Democratic presidential nomination and came to see their dinner show on February 7. Sinatra introduced him from the stage—"the brightest man in the political world, in this country or any country in the world today, and I personally feel that I'm gonna visit himself in that house one day very soon"—as Kennedy stood and took a couple of bows. Sinatra was one of JFK's closest friends and strongest supporters in Hollywood during the 1960 presidential campaign. Lawford was even part of the family. Never before in America had show business and the nation's business been so intimately connected.

The Rat Pack show at the Sands Hotel in January and February of 1960 was a once-in-a-lifetime event, never again to be repeated in Las Vegas with the full original cast. The group did get back together a month later in Miami, joining Sinatra for the last few nights of his engagement at the Fontainebleau Hotel. And they had a brief one-night reunion in Las Vegas on August 3, 1960, at the world premiere of *Ocean's 11*, attended by a who's who of Vegas celebrities (Joe E. Lewis, Sophie Tucker, Tony Curtis, Danny Kaye, Louis Prima, and Keely Smith), along with ten thousand fans who jammed the streets outside the Fremont Theater, where the film was screened at midnight.

The movie got only mixed reviews, but it holds up surprisingly well—an enjoyable heist caper that perfectly captures the Rat Pack camaraderie in the early, fun years. More important, it was a box-office hit, one of the ten top-grossing films of 1960. That ensured there would be a second Rat Pack film, and *Sergeants 3*, a comedy-Western update of *Gunga Din*, reuniting all five of the Rat Pack principles, went into production in the spring of 1961, shot mostly on location in Utah. Las Vegas was too far away for a repeat of the Rat Pack shows, so the stars made separate forays into town: Sinatra, Martin, Davis, and Bishop each did a week at the Sands, promoted by Entratter as "Jackpot Month." The group made one trip into Vegas together in early June, dropping in on the shows of Eddie Fisher and Danny Thomas, and celebrating Dean's forty-fourth birthday at the Sands with a five-foot-tall cake in the shape of a J&B Scotch bottle.

They were the axis of power in Las Vegas, the in-group everyone wanted to be in with. Their clubhouse was the Sands steam room, where they would gather late in the afternoon, to relax and schmooze before their evening shows. Each had a robe with his own moniker: LEADER for Sinatra, DAGO for Martin, SMOKEY for Sammy. After their shows, they would often be found in the casino, dealing blackjack cards (flouting the rules, so that the customers wouldn't go bust), or in the audience for other shows along the Strip. "There was an electricity when they were in town," said Bob Newhart. "The whole town just glowed. There was an excitement in the air that was palpable. And everybody benefited from it. Every act benefited from their being in town."

Their original name, the Clan, was surprisingly persistent, despite its unfortunate echo of that other Klan. Eventually it was retired in favor of the Rat Pack. But under any name, Sinatra always dismissed the notion that it was any kind of organized club. "There is no Clan," he told columnist Earl Wilson. "It's some guys that like each other and get along together. There are no membership cards or anything like that. This whole thing is silly." Sammy, typically, was more willing to embrace his affiliation with the coolest fraternity in show business. "I am a member of the Clan," he told an audience at the Copa in New York. "That's a little group of ordinary guys that get together once a year to take over the entire world."

Sinatra was the king, Vegas' undisputed Most Valuable Player. No headliner brought in more high rollers—the big gamblers who could drop thousands of dollars a night in the casinos. (Sinatra, too, could lose thousands gambling, but the Sands would either extend his credit or just forgive the debt. He was a good investment.) He was the star other Vegas entertainers looked up to, tried to copy, or wanted to hang out with. "If Frank went to a tailor, everyone went to that tailor," said Corinne Entratter. "If Frank drank Jack Daniel's, everybody drank Jack Daniel's." Mia Farrow, who began dating Sinatra in 1965, observed the strange effect he had on people. "I noticed that no matter who was in a room, when Frank entered it, he became the focus," she wrote in her autobiography, *What Falls Away*. "And no one was ever really at ease with him, no matter who they were or how charming he was, because there was something about him that made people uncomfortable. He was absolutely without falseness, without artifice, in a world of pretenders. He had a child's sense of outrage at any perceived unfairness and an inability to compromise. He was tough in his judgments of others, and of himself."

He was thin-skinned and quick-tempered. "With Frank it was like walking on eggshells," said Corinne Entratter. "People would come to me and say, 'Corinne, what mood's Frank in today?' And I'd go, 'Lay low.'" Stories of his bad behavior abounded—waiters he abused for fouling up an order, fans who got a rude brush-off for pestering him, reporters he punched out for writing things he didn't like. Lisa Medford, who worked as a Copa Girl and was dating Sands casino boss Carl Cohen, recalled sitting at a blackjack table with Sinatra one night when a well-dressed woman—"lovely woman, in her late twenties, not a hooker, could have been from Shaker Heights"—rebuffed some of his crude comments and then stormed out of the casino. But not before Sinatra, according to Medford, dropped his gold Dunhill lighter into her purse and then called security to claim that she had stolen it. Sinatra could be generous with friends, modest about his fame, and charming when he wanted to be. "But when he was an asshole," said Medford, "it was in neon."

Jack Entratter, Sinatra's boss at the Sands, was one of the few who could handle him—though some thought it was the other way around.

"Sinatra really had Jack wrapped around his little finger," said Eydie Gormé. "Sinatra in the middle of the casino would pick up a bottle of booze, open the top, and throw it in Jack's face, and Entratter wouldn't do anything about it. This man was tough, but he took a lot of crap from Sinatra. I'll never understand why." Entratter, who had an impressive temper of his own, knew to keep it in check with Frank; let the man blow off steam, he figured, and reason with him later. Once, when Sinatra was in Italy for the filming of *Von Ryan's Express*, his demands got so out of hand that the film's producer made an emergency call to Entratter: get over here fast. Entratter packed his Turnbull & Asser shirts, hopped a plane to Italy, and helped get Frank under control.

Dean Martin needed no such coddling. He was nearly as valuable to the Sands as Sinatra, one of the few stars who came close to him in attracting high rollers. ("Dean Martin is worth his weight in $100 chips—a star who pulls in the big players to the casino," *Variety* noted in July 1960.) But he was as easygoing and laid-back as Sinatra was prickly and high-maintenance. He was affable with friends (everyone was "pally"), polite with fans, more respectful of women. He was the only member of Frank's circle who didn't grovel for his approval, and the only one who could bail out early from his late-night partying. (Dean needed the sleep, so he could get up early and play golf.) But he was remote and inscrutable, and few felt close to him. "He was nice to everyone," said Shirley MacLaine. "He just didn't want nice to go on too long." He had seven children with two different wives, but even they didn't know him well. "The important thing to say about my husband is that I don't understand him," said his second wife, Jeannie, after their divorce in 1973. "He is one of the rare human beings who is not comfortable communicating. He's just not interested."

Sammy, on the other hand, was as inexhaustible offstage as he was on. He loved the Vegas party scene, always surrounding himself with other show people, screening films he had shipped in from Hollywood, then wrapping up the night with breakfast in the Sands Garden Room. "Sammy always had to be with people," said Vera Goulet, who was married to singer Robert. "You needed two months rest after two hours with Sammy." His obsessive partying and showbiz extravagances, along with his white girlfriends—in 1960 he married Swedish actress May Britt—made him controversial in the black community. ("Is Sammy Ashamed He's a Negro?" read a headline in an African American newspaper in the 1950s.) And his fawning relationship with Sinatra, both onstage and off, was unsettling to many. "Over the years I watched Sammy dress like Frank, walk like Frank, smoke like Frank," said Cindy Bitterman, a friend of both. "He wanted to be a little Frank, which I thought was pathetic."

There was, of course, no shortage of people who wanted to be friends with Frank Sinatra. His circle of pals included New York saloon owner Jilly Rizzo, sometime business partner Hank Sanicola, songwriters Jimmy Van Heusen and Sammy Cahn, along with Hollywood friends whom he often cast in his movies, like Richard "Nick" Conte and Buddy Lester. Not to mention a steady stream of girlfriends, a few of them serious (like dancer Juliet Prowse, to whom Sinatra was briefly engaged), along with countless one-night stands. In Las Vegas, performers he liked always got a boost when Frank dropped in to see them—Hank Henry, for instance, a burlesque comic who headlined a show over at the Silver Slipper (Sinatra cast him as the undertaker in Ocean's 11), or Sonny King, Dean Martin's former roommate in New York City, who worked the Sands lounge and had bit roles in two Rat Pack films. But no entertainer benefited more from Frank's favor than a bald-headed insult comic who was causing a nightly ruckus at the Sahara Hotel, Don Rickles.

Sinatra had first seen him at a Murray Franklin's nightclub in

Miami. When Frank sat down at a table, Rickles greeted him with a line heard round the showbiz world: "Make yourself comfortable, Frank. Hit somebody." Luckily Sinatra laughed. Later, when Rickles became a regular in the Sahara lounge, Sinatra would often come in with friends to see him. Rickles's barbs became the talk of the town. To Frank: "I saw you in *The Pride and the Passion*. The cannon was great." To Sammy: "You tell everybody he's your best friend. Then you go backstage and bust all his records." Rickles soon became part of Sinatra's circle, a regular at the Sands steam room, where he got his own robe (with a rhino head on the back—because that's what he looked like) and his own share of abuse. Once, as a gag, the gang stripped off his towel and pushed him out into the pool area, in front of all the guests, stark naked. Good times.

The Rat Pack's triumph in the early 1960s was also a triumph of the Great American Songbook—the pop standards of Cole Porter, Richard Rodgers, Harold Arlen, and others that were the core repertoire for nearly all the top nightclub singers of the era. These popular vocalists formed a bulwark against the advancing threat from another kind of music that was dominating the radio airwaves and grabbing the attention of the younger generation: rock 'n' roll.

Sinatra hated rock 'n' roll. As a young singer back in the forties he had made the bobby-soxers swoon, but the screaming frenzy that greeted Elvis Presley in the mid-1950s was of a different order. Frank couldn't understand it. He would sit alone in his den, his valet George Jacobs recalled, listening over and over to Elvis songs like "Don't Be Cruel" and "All Shook Up," "trying to figure out just what the hell this new stuff was." He would joke to friends about Elvis, "If I want a nigger,

I'll get a *real* nigger." (This, too, according to Jacobs, who was black.) In a 1957 article for a French magazine, Sinatra unleashed a scathing attack on the whole genre, denouncing rock 'n' roll as "the most brutal, ugly, degenerate, vicious form of expression it has been my displeasure to hear.... It fosters almost totally negative and destructive reactions in young people. It smells phony and false. It is sung, played, and written for the most part by cretinous goons and by means of its almost imbecilic reiterations and sly, lewd—in plain fact—dirty lyrics, it manages to be the martial music of every sideburned delinquent on the face of the earth."

Elvis, the sideburned delinquent who was Sinatra's chief target, was considerably more temperate in response. "I admire the man," he said when asked about Sinatra's remarks at a press conference in Los Angeles. "He has a right to say what he wants to say. He is a great success and a fine actor, but I don't think he should have said it. He is mistaken about this. This is a trend, just the same as he faced when he started years ago. I consider it the greatest in music."

Elvis was in Germany when the Rat Pack took Vegas by storm in early 1960. But he was due to be discharged from the Army in March, and the nation was already gearing up for the most heralded homecoming in show-business history. Few would have guessed that the host for that homecoming—Elvis's first appearance on national TV after his return from the Army—would be, of all people, the man who had bad-mouthed his music so viciously three years earlier: Frank Sinatra.

Television was the one medium Sinatra could never conquer. He starred in a CBS variety series in the early 1950s, but it lasted only two seasons. He landed another series on ABC during the 1957–58 season, but that one, too, was canceled because of low ratings. He did four specials for ABC, sponsored by Timex, in the 1959–60 season, but they were not exactly setting the world on fire. Then, in the fall of 1959,

Sinatra negotiated with Colonel Tom Parker to pay Elvis $125,000 (more than Sinatra himself was getting) to make a guest appearance on Frank's last ABC special of the season. "After all," Sinatra rationalized to the press, "the kid's been away two years, and I get the feeling he really believes in what he's doing." The kid's comeback also promised to be a ratings bonanza.

Frank Sinatra's Welcome Home Party for Elvis Presley was taped in Miami in March 1960, just after Sinatra finished up his engagement at the Fontainebleau. Sinatra packed the show with old friends, including three Rat Packers—Sammy Davis Jr., Joey Bishop, and Peter Lawford—as well as his nineteen-year-old daughter, Nancy, who was engaged to marry her own rock 'n' roll star, Tommy Sands. It may have been Elvis's homecoming, but Sinatra was going to make sure everyone knew who was still head of the household.

The special, which aired on ABC in early May, is a fascinating glimpse of the culture clash between two generations of American popular music. Sinatra opens the show with Sammy Cahn's "It's Nice to Go Traveling," with special lyrics for the occasion, and Elvis comes out in full-dress Army uniform to intone the final lyric: "But it's so, so nice to come home." Elvis then retreats for most of the hour, as Sinatra presents a look back at what Elvis missed in the two years he was away. What he missed, it turns out, was a Sinatra hit single (Frank sings "Witchcraft"), the movie *Porgy and Bess* (Sammy performs his big number from the film, "There's a Boat That's Leavin' Soon for New York"), and the 1959 Academy Awards (Sammy does some impressions, while Frank and Joey heckle him, Rat Pack–style, from the sidelines).

Elvis returns for a mere eight minutes near the end of the show. Now dressed in a tuxedo, hair greased up and standing at attention high on his head, he sings two numbers from his new album: the ballad "Fame and Fortune" and the more rocking "Stuck on You." He is in good form, a little tense at first, then loosening up with some vintage head- and hip-shaking that draws screams from an audience stocked with teenage girls. "I'm glad to see the Army hasn't changed you," says Sinatra, not very convincingly, as he greets Elvis after the number. "First time I ever heard a woman screaming at a male singer," offers Bishop, in a painfully obvious setup for Sinatra—who responds with a mock-annoyed expression, hands on hips, "Don't you remember *me* there, Charlie?"

Bishop then supplies the lead-in for the show's big number: "Mr. Presley, would you think it presumptuous of Frank to join you in a duet?" "I would consider it quite an honor," Elvis replies, and they launch into a two-song medley: Frank doing a swinging version of "Love Me Tender," and Elvis taking a crack at Sinatra's "Witchcraft," the two singers alternating verses before harmonizing together prettily on the last couple of bars of "Love Me Tender." Frank comes off better than Elvis; it is clearly Sinatra's turf, and Elvis never really seems comfortable. But it was a win for both: the show drew a phenomenal 67 percent of the viewing audience, the highest rating ever for a Frank Sinatra show, and proof that Elvis's two-year absence had not dimmed his enormous drawing power.

Sinatra and Elvis had relatively little contact after that and were never close. But Elvis had strong ties to two other members of the Rat Pack. He and Sammy had gotten to know each other in Hollywood before Elvis went into the Army; they ran around with the same crowd of young actors and were even once mentioned for the costarring roles in Stanley Kramer's *The Defiant Ones*, a racial allegory about black and white convicts chained together after a prison escape. (Kramer eventually made a wiser choice and cast Sidney Poitier and Tony Curtis.) Elvis also had much admiration for Dean Martin. "People call me the king of rock," he told Martin's daughter Deana, when he met her on the

Paramount lot. "But your dad is the king of cool." One can see the influence—in their sultry, chesty baritones, as well as in Elvis's song choices after he came out of the Army, which included the Italian-flavored love song "It's Now or Never," an anglicized version of "O Sole Mio."

The other thing Elvis shared with the Rat Pack was a love of Vegas partying. After returning from the Army, Elvis resumed his regular visits to Las Vegas, always with a retinue of friends and plenty of women. "It was a party like you wouldn't believe," said Joe Esposito, a former Army buddy from Chicago who became part of his entourage. "Go to a different show every night, then pick up a bunch of women afterwards, go party the next night. . . . We'd stay there and never sleep, we were all taking pills just so we could keep up with each other." In June 1960, on a weekend in Vegas after finishing work on his first post-Army movie, *G.I. Blues*, Elvis and his entourage were such a frequent sight along the Strip, in their black mohair suits and sunglasses, that a local columnist dubbed them the "Memphis mafia." The name stuck: a country-fried, rockabilly version of the Rat Pack.

But Elvis came back from the Army a changed, much diluted performer. After a benefit concert in Hawaii in March 1961, he withdrew from live performing, either in concerts or on television, for nearly the entire decade. Instead, he churned out movies—which quickly degenerated into sappy, formulaic drivel. His music, too, became slicker and more disposable—a few chart-toppers early in the decade, like "Good Luck Charm" and "Return to Sender," followed by a string of mostly forgettable movie songs.

It wasn't just Elvis. After upending the music world in the mid-1950s, many of the pioneers of rock 'n' roll were, by the early sixties, sidelined or out of the picture. Chuck Berry spent a year and a half in prison; Little Richard turned to religion; Buddy Holly was killed in a 1959 plane crash. In their place were a gaggle of clean-cut, and largely white, teen idols—singers like Frankie Avalon, Bobby Darin, Bobby Rydell, and Paul Anka—who were more apt to see the Rat Pack as role models, not rivals. "As kids we looked at them and said, 'We wanna be like those guys,'" said Anka, the Canadian-born singer-songwriter of hits like "Lonely Boy" and "Put Your Head on My Shoulder." "We knew they were the coolest, suavest cats on the planet." And for a little while longer, they were.

The troubles began with hubris. After they finished filming *Sergeants 3* in the summer of 1961, Sinatra and his pals descended on Eddie Fisher's opening at the Cocoanut Grove in Los Angeles. With dozens of celebrities in the audience, eager to support Eddie after his wife, Elizabeth Taylor's hospitalization for a near-fatal bout of pneumonia, Frank and Dean started heckling him from the audience, then barged onstage, joined by Joey and Sammy. "They took over," the AP reported, "doing imitations, limericks, racial jokes and songs—while Fisher sat on the bandstand, somewhat forlornly." For the first time, the Rat Pack got bad reviews. Milton Berle called their antics "a disgusting display of ego." Hedda Hopper was appalled: "Frank and his henchmen took over and ruined Eddie's performance."

Then came a major change in the club's membership roll.

Peter Lawford always seemed the most superfluous member of the Rat Pack. Unlike Frank or Sammy or Dean (or even Joey), he had no particular talent as a nightclub performer. His importance to the group, as everyone knew, was his connection to the glamorous Kennedys. But once JFK took office—and his younger brother Bobby, the newly appointed attorney general, launched a major investigation of organized crime—the White House began to put some distance between the president and Sinatra. It wasn't just that Sinatra's ties to Mafia figures were potentially embarrassing. The Kennedys learned (from FBI director J. Edgar Hoover) that JFK and mob boss Sam Giancana were sharing a girlfriend, an LA beauty named Judith Campbell—who, in fact, had been introduced to Kennedy in Las Vegas by Frank Sinatra.

Sinatra noticed the growing chill in his relations with the Kennedys. Still, when JFK scheduled his first trip to the West Coast as president, in March 1962, his itinerary included a one-night stay at Sinatra's house in Palm Springs. Sinatra, who had hosted Kennedy there once before, in 1959, was excited about the visit and spent weeks getting the place ready, expanding a guest bungalow for the Secret Service and even adding a heliport. But a few days before the trip, Kennedy's advisers convinced him that staying with Sinatra would be bad optics, and the visit was abruptly canceled. Kennedy would stay with Bing Crosby—a Republican, no less—instead.

Lawford was assigned to break the bad news to Sinatra. It was not a pleasant phone call. Lawford tried to blame the change of plans on security concerns, but Sinatra knew better. First he phoned Bobby Kennedy and tried to get the visit reinstated. When that failed, Sinatra called Lawford back and exploded. "Frank was livid," Lawford would recall. "He called Bobby every name in the book and then rang me up and reamed me out again. He was quite unreasonable, irrational really." George Jacobs recalled that Sinatra, after hanging up the phone, went on "the most violent rampage I had seen," smashing his collection of Kennedy photos, ripping up Lawford's clothes, and trying (but failing) to tear the KENNEDY SLEPT HERE sign from the guest bedroom. It was hardly Lawford's fault, but the messenger took the blame. Sinatra cut him off completely.

Bishop, an on-again, off-again participant in the Rat Pack

get-togethers, was also subject to Sinatra's whims. Joey was cast in the third Rat Pack movie, *Robin and the 7 Hoods*, scheduled to begin filming in the fall of 1963, but after some sort of fight with Sinatra was dumped from the cast, and Sinatra didn't talk to him for a year. For the rest of its heyday, the Rat Pack essentially boiled down to its three principals—Sinatra, Martin, and Davis. In November 1962 they were back together for a weeklong engagement at the Villa Venice, a new hotel and gambling club in the Chicago suburbs, owned by Sam Giancana. Then, for the first time since the original Summit shows, they brought the act back to Las Vegas, appearing at the Sands in January 1963, and again in September for an engagement advertised, with unnecessary coyness, as "Dean Martin. Maybe Frank. Maybe Sammy."

Several nights of the September engagement were recorded, for an album that was, once again, shelved and released only after Sinatra's death. *The Rat Pack Live at the Sands* is the best account we have of their mature act, which had acquired somewhat more polish and discipline since the 1960 Summit free-for-all. Martin opens the show with his by now well-honed drunk routine ("How long I been on?" he says, just after woozily taking the stage), with a little singing interspersed. Sinatra follows with a half dozen numbers of his own, before Martin returns with a drink cart and some obviously scripted repartee. (Sinatra: "I want to talk to you about your drinking." Martin: "What happened, did I miss a round?") Sammy's role, once again, seems to be primarily to take abuse from the other two. But the gags at least have a little more structure and self-awareness. When Sammy wants to do another song, Dean and Frank tell him no—"It's over, you've had it." Sammy suddenly gets indignant: "I'm a little sick and tired of being the one that's always picked on," he cries. "I like this audience, I like this room, and I'm going to stay out here until I'm good and ready!" After the applause dies down, Frank says, "Are you ready?" Sammy, meekly: "Yeah, Frank."

There are still plenty of juvenile groaners and painfully racist wise-cracks. (Frank: "Better keep smilin', Sam, so everybody knows where you are.") But musically, the album is first-rate. Sinatra is solidly on his game with old reliables like "I Only Have Eyes for You" and new additions like "Call Me Irresponsible." Martin displays his seductive baritone to good effect in a medley of Italian love songs—"Via Veneto," "Volare," and "An Evening in Roma." Sammy ignores the heckling long enough to show off some nifty musical impressions (no one did a bet-ter Nat King Cole). The highlight of the show, however, is Sinatra and Martin's dueting on two songs from *Guys and Dolls*: the title number and "The Oldest Established (Permanent Floating Crap Game in New York)." They are two such different singers—one puts you on edge, the other nearly puts you to sleep—that it's startling to hear how simpatico they are on Frank Loesser's vibrant, street-smart show tunes. It's the ideal showcase for a unique musical partnership.

Sinatra had some major distractions during that September 1963 engagement, however. He was trying to fend off a state investigation into the Cal-Neva Lodge, the Lake Tahoe resort in which he had ac-quired a 50 percent ownership stake the year before. The hotel was drawing scrutiny for a visit that Sam Giancana, a shadow owner of the resort, had made there in July, along with his girlfriend, singer Phyllis McGuire. Giancana's presence at Cal-Neva was a no-no, since his name was listed in the notorious Black Book of mob-connected figures who were not allowed to set foot in a Nevada casino. Giancana made the visit even harder to ignore when he got into a late-night brawl with McGuire's road manager—with Sinatra himself present.

Sinatra soon got a phone call from Ed Olsen, chairman of the Ne-vada Gaming Control Board, asking him to explain Giancana's presence at the hotel. Sinatra tried to dodge the question and claimed to know nothing about the brawl. But the investigation continued, and when it leaked to the press, Sinatra called Olsen back and invited him for an off-the-record conversation over dinner at Cal-Neva. Olsen declined, saying it wouldn't be appropriate in the midst of an investigation. That set off Sinatra's always volatile temper.

"I'm never coming to see you again," he snapped, in a conversation recorded on tape.

"If I want to see you, I will send a subpoena," said Olsen.

"You just try and find me. And if you do, you can look for a big, fat, fucking surprise. . . . Don't fuck with me."

"Are you threatening me?"

"No, just don't fuck with me, and you can tell that to your fucking board and that fucking commission too!"

On September 11, 1963, Olsen formally charged Sinatra with violating Gaming Control Board rules by associating with Giancana at Cal-Neva and gave him two weeks to respond or else have his gambling license revoked. The news was a bombshell in Las Vegas. Some sprang to Sinatra's defense, including *Las Vegas Sun* editor Hank Greenspun, who argued in a front-page column that revoking Sinatra's license would be "a rotten, horrible, mean, and cheap way to repay this man for all the good he has brought this state." Even President Kennedy, in Las Vegas to give a speech, tried to put in a word for his friend with Governor Grant Sawyer: "Aren't you people being a little hard on Frank out here?" But rather than fight the charges, Sinatra announced in October that he would sell his stake in the hotel. He spun it as a voluntary business decision, but it was a public humiliation for Sinatra—and a revealing peek, for all the world, into the darker side of Vegas' most celebrated star.

The incident had a startling coda. A few months after the contretemps, Olsen ran into Sammy Davis Jr. at the Sands Hotel. When Sammy approached, Olsen braced for a tense encounter with Sinatra's famous friend. But the response was unexpected. "That little son of a bitch," Sammy said, according to Olsen. "He's needed this for years. I've been working with him for sixteen years, and nobody's ever had the guts to stand up to him."

A month later the Rat Pack suffered a much different and more cataclysmic blow. Sinatra and crew were on the Warner Bros. lot, shooting a scene from *Robin and the 7 Hoods*, on Friday morning, November 22, 1963, when the awful news came in from Dallas: President Kennedy had been shot and killed by Lee Harvey Oswald. Work stopped for half an hour, then resumed for the rest of the day. After it was finished, Sinatra retreated to Palm Springs, where he spent the weekend watching TV coverage of the assassination, devastated. His relations with the Kennedys had been deteriorating for a couple of years, but now the entire Camelot connection, so much a part of the Rat Pack mystique, was permanently shattered.

Sinatra didn't even get a chance to attend the funeral. "It just wasn't possible to invite him," said Peter Lawford. "He'd already been too much of an embarrassment to the family."

Sinatra's annus horribilis continued a couple of weeks later, when his son, Frank Jr.—who was trying to launch his own career as a singer, accompanied by Tommy Dorsey's band—was kidnapped in Lake Tahoe. In the tense two days that followed, the kidnappers (a trio of fairly bumbling amateurs) demanded a ransom of just $240,000, and Sinatra agreed to pay it. The episode had a happy ending, with Frank Jr. released unharmed, the money recovered, and the kidnappers arrested. Sinatra appeared at the Sands' eleventh anniversary celebration the following weekend and got a standing ovation. But even the sympathy generated by the narrowly averted family tragedy was tempered. Rumors circulated that the kidnapping was merely a publicity stunt to help Frank Jr.'s career (which, in fact, was the kidnappers' defense at their trial, where they were convicted and sentenced to prison). Though surely untrue, it was a testament to Sinatra's dodgy reputation that some were ready to believe it.

By 1964 the Rat Pack was largely a spent force. Kennedy was gone, and the Beatles had arrived—and with them the first stirrings of a cultural revolution that would make the tuxedo-clad, Scotch-drinking Rat Packers look dated and last generation. There would still be a couple of get-togethers. In June 1965, Sinatra, Martin, and Davis convened for one night at the Kiel Opera House in St. Louis, a benefit performance for Dismas House, a halfway house for released convicts. Joey Bishop was supposed to be there, too, but he hurt his back, and Johnny Carson replaced him. (Carson quipped that Joey had "slipped a disk backing out of Frank's presence." Bishop resented the joke.) The following year, Joey was back for a last hurrah with Frank and Dean at the Sands, billed as Dean Martin and His Friends. (Minimum tab: $12.50, beating the previous Vegas record of $10, set by Sinatra alone.) The show began with Bishop and Sinatra talking over offstage microphones, wondering where Dean was. Sinatra opened the show in his place, before Martin wandered out, drink in hand: "I heard Dean Martin being announced. You know how crazy I am about him."

The Rat Packers were managing quite nicely on their own. Martin recorded a single, "Everybody Loves Somebody Sometime," in 1964 that knocked the Beatles' "A Hard Day's Night" out of the No. 1 spot, and in September 1965 he launched an NBC variety show that would run for nine seasons. His Vegas appearances, meanwhile, became as much comedy act as music showcase. He had a habit of lazily breaking off his songs before finishing them (if you want to hear the whole thing,

he'd tell the audience, "buy my albums") and filled his act instead with
drinking gags, jokes about his wife and family, and sheer Vegas foolish-
ness. ("Last night a girl was banging on my door for forty-five minutes.
But I wouldn't let her out.") His time with Jerry Lewis had not been
spent in vain.

Sammy Davis took a two-year break from Las Vegas in 1964 to star
in the Broadway musical *Golden Boy*. He returned to the Sands in May
1966 with a splashy show divided into two forty-minute acts, separated
by Lola Falana. His dynamic stage presence is nicely captured in a live
album he recorded at the Sands that year, *Sammy Davis Jr./That's All*.
His crisp, brassy voice never had the subtlety of Sinatra's, but he could
put across a Broadway showstopper like "What Kind of Fool Am I?" or
"As Long as He Needs Me" and swing with gusto on an old rouser like
"Birth of the Blues," the number that often closed the Rat Pack shows.
Without Frank or Dean lording over him, Sammy came into his own
as a Vegas powerhouse.

After suffering through the private and public traumas of 1963,
Sinatra also made an impressive career rebound. He began to update
his repertoire with reflective, late-career numbers like "It Was a Very
Good Year" and "That's Life." His fiftieth birthday year, 1965, brought
a raft of tributes, magazine covers, and TV specials. Then, in January
1966, he recorded a live album that would serve as a capstone to his
classic Vegas period—*Sinatra at the Sands*, accompanied by Count
Basie and his orchestra, conducted by up-and-coming arranger Quincy
Jones.

Sinatra at the Sands is justly revered by Sinatra scholars and fans.
Pop-music critic Will Friedwald calls it "one of those miraculous moments in American music that explain why so many of us became Sinatra fans to begin with." Basie and his swinging outfit (who had worked
with Sinatra once before at the Sands, in November 1964) obviously

inspired and invigorated Sinatra. "Now this man here," Frank says at the outset, in his *Amos 'n' Andy* cadences, "is gonna take me by the hand, and he gonna lead me down the right path to righteousness, and all that other mother jazz—in the right tempo!" The tempos are always right, as Basie brings out Sinatra's muscular, hard-charging best on such numbers as "You Make Me Feel So Young," "I've Got You under My Skin," and (the song from *Robin and the 7 Hoods* that would become a staple of his nightclub act) "My Kind of Town." The album is marred a bit by Sinatra's self-indulgent patter, overfilled with drinking anecdotes, ethnic jokes, and tough-guy attitude. Some alternate takes of the session (released on the 2006 boxed set *Sinatra: Vegas*) reveal even more of the edge and ego that were starting to afflict his Vegas performances. "When I on dis stage, I da boss," he says, after snapping at a couple of audience members who have spoken out of turn.

It was, perhaps, a foreshadowing of things to come. A year and a half later, Sinatra would have a blowup at the Sands that would bring an end to his long relationship with the hotel, force the Rat Pack to go their separate ways, and put a final period on the most celebrated buddy act in Vegas history.

It was a great ride—the "Mount Rushmore of men having fun," as critic James Wolcott put it. To audiences looking for an escape from the straitlaced 1950s, the Rat Pack represented a kind of bent fantasy of what the rich and famous could do when there were no restraints—smoke, drink, make tasteless jokes, get beautiful women. And Vegas was the fantasyland where all that could take place, even for people who weren't rich and famous. "Their desert hijinks grabbed the imagination of the world, gave Las Vegas more romantic cachet than perhaps it ever deserved," wrote Bill Zehme in *The Way You Wear Your Hat: Frank Sinatra and the Lost Art of Livin'*. "They brought a better class of sin to Sin City."

But they needed to leave the stage before a new kind of Vegas entertainment could emerge. Frank Sinatra and Elvis Presley represented two opposite poles in American popular music: the suave, largely urban, jazz-influenced tradition that dominated radio, recordings, and nightclubs for decades, and the unruly, largely rural, blues-and-country-influenced music that would first catch on in the mid-1950s and virtually take over in the next decade. That seismic shift, in music as well as in the rest of the culture, was mirrored in the changes that would come to the Las Vegas Strip. In a sense, it took the Rat Pack's breakup and Sinatra's flameout to make Las Vegas safe for Elvis Presley.

But first, there was a lot of livin' to do.

Four

THE ENTERTAINMENT CAPITAL

The Rat Pack show at the Sands Hotel was just one of several events that made 1960 a pivotal year in Las Vegas' emergence as the nation's live-entertainment capital. In August 1960, TWA inaugurated nonstop flights from Chicago to Las Vegas—the beginning of transcontinental jet service that would make Vegas much more accessible to visitors from the East Coast and give a fresh boost to tourist traffic into the desert city. In June, El Rancho Vegas, the oldest hotel on the Las Vegas Strip, was destroyed in a fire, a disaster that marked a symbolic end to the city's formative early years and the dawn of a new era. The Chez Paree in Chicago, one of the country's most celebrated nightclubs, closed its doors in 1960—a distant event with no direct impact on Vegas, but another milestone in the steady demise of nightclub entertainment, leaving Las Vegas as one of its last remaining outposts.

Television was, meanwhile, strengthening its hold on the American public. In 1952, when the Sands and Sahara hotels opened, 34 percent of US households had a television set. By 1960 over 87 percent did. Though competition from television was a big reason why nightclubs were losing their audience, the new medium was a net plus for Las Vegas, since it created a bigger pool of potential stars to help fill the showrooms, from veteran prime-time favorites like Milton Berle and Red Skelton, to relatively new, TV-created personalities like Johnny Carson.

As Las Vegas moved into the 1960s, its long tradition of racial segregation was starting to break down as well. Through the 1940s and '50s, African Americans were not welcome to stay at the major Strip hotels, or to work there in any but the lowest-level jobs. There were no black chorus girls or black dealers in the casinos. African American entertainers at the Strip hotels were no longer forced to stay in segregated housing across town (the Sands in 1955 became the first resort to allow its black performers to stay at the hotel while they were appearing there), but even they still faced barriers.

Ruth Gillis, a showgirl-turned-singer from Chicago, found that out when she was appearing in the Sands lounge in the late 1950s, alternating sets with jazz singer Ella Fitzgerald. The two got friendly, and one day Ella asked Ruth if she would take her to see Pearl Bailey, who was headlining at the Flamingo. Ruth called up a friend at the hotel, who got them comp seats and told her to come in through the front door. Gillis was puzzled at the remark, but after they saw the show—from great seats, where they were introduced by Bailey from the stage—she understood why.

"We left the showroom, walked back out through the front door," Gillis recalled. "Ella turned to me and said, 'I'm your friend for life.' I asked her why. She said, 'You took me through the front door.' I hadn't realized until then that black people were not allowed to enter through the front door."

That benighted era ended, at least officially, on March 26, 1960, when the City of Las Vegas, following threats of protests by the local NAACP chapter, agreed to outlaw segregation in all public places. Though the Strip hotels were outside the city limits and thus not in its jurisdiction, they voluntarily agreed to abide by the agreement. Unequal treatment of racial minorities would linger through the 1960s, until a 1971 consent agreement finally outlawed discrimination in accommodations and hiring. Yet by 1960 Las Vegas was at least beginning to move beyond its Jim Crow past.

Five big hotels on the east side of the Strip were the primary competitors for big-name talent in the early 1960s. First among equals was the Sands, where Jack Entratter assembled the most impressive lineup of stars on the Strip: not just the Rat Pack, but also Jerry Lewis, Danny Thomas, Red Skelton, Nat King Cole, and the husband-wife singing duo of Steve Lawrence and Eydie Gormé. The Sahara, the first hotel on the Strip heading south from downtown, was probably its closest competitor, known especially for top comedians like George Burns, Victor Borge, Buddy Hackett, Bob Newhart, and the bullet-headed insult machine who ruled over the Casbar Lounge, Don Rickles.

The Desert Inn was something of the grande dame of the Strip, known for its high rollers and a classy lineup of old-school stars such as Jimmy Durante, Danny Kaye, and Eddie Fisher. The elegant, nine-story Riviera was home to Liberace, Debbie Reynolds, and, for years, lounge-show wild man Shecky Greene. The Flamingo no longer enjoyed the preeminence it had in the old Bugsy Siegel days, but was still a formidable competitor, booking top acts ranging from Bobby Darin to Ethel Merman, the Broadway star who made her one Vegas appearance there in 1962.

Other Strip hotels, like the Dunes, Thunderbird, and Tropicana, also booked major stars, but they were more apt to counterprogram with splashy production shows, like the *Lido de Paris* and *Folies Bergere*, or the occasional Broadway musical, like *Flower Drum Song*, the Rodgers and Hammerstein show that had a successful ten-month run at the Thunderbird in 1961. The hotels downtown were still focused primarily on gambling, but they were beginning to book entertainers, too, among them a teenage singer named Wayne Newton, who debuted with his brother, Jerry, in the Fremont Lounge in 1959.

Despite the intense competition, salaries for top stars were relatively stable in the early sixties. The Riviera had paid Liberace a record $50,000 a week to open the hotel in 1955, and Judy Garland surpassed him when she got $55,000 from the Sahara a year later. But for the next several years, the salary inflation abated, mostly topping out at $25,000 to $30,000 a week. Whether due to collusion or just good business sense, bidding up salaries "is now virtually unknown in Las Vegas," the Sahara Hotel's Stan Irwin told *Variety* in 1961. The Sands' Entratter even bragged that he was able to pay *less* for top stars because they preferred to remain loyal to him and his hotel.

Still, Vegas was the big-money payday for nightclub entertainers. Along with top salaries, they could expect luxury accommodations, lavish perks, and usually a little extra under the table—easy to do at the mob-run hotels, where skimming money from the casino take was standard operating procedure. "Everybody had two salaries," said George Schlatter, who booked acts for the New Frontier. "Your official salary, and a little salad on the side."

Nearly everybody wanted to play Vegas in those years. For an entertainer on the rise, it was a high-profile gig that brought you to the attention of agents and producers, which in turn could lead to TV guest appearances, concert tours, even movie and Broadway roles. "I think the fact that you were playing Vegas put you at a certain level," said Bob Newhart. "There was a pecking order, and playing Vegas was part of the pecking order." For a touring performer, moreover, Vegas was a welcome chance to get off the road and settle down in one place for a while. "For four weeks you had a normal life," said Newhart, "or as normal a life as Vegas gets. It was like your second home."

Most important, Vegas was a place to *work*—to hone your craft in front of live audiences, night after night, week after week. "You really found out who you were as an entertainer," said Paul Anka. "What you were capable of doing, how to get up there and feel comfortable, to really work an audience and all that goes with it. Because you're only going to be as good as the mileage."

For a singer, Vegas offered the best of everything: top facilities, fine acoustics, first-class musicians. Each hotel had a house orchestra, usually sixteen or eighteen pieces, often augmented by the singer's own conductor or arranger and sometimes extra players. "There isn't any deal that you can't have if you're a performer to make sure the job is done right," said Tony Bennett. "The sound, the carpenters, the lights, the orchestras—there's not one bad organization on the Strip."

Bennett knew practically all of them. He may well hold the record for headlining in more hotels than anyone else in Vegas history. Discovered in 1950 by Bob Hope, who took him on his first national tour, Bennett began his Vegas career at El Rancho Vegas in the early fifties and later played the Dunes, the Sahara, the Sands, the Riviera, and eventually Caesars Palace, which gave him a "contract for life" in 1969. He recorded an album in Las Vegas, *Live from the Sahara*, in 1964, and his signature hit, "I Left My Heart in San Francisco," was covered by dozens of Vegas singers in the sixties. He was one of the few singers of the era who managed to keep his jazz credibility while also turning out popular hits, and a rare Italian American vocalist who seemed relatively free of Frank Sinatra's influence—Sinatra without the angst, or the attitude.

Vic Damone, on the other hand, openly acknowledged his debt to Sinatra. He grew up in Brooklyn trying to imitate Sinatra, filled in for him once on radio's *Your Hit Parade*, and years later became part of Sinatra's steam-room cabal at the Sands (nicknamed Little Dago, to distinguish him from Big Dago, Dean Martin). Damone had a smooth, appealing baritone and good taste in accompanists. His first music director was future pop songwriter Burt Bacharach. Later, after Bacharach left to work with Marlene Dietrich, Damone replaced him with a young pianist named John Williams—years before he became one of the top movie composers in Hollywood.

Sinatra once said Damone had "the best pipes in the business." But he never had Sinatra's stage charisma or emotional conviction, and Vegas could give only so much gas to a career that had trouble surviving rock 'n' roll. Damone turned down the role of Johnny Fontaine, the Sinatra-like singer in *The Godfather* (he thought the part was too small to justify the long break it would have meant in his touring), and had to declare bankruptcy after his savings were cleaned out by two shady investors he had enlisted to help launch his own record label. But Vegas came to the rescue: Damone signed a long-term contract with the Frontier Hotel, guaranteeing him $30,000 a week to appear in the lounge for sixteen weeks a year—a steady gig that helped save his career.

The lounges were an increasingly important venue for singers in the 1960s. After the success of acts like the Mary Kaye Trio and Louis Prima and Keely Smith, the hotels began to see the lounges as traffic drivers. Patrons could come and go as they pleased, which kept the crowds circulating in and out of the casinos. And with shows scheduled continuously through the night, the showroom stars would often stop in after their own sets were finished, thus bringing more attention and buzz to the lounges.

"The cocktail lounges no longer take second place to the major rooms as far as b.o. [box office] is concerned," *Variety* reported in 1965. "In many cases they have become the major operation." Several hotels enlarged their lounges and gave them new names to reflect their enhanced status. The Flamingo's lounge became the Driftwood Room and booked top jazz artists like Sarah Vaughan, Billy Eckstine, and Lionel Hampton. The Tropicana Hotel brought in Maynard Sloate, the owner of a jazz club in LA, to take over its five-hundred-seat lounge, which he renamed the Blue Room and filled with such jazz and big-band luminaries as Louis Armstrong, Woody Herman, Benny Goodman, and George Shearing.

The Vegas lounges were a launching pad for some, a full-time home for others. One of the most durable lounge performers in Vegas was Sonny King, a thick-necked former boxer from Brooklyn, who once roomed with Dean Martin, and for years appeared in Jimmy Durante's stage shows as his singing "junior partner." King spent thirteen years in the Sands lounge, where Sinatra and the Rat Pack would often come in to heckle him. He was a schmaltzy, old-style performer, who would flash his cuffs like Jolson and dish out the sentiment with songs like "You're Nobody Till Somebody Loves You." "He could sing 'My Way' in a way that made you forget Sinatra; it was gut-wrenching," said Dennis Klein, who saw King often while writing for Vegas comedians in the sixties. "He captivated a room."

Buddy Greco was another singer who flourished in Vegas lounges, but who also graduated to a substantial TV and recording career. Born in Philadelphia, Greco spent four years as a pianist with Benny Goodman's orchestra and had a jazzy, easygoing vocal style that he parlayed, most memorably, into a hit 1960 recording of "The Lady Is a Tramp."

But his supercool, finger-snapping image became a prototype for the kind of lounge-lizard slickness parodied by Bill Murray on *Saturday Night Live*—and the model, reputedly, for Jerry Lewis's smarmy Buddy Love character in *The Nutty Professor*. (Greco was a golfing buddy of Jerry's at the time and claimed that Lewis wrote the part for him, before deciding to play it himself.)

Virtually every major popular singer of the era played Vegas during the sixties: jazz singers like Peggy Lee and Mel Tormé; 1950s hit-makers like Patti Page and Kay Starr; easy-listening favorites like Andy Williams and Johnny Mathis; the romantic belter Robert Goulet, who segued from Broadway's *Camelot* to Vegas showrooms, making his hit song from that show, "If Ever I Would Leave You," his ubiquitous closing number; the husband-wife team of Steve Lawrence and Eydie Gormé, who got married at El Rancho Vegas in 1957 and became part of Jack Entratter's powerhouse stable at the Sands.

Audiences got to know the performers up close and personal, and some of them brought their offstage soap operas with them. Judy Garland played Vegas often during the fifties and sixties, in between her bouts with drugs, alcohol, and marital problems. She walked out of an engagement at the Flamingo Hotel on New Year's Eve 1957 when she couldn't handle the rowdy crowd. She appeared at the Sahara in 1962, but was so nervous that Stan Irwin, the hotel's entertainment director, would put her in a hypnotic trance (a skill he had learned in his days as a comedian) to calm her down before each night's show. Garland got standing ovations and did such strong business that her four-week engagement was extended by two weeks—just one show a night at two thirty in the morning, to accommodate her insomniac schedule.

Yet when Garland returned to the Sahara in 1965, she was so shaky that spotters were stationed on either side of the catwalk on which she entered, to make sure she didn't fall off. "There are times when her voice assumes somewhat of a brittle quality that is not reminiscent of the old Garland voice, but this is comparatively inconsequential," *Variety's* reviewer observed diplomatically. "She is the Crown Princess of Song, and there is hardly anything that she can do wrong." Her last Vegas engagement, at Caesars Palace in December 1967, was even more fraught. Before one show, she learned of the death of Bert Lahr, the Cowardly Lion from *The Wizard of Oz*, and refused to go on. Another night she caught a glimpse of her ex-husband Sid Luft in the wings (she had banned him from the premises) and lashed out onstage at her bosses: "Ladies and gentlemen, I need help. I am working for two people who are worse than Goebbels and Göring." *Variety* called her show a "curiously unsettling experience," but still made allowances: "Whether in voice or not, there is always a supercharged authority present in sometime awkward, often disturbing, yet never dull or lackadaisical delivery of any song, ballad or uptempo." A year and a half later she was dead of a drug overdose.

Eddie Fisher was another Vegas star whose offstage antics seemed to shadow his performances. The Philadelphia-born singer, the son of Russian Jewish immigrants, began turning out hits like "I'm Walking behind You" and "Oh! My Papa" in the early fifties, displaying a rich, romantic tenor that made teenage girls swoon the way Sinatra had a decade earlier. In Vegas Fisher would typically open his show by strolling down the aisle from the rear and canoodling with women in the crowd. But it was his own complicated love life—he married Hollywood sweetheart Debbie Reynolds, left her for Elizabeth Taylor, only to have Liz dump him for Richard Burton—that seemed to follow him around onstage.

When Fisher played the Tropicana in 1957, Debbie surprised him one night by donning a headdress and gold-lamé top and joining the line of chorus girls. She thought it was a hoot; Eddie was furious with her for upstaging him—another fight in a marriage that was hitting the rocks. Two years later, after their split, he was back at the Tropicana, serenading Liz Taylor at a front-row table with songs like "Tonight" and "Makin' Whoopee." They got married in Las Vegas on the last day of his engagement. (When Eddie discovered he had no cash for the license, he tried to pay with casino chips.) A couple of years later, after Taylor and Burton's much-publicized affair on the set of *Cleopatra*, Fisher was back at the Desert Inn making jokes about it. "They started that *Cleopatra* picture so long ago they could have used the original cast," he said. "And I wish they had."

Fisher's offstage troubles went beyond his messy love life; he was also a prolific gambler, drinker, and, in later years, coke and meth addict. Yet he continued to be one of Vegas' top-earning stars, and Caesars Palace signed him to a three-year contract in 1966. By the end of the sixties, however, he was forgetting song lyrics and playing to half-empty houses. Caesars dumped him in 1969, and he declared bankruptcy the next year—a poster boy for Vegas' perils as well as its promise.

Garland and Fisher were the kind of out-there, heart-on-their-sleeve performers that Vegas embraced. The young Barbra Streisand was different. The Brooklyn-born singer was making a splash in New York nightclubs, on Broadway in *I Can Get It for You Wholesale*, and in TV guest appearances. But when Liberace brought her to Vegas in July 1963 as his opening act at the Riviera, her spare New York style didn't go over well with a crowd accustomed to Vegas pizzazz. "Instead of warming up the audience, her designated job," said one observer, "Barbra left Liberace with a cold stage and a frigid, frustrated crowd."

But Liberace liked Streisand, and the old showman figured out a way to help. Instead of letting her open the show cold turkey, after a couple of nights Liberace began opening the show himself, with a couple of upbeat numbers, then giving her a big buildup, introducing

Streisand as his new "discovery" from New York. Given proper warning, and Liberace's endorsement, the Vegas crowd suddenly warmed to her. In the middle of her four-week engagement, Streisand was signed to star in the new Broadway musical *Funny Girl*, and the Riviera offered her an open-ended contract to return.

But she wouldn't be back to Las Vegas for six years. And it wouldn't be at the Riviera, but as the opening headliner at the brand-new International Hotel. Even then, she was still, in a sense, just an opening act. The headliner who followed her was Elvis Presley.

For most of the 1960s, Elvis had little thought of playing Las Vegas. Colonel Parker's friend Milton Prell once offered $75,000 a week for Elvis to appear for two weeks at the Sahara Hotel, but the Colonel turned him down—as he did almost everything else in those years. Shortly after Elvis's return from the Army in 1960, in one of the great career miscalculations of all time, Colonel Parker decided that Elvis would do no more live performing, but would instead become a movie star.

It was a bad idea, but not necessarily an absurd one. What's easy to forget is that in the early years of rock 'n' roll, no one was quite sure that the new music would be anything more than a passing teenage fad. Many young rock 'n' roll singers figured they would eventually need to pivot to something else if they wanted to have a long career. Hollywood seemed a logical next step for Elvis. He loved movies and wanted desperately to be a serious actor, like James Dean or Marlon Brando. Elvis made four passably entertaining musical films before the Army—one, *King Creole* in 1958, possibly better than that. But after his return from Germany (and two unsuccessful attempts at straight dramatic roles, in *Flaming Star* and *Wild in the Country*), his movies devolved into a conveyer belt of low-grade formula musicals, which did well at the box office but left him frustrated and bored.

Las Vegas was his refuge. When his movie shoots were finished, he would typically grab a few of the guys and race to the desert town for some R&R. He would stay at the Sahara Hotel for a weekend or a week or even several weeks. He went to Vegas for the Christmas holidays in 1961 and stuck around for an entire month, celebrating his twenty-seventh birthday on January 8 at the Sahara with a cake from Milton Prell. In many ways Elvis was the perfect Las Vegas tourist. He wasn't a big gambler, but he loved the shows, the all-night activity, the chance to escape. "He loved Las Vegas for one reason above all: time was meaningless here, there was no clock, there were no obligations," wrote his biographer Peter Guralnick. "It was a place where you could lose yourself, a place where you could indulge your every fantasy—it was, for Elvis, momentary respite from all the self-doubt, from all the questions lying in wait, lurking in the shadows, waiting to assault him."

When Priscilla Beaulieu, the girlfriend he left behind in Germany, came to visit him in June of 1962, the first thing he did after she arrived in Los Angeles was take her to Las Vegas. They drove all night in his newly customized RV and got to the Sahara at seven in the morning. After a little sleep, Elvis took her shopping and had the hotel hairdresser give her a new beehive do and slather on makeup—"so heavily that you couldn't tell if my eyes were black, blue, or black and blue," Priscilla recalled. Then they went to see Red Skelton's show at the Sands, nearly getting trampled by fans when they didn't make their exit fast enough. For the next two weeks Elvis showed Priscilla the town, took her to shows, and introduced her to the drugs he was taking to stay up all night and get to sleep in the morning. He wouldn't consummate the relationship, saying he wanted her to stay a virgin until they married. Elvis was old-fashioned that way.

In July of 1963 Elvis was back in Las Vegas, but this time without Priscilla and, for the first time since his 1956 gig at the New Frontier, for work, not play: two weeks of location shooting for his fifteenth movie, *Viva Las Vegas*.

The films by this point had fallen into a depressing rut, most of them sappy musical travelogues like *Fun in Acapulco* and *It Happened at the World's Fair*. *Viva Las Vegas* was very much in the same vein, but it held out a little more promise. It had the biggest budget of any Elvis film to date. The director was George Sidney, a respected veteran of such Hollywood musicals as *Anchors Aweigh* and *Show Boat*. And Elvis's costar was one of the hottest young talents in Hollywood—Ann-Margret, the Swedish-born singer-dancer who had just made a splash with her kittenish performance as the starstruck teen in the musical *Bye Bye Birdie*, which Sidney had also directed. Sammy Davis Jr. was even signed to play Elvis's sidekick in the movie, but the Colonel—most likely wary of another star competing for attention with Elvis—nixed him, much to Sidney's dismay.

After three days of sound recording in Los Angeles, the production moved to Las Vegas on July 15. Elvis and his entourage stayed at the Sahara, with most of the filming done at the Flamingo and Tropicana, as well as at various outdoor locations around the city. Elvis plays a race-car driver who is working in a garage to raise money so he can compete in the Las Vegas Grand Prix. Ann-Margret is a hotel swim instructor who brings her car to be repaired and falls for him. The rest is a pretty typical boy-chases-girl romp, which climaxes with a talent-show competition (they tie for first place, but he gets the top prize on a coin flip) and the big car race (he wins, she watches).

The two costars were soon a romantic item offscreen as well. They flirted with each other between scenes, rode motorcycles together, and shooed away Elvis's entourage so they could spend long hours alone in his suite. The romance continued when they returned to Los Angeles for several more weeks of shooting on the MGM lot. Elvis's pals liked Ann-Margret and saw a real connection between the two. "I knew what was going to happen once we got to know each other," Ann-Margret wrote in her memoir. "Elvis did too. We both felt a current, an electricity that went straight through us. It would become a force we couldn't control."

The only problem was the girl back home. Priscilla was now living in Memphis, taking modeling and dance classes while waiting for Elvis to make good on his promise of marriage. When she started seeing gossip-column items about Elvis and Ann-Margret, she called him up and demanded to know what was going on. Elvis denied everything. "She comes around here mostly on weekends with her motorcycle," he said. "She hangs out and jokes with the guys. That's it." But when Priscilla asked if she could come out to LA for a visit, Elvis kept putting her off, telling her there were too many "problems on the set."

In that, at least, he was not lying. Colonel Parker was not happy during the filming of *Viva Las Vegas*. The production was going over budget, and director Sidney (who was rumored to have had his own affair with Ann-Margret while shooting *Bye Bye Birdie*) was giving Ann-Margret too many close-ups and too much screen time, threatening to upstage Elvis. The script originally included three duets for the two stars, but at the Colonel's insistence one of them was cut, and another was turned into a solo for Elvis. Still, for the first time Elvis had a costar who could hold her own with him on-screen.

Viva Las Vegas is a pretty bad film, tolerable only in comparison with the even cheesier ones that came before and after. ("About as pleasant and unimportant as a banana split," wrote Howard Thompson in his review for the *New York Times*.) Elvis and Ann-Margret have a sweet duet, "The Lady Loves Me," in the old Hollywood-musical mode,

and a couple of the big production numbers are staged with more pa-
nache than usual in Elvis films—an up-tempo wingding in the school
gym, "Come On, Everybody," and Elvis's hard-charging cover of Ray
Charles's "What'd I Say." But the script (by Sally Benson, who also
wrote Hitchcock's *Shadow of a Doubt*) is ludicrous, the direction lackadaisical, and Elvis's acting as glazed and stilted as ever. Ann-Margret,
with her head-snapping, hip-shaking, go-go-dancing energy, really does
outshine him.

Yet *Viva Las Vegas* has endured as the quintessential Las Vegas
film. From its opening aerial shots of the Strip, through its tour of Vegas
floor shows (as Elvis scours the hotel chorus lines for the girl he's just
met), the movie serves as a good travel brochure for Vegas in its classic
era. But *Viva Las Vegas* has attained its iconic status mainly because of
its title song, written by Doc Pomus and Mort Shuman. Its lyrics are
some of the clunkiest in the Elvis canon ("There's a thousand pretty
women waitin' out there / And they're all livin' devil-may-care"—three
*there*s in two lines!). But the bongo-driven beat, catchy melody, and Elvis's energetic vocal performance seemed to perfectly capture the fun-
loving, high-flying spirit of Vegas in its golden age.

Viva Las Vegas finished shooting in September 1963, but MGM
didn't release it until the following May. The movie did reasonably well
at the box office, ranking thirteenth among the year's top grossers. But
in the meantime, there was an earthquake.

In February 1964, the Beatles arrived in New York City, for their
era-defining US television debut on *The Ed Sullivan Show*. By April,
their songs occupied all five of the top five spots on the *Billboard* Hot
100 chart. In August they returned to the United States for the start
of their first American tour. The riotous reception they got surpassed
even the frenzy that greeted Elvis back in the mid-1950s.

Las Vegas, strangely enough, was the second stop on their US tour.

Stan Irwin—one of the few Vegas impresarios who knew who the heck the Beatles were—booked them for the Sahara Hotel, but when demand for tickets outstripped the showroom's capacity, the concert was moved to the Las Vegas Convention Center. Irwin offered complimentary tickets to all the hotel owners in town, but didn't get much of a response until a few days later, when they started calling him back: their high rollers all wanted tickets for their kids.

The Fab Four began the tour in San Francisco and flew to Las Vegas in the early morning hours of August 20. They were whisked from McCarran Airport to the Sahara, where screaming fans surrounded the hotel and the Beatles had to slip in through the freight elevator. They spent the night in an eighteenth-floor suite, furnished with two slot machines to keep them occupied. Eight thousand people jammed the convention center the next day for each of their two shows, at 4:00 p.m. and 9:00 p.m. The Beatles performed a dozen songs—the same set they did on all their tour stops, with the addition, just for Vegas, of the Broadway ballad "Till There Was You." After a brief press conference, they spent another night at the hotel and then were off to Seattle.

The *Las Vegas Review-Journal*'s front-page headline the next morning read "Las Vegas Survives Beatles—Barely."

Vegas survived quite nicely, at least for a while. Business was booming. Stars continued to flock to the city's showrooms. And when there weren't enough stars to go around, the hotels came up with even splashier alternatives. This was the heyday of the Vegas production show.

The *Lido de Paris* and *Folies Bergere* had proven to be durable hits at the Stardust and Tropicana, respectively, since opening there in the late fifties. Then, in 1963, the Dunes introduced a third French-flavored

production show, the *Casino de Paris*. Named for a Paris music hall that
dated back to the 1890s, it was the most stylish and contemporary of
the French-inspired shows, with choreography by the highly regarded
Ron Lewis, chic and colorful costumes by Spanish designer José Luis
Viñas, and with a real French star imported from Paris, singer Line
Renaud. The *Casino de Paris* became Vegas' third big production-show
hit and settled in for a long run. Some Vegas watchers even began to
speculate that the production shows would eventually take over most
of the big showrooms, relegating all but the biggest stars to the lounges.

It never happened. But for hotel entertainment bookers, the
production shows offered some big advantages. They were costly to
produce, but the same show could run for a year or longer—thus am-
ortizing the costs, before a new edition was brought in to replace it.
(The imported sets and costumes, however, all had to be disposed of
after three years, to avoid paying duty. Because it was too expensive to
ship them back to Paris, most were simply taken out into the desert
and burned—much to the chagrin of the directors and designers who
created them.) Instead of high-priced stars, the shows offered glamorous showgirls (sometimes uncovered), lavish sets and costumes, and a
parade of "specialty acts"—magicians, acrobats, dance teams, jugglers,
hypnotists, cyclists, and other performers drawn from the vaudeville
and circus traditions. (Among them were Siegfried and Roy, two German illusionists who made a live cheetah appear and disappear in an
eye-popping magic act that made its Vegas debut as part of the 1967
edition of the *Folies Bergere*.)

But most of all, the shows offered spectacle. And the master of
Vegas spectacle—the city's own Florenz Ziegfeld, Busby Berkeley,
and Steven Spielberg rolled into one pair of pants—was an innovative,
high-strung director-choreographer named Donn Arden.

He was born Arlyle Arden Peterson in St. Louis in 1917 and

was dancing for $5 in local movie theaters while still in grade school. After studying with choreographer Robert Alton—later a prominent Broadway choreographer of such shows as *Anything Goes* and *Pal Joey*—Arden began staging dance numbers for nightclubs around the Midwest and East. Moe Dalitz, who owned some of the clubs, brought him out to Las Vegas, and by the 1960s Arden was everywhere. He created opening production numbers for the Desert Inn (themed song-and-dance confections that preceded the main show, with titles like "Now We're in Tripoli" and "A Girl by Any Other Name"); staged new editions of the *Lido* show every two years; and in 1964 created his first completely original full-length show for the Desert Inn: *Hello, America!*, a nostalgic, family-friendly (no nudity) look back at turn-of-the-century America.

With each new production, Arden tried to top himself with more dazzling stage effects. His shows had rainstorms, fireworks, ice-skaters, flights of doves, Tyrolean bell ringers, musketeers on horseback. The highlight of his 1962 edition of the *Lido de Paris* was a giant dam bursting and flooding a small French village—the onrushing water flooding over houses and bridges and straight toward the audience. "It's not entertainment of the accepted nitery genre," said a rather shaken *Variety* critic. "In fact it's downright frightening." For the 1964 *Lido* show, Arden staged a train collision and the eruption of Mount Vesuvius. For *Hello, America!* he re-created the 1906 San Francisco earthquake and the sinking of the *Titanic*, and for a sequel two years later the explosion of the *Hindenburg*. "Competition among big shows in Las Vegas is so intense that we must come up each year with more unique and costly stage innovations," Arden said in 1965. "Where will it all end? Well, the boys who spend the money for these super-expensive colossals will decide that."

They were still spending in 1967, when Arden created perhaps his most acclaimed show, *Pzazz '68*, at the Desert Inn. No disasters this time. Just a glitzy celebration of Hollywood's past, including a tribute to female stars of three different eras (Mae West, Carmen Miranda, and Julie Andrews—flying through the air as Mary Poppins, naturally), and other segments paying homage to Fred Astaire, the Hope-Crosby *Road* pictures, and *Beau Geste*–style foreign-legion epics. "From the rousing opening to the resplendent closing, the audience sat electrified and entranced," raved *Las Vegas Sun* editor Hank Greenspun, "knowing they were watching one of the greatest shows ever produced in Las Vegas, or anywhere else for that matter." *Los Angeles Times* film critic Charles Champlin, a more temperate outside observer, called *Pzazz '68* the best Vegas show he had ever seen.

Arden not only invented the Vegas spectacle; he was largely responsible for creating the look and style of the Vegas showgirl. The dancers in his shows had to be tall (at least five feet eight inches), with "small and firm" breasts ("tight and firm" butts on the men). They also had to know how to move. "There's a certain way a girl can walk, particularly when you're going across the stage," Arden explained. "By simply twisting the foot, it swings the pelvis forward, which is suggestive and sensual. When you're crossing your feet and you're going across, if you twist right and swing that torso, you get a revolve going in there that's just right. . . . It isn't the way a woman should walk, necessarily, unless she's a hooker. You're selling the pelvis; that's the Arden walk."

He could be a terror to work for—an exacting, temperamental taskmaster, who could inspire dancers or bring them to tears. He would berate his girls for putting on too much weight, or blowing a step, or simply not having their hair pinned up during rehearsals. It was usually worse in the afternoons, after a couple of martinis. "He would scream and holler, break the girls down in tears. I've never heard anything so abusive in all my life," said Sonia Kara, a British-born Bluebell Girl, who came to Las Vegas in 1967. "It was scary. He would come in with a hangover so bad and just go for the gullet."

Some dancers considered Arden a pushover, however, compared to the dark genius of Vegas choreography, Ron Lewis. During rehearsals Arden would shout out insults from the audience; Lewis was known to hound girls on the stage, following them around screaming, even throwing things. He began as an assistant to French choreographer Frederic Apcar on the first *Folies Bergere* show in 1959. But he came into his own with his stylish and sexy choreography for the long-running lounge show *Vive Les Girls* at the Dunes, as well as the *Casino de Paris* shows in the main room. For many years he worked with Liza Minnelli, choreographing her TV specials and her 1977 Broadway show, *The Act*. But Las Vegas remained his home base, and he was by common consent the gold standard of Vegas choreography in the golden age.

A disciple of jazz-dance pioneer Jack Cole, Lewis brought a vibrant, jazzy style to Vegas dance: heavily accented movements, stylized hip thrusts and head rolls, precise placement of hands, fingers, knees—a style some compared to Bob Fosse's (though Fosse may have taken some of his moves from Lewis). "Ron was slim, sinewy, and had nitroglycerin in his veins," said Ron Walker, a swing dancer in *Casino de Paris*. "Dancers loved him because his work was never contrived, always original, and extremely fun to do." "When you were a Ron Lewis dancer," said Sal Angelica, who worked for Lewis in *Casino de Paris*, "you were the crème de la crème. He was tough as nails. You never knew what he was going to throw at you. But he was the best."

Vegas had other talented (and easier-to-work-with) choreographers, such as Jerry Jackson, a former lounge-show dancer who began choreographing numbers for *Vive Les Girls* and *Folies Bergere* and took over as the *Folies'* director in 1975. Top choreographers from Hollywood and Broadway also made their way to Vegas: Hermes Pan,

famous for staging Fred Astaire dance numbers in the 1930s, directed a
Folies Bergere show in the mid-1960s, and Ron Field, the Tony-winning
Broadway choreographer of *Cabaret*, staged acts for a number of Vegas
headliners. Vegas choreography was often dismissed as schlocky, and
some of it surely was. But at its best, it had a mix of precision, style, and
splash that outsiders often missed. "People from New York or Los Angeles thought they were so much better than Vegas," said Jerry Jackson.
"Very often they would come in and say, 'Anything I could do is better
than what they have.' And they would bomb out. You can't just throw
people doing generic dance steps onstage. They didn't understand what
Vegas was and how difficult it was."

Dancers, too, were proud of their work in Vegas. "I came to Las
Vegas from New York in 1965 for six months. I stayed forever," said
Sal Angelica, who danced for years with Juliet Prowse. "From the day
I got here I never stopped working. Broadway is actually less stressful
than Vegas. On Broadway, the dancing isn't the star. Here, dancing was
the star."

Big stars, great singers, lavish production shows, bare breasts—all of
them helped make Las Vegas the nation's hottest entertainment center
in the 1960s. But what gave Vegas its special sizzle was comedy.

Many of Vegas' top headliners were longtime funnymen from the
movies, radio, and television. Jack Benny, Milton Berle, and George
Burns were all Vegas regulars in the sixties, headlining TV-style variety
shows in which they would often introduce new talent. Jerry Lewis,
after his breakup with Dean Martin, continued as a solo headliner at
the Sands Hotel with an act that featured slapstick, songs, audience-
participation stunts, and Jerry's sometimes overbearing ego. Danny

Thomas, the nightclub entertainer from Toledo, Ohio, who became one of TV's best-known fathers in the 1950s sitcom *Make Room for Daddy*, was a favorite at the Sands for years, as was Red Skelton, the genial clown who reprised many of the characters and pantomime bits from his popular CBS comedy show.

Television was the springboard for other, more unlikely Vegas comedy stars. Carol Burnett had just won an Emmy for her sketch-comedy work in Garry Moore's comedy-variety series on CBS when she came to Vegas in the summer of 1962 with her own show—featuring sketches, songs, parody numbers, and some of her familiar characters from TV—and set an advance-sale record at the Sands. But nothing demonstrated more clearly the power of television to create new Vegas stars than Johnny Carson's smash debut at the Sahara Hotel in July of 1964.

Carson had been host of the *Tonight* show for less than two years and had virtually no experience as a nightclub entertainer. He was strictly a television phenomenon; some were skeptical that he would be able to sustain a Las Vegas show. But when the Sahara's Stan Irwin (who also produced the *Tonight* show for two years) brought Carson to Vegas for a four-week run, he broke the hotel's attendance record, previously set by Judy Garland.

Carson put together a Vegas act that expanded nicely on his familiar *Tonight* show monologues and sketches. He had new set pieces, including a takeoff of Edward R. Murrow reading "The Three Little Pigs," and a showcase bit, "Deputy John's Fun House," in which he played a sour children's show host battling a hangover. He could be just a bit naughtier on the Vegas stage than he was on TV. (He joked about the hotel maid who burst into his room when he was coming out of the shower in flagrante. Quipped Carson, "Have you ever tried to hide behind a silver dollar?") Carson would return to the Sahara for four weeks every summer during his *Tonight* show break—selling out shows, dropping in on lounge performers like Don Rickles, and creating more buzz in town than anyone but Frank Sinatra.

The patron saint of Vegas stand-up comics—a regular at El Rancho Vegas throughout the 1950s—was Joe E. Lewis, a doughy, slow-paced nightclub comic who would amble out onstage with a glass of Scotch and make jokes about his gambling and drinking. (Dean Martin, who modeled much of his drunk act on Lewis, loved to quote one of his lines: "You're not drunk if you can lie on the floor without holding on.") But the stand-up comedians who succeeded Lewis in the 1960s were a louder, faster, more in-your-face bunch. They had honed their skills in the nightclubs and presentation houses of New York and the resort hotels of the Catskills, known as the Borscht Belt. In Vegas they mostly worked the lounges, or as opening acts in the main room, though a few became headliners. They had to battle restless crowds and drunk hecklers and rival comics stealing their material. "The audiences in Vegas demanded a certain kind of energy," said comedy writer Dennis Klein. "They didn't like comedians who take their time and relate to the audience in a personal way. To them, subtle comedians were comedians who weren't funny enough."

Jack Carter, who headlined at the Flamingo for several years, was perhaps the archetype: an aggressive, neurotic, raspy-voiced tummler who did songs, impressions, put-downs of the audience, and a barrage of jokes about wives, kids, gamblers, hookers, and any ethnic group he could get his hands on. ("Did you hear about the Polish rapist? He was standing in the lineup, they brought in the girl, and he says, 'That's her!'") For insult comedy, there was the portly, acerbic Jack E. Leonard ("Hello, opponents," he would say, by way of greeting). For manic improvisation, Dick Shawn, a singer-dancer-comic who had a popular Vegas act well before Mel Brooks cast him as Hitler in *The Producers*.

For a change of pace, the gentle, Yiddish-dialect storyteller Myron Cohen. For the rest, a gaggle of seemingly interchangeable Jackies, Buddys, and Mortys. (Women were rare. The few who did well in Vegas were self-deprecating gagsters like Phyllis Diller, who joked about her string-bean figure and ineptitude at housework, and Totie Fields, who traded mostly in fat jokes. Sample: "I've been on a diet for two weeks, and all I've lost is two weeks.")

Yet Las Vegas also welcomed many of the more cerebral, "new wave" stand-up comedians who emerged in the late 1950s and early '60s. Bob Newhart, the Chicago comic who specialized in deadpan satirical bits with telephone in hand (a PR man advising Abraham Lincoln on the Gettysburg Address, for example, or a night watchman at the Empire State Building on the night King Kong climbs up), found that he had to cut them down a little to suit the shorter attention span of Vegas audiences. Reviewing his Sahara debut in October 1963, *Variety* thought his material "possibly will zoom over the head of the non-hip." But Newhart worked successfully in Vegas throughout the decade. Shelley Berman, another conversational satirist with roots in Chicago improv theater, also became a Vegas headliner—though the famously volatile comedian would throw screaming fits in his dressing room out of frustration with the audiences. (Maynard Sloate, who booked him at the Tropicana, called Berman "vicious" and "temperamental without hope.")

Even Woody Allen played Las Vegas. His Jewish-neurotic-shlemiel stand-up act was gaining a hip following in New York nightclubs, on record albums, and from his TV guest appearances when Caesars Palace booked him as a headliner in 1966. Though Vegas might have seemed an unlikely venue for him, Allen found the offer hard to refuse. "It was an achievement," he said. "Because I'd started out in the Village, and people thought, 'Oh, this guy will never get out of the Village.'

Then when I was playing uptown places like the Blue Angel, they said he'd never get out of New York. So it was an achievement for me to go into places like Caesars in Las Vegas."

Allen got good reviews, and he returned for several more appearances at Caesars. But he was disappointed that he was never able to fill the house. Chagrined at the many empty seats during his first engagement, he offered to give back part of his salary. "I felt guilty about taking their money," he said—surely a Vegas first.

But comics like Woody Allen and Bob Newhart were the outliers. Vegas comedy in the 1960s was defined mainly by a triumvirate of comics who made Vegas their home base; had acts that perfectly suited the raucous, anything-goes environment; and were among the city's top attractions for decades.

Stan Irwin, entertainment director at the Sahara, was a former comedian himself and a good judge of talent. But he had to see Don Rickles five times in Los Angeles before deciding to take a chance and book him into the Sahara's lounge. Rickles, a native of Queens who served in the Navy during World War II, had spent more than a decade bouncing around clubs up and down the East Coast. He made his first appearance at the Slate Brothers' club in LA in 1957 as a last-minute replacement for Lenny Bruce, who was fired for cursing out the audience. Rickles was soon a regular at the club, building an act out of insult jokes, aimed at members of the audience as well as the many celebrities, like Frank Sinatra, who came to see him.

Brought into the Sahara's Casbar Lounge in 1960 to alternate sets with Louis Prima and Keely Smith, Rickles caused almost as much tumult as they did. He would pummel the audience with barbs playing on every racial, religious, and ethnic stereotype imaginable. "I know you're Italian—nothing matches," he'd say to a man in the front row. Or: "You gotta be a Jew, lady; you're the only one with a stole on." Black people ate watermelon and sang spirituals; Mexicans always had the runs. A fat guy in the audience? "Hey buddy, there's a new thing out there. It's called a diet." A really tall woman? "Give her a basketball and let her dribble around." To a gentleman sitting with a pretty younger woman: "Is that your wife? Oh, I didn't recognize you, Trixie."

Some claimed that Rickles stole his act from Jack E. Leonard, the leading insult comedian of an earlier day. (Leonard apparently agreed: "He's doing me!" he would complain to friends.) But Rickles's comedy was both more incendiary and more canny. He got away with his crude, politically incorrect jokes because they were so brazen, so all-embracing, so obviously *an act*. He loved shocking the straitlaced crowd—"That's right, lady, you heard it. What the hell you think you're gonna see here, high mass?"—and then reassuring them that it was all in fun. He would typically close his slash-and-burn sets by thanking his mother and making a plea for tolerance and understanding. "Laugh at bigotry, that's what I do," he'd say, harking back to his experiences in the Navy, where all races, creeds, and colors worked together for one purpose. "When our time is up, we'll all be on one team. So why do we need bigotry and nonsense?"

Rickles knew that the key in Vegas was not to cross the line between irreverent and threatening. It was the same strategy employed by another top Vegas comic—a more versatile performer than Rickles, a veteran of TV, movies, and Broadway, who sounded like a Brooklyn cabdriver crossed with Betty Boop and looked like a Munchkin who had eaten too many lollipops. But he became known as the dirtiest comic in Vegas.

Buddy Hackett—another Jewish New Yorker, born in 1924 in Brooklyn, the son of an upholstery salesman—began his career in the Catskills in the late forties and made his Vegas debut in 1952 at the Desert Inn, as part of something called the *International Revue*. His most famous early routine was an impression of an exasperated waiter in a family Chinese restaurant, trying to get the wonton- and egg-drop-soup orders straight. But eventually he developed a more fractured, free-form style, often juggling three or four stories at the same time—like flipping channels with a TV remote, he liked to say. By the 1960s Hackett was headlining at the Sahara, one of the hottest comedians in town. After the death in 1966 of his friend Lenny Bruce—the taboo-busting comedian who was often under fire for his "obscene" material—Hackett's material took a blue turn. "When he worked clean, everybody started stealing his material," explained his son, Sandy Hackett. "So he said, 'I'm gonna do stuff nobody's gonna steal.'"

He started out mildly enough, riffing on the word *ass*, wondering why people considered it dirty. *Hand* can be a dirty word, if it's holding a gun, Hackett would say: "Guy has a gun in his ass, not so frightening." Before long he was spouting nearly all the forbidden four-letter words, and by 1968 the hotel was advertising his shows as "adults only." "Hackett has a definite mission in his nitery life now," wrote *Variety's* Bill Willard in January 1969. "He obviously opts to break all the forbidden word barriers, to be the spokesman for the new nitery morality. . . . Withal, he's very funny doing his little naughty word thing, and all his ephemera convulses the majority of the audience."

His impish personality helped him get away with it. At the end of his act he would apologize for his rough material with a humble mea culpa, like a little boy apologizing to his schoolteacher. Noted Shecky Greene, his friend and sometime rival, "Buddy had the ability to say *fuck* onstage, and then say, in that endearing voice, 'I really didn't mean to sound that way, I hope you people forgive me.' That little-boy quality sucked you in." As Hackett once put it, "I want to get the audience to hate me—and then see how long it takes to win them back."

Hackett reputedly pulled in more high rollers than anybody else in Vegas but Sinatra, and he understood the business. In 1969 Sahara owner Del Webb made him a vice president of entertainment for the hotel, where he worked at least fifteen weeks out of the year and had a house next to the seventh green on the golf course. But offstage, Hackett's wild behavior became the stuff of Vegas legend. He collected guns, always carried one around with him, and sometimes used it. Pete Barbutti claimed he was once in the Sands greenroom when Hackett, unhappy to hear that Totie Fields was doing good business, shot her picture off the wall. Hackett and Shecky Greene once got in an argument that ended with Greene tossing Buddy's gun and car keys into the desert in the middle of the night. Hackett called him up at seven the next morning to say he didn't mind losing the gun—he had plenty more at home—but still couldn't find his keys. "He was like the devil," said Shecky. "You never knew what was going to happen with Buddy. But he was a brilliant comedian."

Pretty much the same could be said of Shecky Greene. Unlike Rickles and Hackett, Greene was almost entirely a Las Vegas creation. He lived in Vegas, worked nearly full-time there, and (unlike Hackett and Rickles, both of whom had more successful TV and movie careers) never made much of a mark anywhere else. His wild, improvisational material changed every night, and none of his Vegas performances were ever recorded. As a result, his gift is the most difficult to pin down. But for many Vegas aficionados, Shecky Greene represented the high point of Las Vegas comedy.

He was born Fred Sheldon Greenfield in 1926 on the north side of Chicago. He learned to do dialects from his older brother, began playing clubs in the Midwest, and spent six years at the Prevue Lounge in New Orleans, before the club burned down. He worked in Reno (where he met his first wife, a blackjack dealer, who, he claimed, turned him into an alcoholic) and made his first appearance in Vegas at the

Last Frontier in 1953. He moved to the Riviera lounge in 1957, was hired away by the Tropicana in 1960, and returned to the Riviera five years later. Wherever he went, business picked up.

In the lounge, Greene was a free-form, improvisational force of nature—mixing jokes, songs, parodies, impressions, dialect stories, and spontaneous mayhem. An opera lover with a beefy frame and a booming voice, Greene might break into a burlesque of *Madama Butterfly*, or a takeoff of *Fiddler on the Roof*, or wheel himself around in a trolley in a parody of *Porgy and Bess*. "His act had no beginning, no middle, and no end," said Pete Barbutti, who first saw Greene at the Tropicana in 1960. "He did everything wrong. Going from point A to point D and back to C and F, starting a story about rabbits and going into his Jewish mother and the Army and something he did with Buddy Hackett. He's the funniest human being I've ever seen. There's never been anybody that powerful onstage." "When you saw a Shecky Greene show, you had the sense that this was a onetime performance, never to be repeated," said Dennis Klein. "He was very immediate, very visceral, very big. Onstage he was on fire. He would overpower an audience. He was to comedy what Jerry Lee Lewis was to music."

Greene could craft a great line, or ad-lib an even better one. One of his oft-repeated jokes was about the time Frank Sinatra saved his life. Some thugs were beating him up, Shecky said, and Sinatra finally told them, "OK, boys, that's enough." The former king Edward VIII of England and his wife, Wallis Simpson, were once in the audience for Greene's show in Miami and left in the middle of his act. "I don't feel bad," Greene called out as they departed. "You walked out on a whole country." He was doing a show in 1972, around the time Sammy Davis Jr.—an African American convert to Judaism—was photographed hugging Richard Nixon, and Greene spotted Pearl Bailey in the audience.

"Are you proud of Sammy Davis?" he asked her from the stage. "Because we're not."

Offstage, however, Greene could be a terror: a manic-depressive who seemed to undergo a Jekyll-Hyde personality change when he was drinking. He went on binges, got into fights, and was constantly feuding with his bosses at the Riviera, who fired him more than once. In January 1965 the hotel called the police and had him arrested for insulting guests. One night when Shecky went on a tear and was turning over blackjack tables in the Riviera casino, Milton Berle tried to calm him down and Shecky flattened him with a punch in the jaw. Then there was the night Shecky was driving drunk on the Strip, lost control of his car, and wound up in the fountain at Caesars Palace. When the police got there, Shecky quipped, "No spray wax." (Some thought the line was apocryphal—but who cared?)

Greene always felt misunderstood as a comedian. People compared him to Rickles, but he wasn't an insult comic. "I never worked like Rickles," he said. "I do dialects, I do singing, I do all kinds of things—Rickles never had one fuckin' iota of my talent." People thought Greene worked dirty, like Hackett, but Shecky used four-letter words in his act only rarely. He eventually graduated from the lounge to the main showroom, but he didn't like it: "I couldn't be Shecky. I couldn't be free." Years later he sobered up and looked back with regret on his crazy Vegas years: "Vegas was very, very good for me. But Vegas was very, very bad for me. I drank in Vegas. I got a reputation. When I think of my life, I get frightened. I got a check once for six thousand dollars, went to the table, and blew it—lost the six thousand dollars in fifteen minutes. As much as this town was good for me, that's how much I hated it. I hated what it did to me. I hated what I saw happen to other people. Millions of guys in the garment business came to this town and lost their business because of the gambling. I would like to bomb every one of these fuckin' places. And you can quote me on that."

Shecky Greene was hardly the only entertainer who had to battle the temptations of Las Vegas. Many stars couldn't resist gambling away the money they earned from their well-paying jobs. "A lot of entertainers were playing Vegas for nothing," said the impressionist Rich Little. "I remember arriving at the Sands for the first time, and Don Adams showed me around. He was gambling, and in the course of an hour he lost twenty thousand dollars. And I found out that he and a lot of the performers were so in debt to the hotel that they were working essentially for free." Jack Benny once joked, "I make approximately the same salary as the other entertainers who work in Vegas. The only difference is that I'm going to take mine home."

Along with the gambling, there were the women: well-endowed showgirls, ambitious cocktail waitresses, high-priced hookers. What happened in Vegas didn't necessarily stay in Vegas, and few marriages seemed to survive long in this freewheeling Sin City. "There was one rule: No wives or girlfriends in the hotel or casino. You never saw a wife on the Strip," said Henry Bushkin, Johnny Carson's lawyer, who accompanied the *Tonight* show star on his Vegas revels. "Nowhere was Johnny more pampered, more doted on, more satisfied, and freer to explore and indulge the far boundaries of his Johnnyness than when he was in Las Vegas. It was his Shangri-la."

To an outsider like Mia Farrow, the Hollywood flower child who started dating Frank Sinatra in 1965, the male-dominated, *Mad Men*–era culture was an alien land. "The women, who didn't seem to mind being referred to as 'broads,' sat up straight with their legs crossed and little expectant smiles on their carefully made-up faces," she wrote in her memoir. "They sipped white wine, smoked, and eyed the men, and laughed at every joke. A long time would pass before any of the women dared to speak, then under the males' conversation they talked about their cats, or where they bought their clothes; but more than half an ear was always with the men, just in case. As hours passed, the women, neglected in their chairs, drooped; no longer listening, no longer laughing."

In the background, always, was the mob. The presence of organized crime in Las Vegas was an open secret for years, but it grabbed the nation's attention most forcefully in 1963 with the publication of *The Green Felt Jungle*, a bestselling exposé written by two Vegas investigative reporters, Ed Reid and Ovid Demaris. Most entertainers were well aware of the mob figures behind the scenes—and sometimes on the scene—but were careful to keep their distance. "The one thing you learned," said Bob Newhart, "you never asked them what line of work they were in previously. You didn't want to know the answer to it."

Yet "the boys," as the locals called them, were largely accepted, even admired, in the entertainment community. They treated you with respect, stuck by their word, and kept a tight rein on the city. "I loved being around those guys," said Paul Anka, who mixed with mob figures but insisted he never took any favors from them. "If they respected you, they protected you. With the mob in control, Vegas was the safest place to be. Even walking around in the middle of the night you didn't have to worry about being mugged."

"They would bring their girlfriends on Friday night, their wives on Saturday, and on Sunday they'd bring their mothers or their family," recalled singer Lainie Kazan, who saw them often in her audiences at the Flamingo. "They invited me to weddings, home for pasta. And I went. I was intrigued. I found them to be very interesting characters." Nelson Sardelli, a lounge singer from Brazil who specialized in Italian love songs, got friendly with many of them, went to their homes for dinner, and once turned down a local thug's offer to put a hit on a manager he was having a feud with. "Because I sing 'Come Back to Sorrento,' the Italian guys come, they cry," Sardelli said. "There was always respect. I never asked them for anything."

Some stars had the juice to stand up to them, or at least claimed to. Shecky Greene liked to tell the story of his meeting with the formidable mob lawyer Sidney Korshak (described by the Justice Department as "one of the five most powerful members of the underworld"), who flew out from Chicago to mediate a dispute between Greene and Riviera boss Ross Miller. Korshak took the two to lunch and ordered Miller to shake hands with Greene and make up. When Miller refused, according to Greene, Korshak threatened to fire him. Shecky was more valuable to the hotel.

Vic Damone's relationship with "the boys" was closer than most. When he was just starting out in nightclubs in New York, he was engaged to marry the daughter of a mob boss from Buffalo. After Damone broke off the engagement (because she refused to cook for his mother), the jilted father of the bride lured him to a fourteenth-floor suite at the Edison Hotel and tried to push him out of a window. As Damone tells the story in his autobiography, he was dangling from the window when his agent burst into the room and pulled him to safety. The feud was finally settled, according to Damone, at a mob meeting chaired by Frank Costello—who gave Damone the thumbs-up and told the mobster to lay off.

"I became very friendly with the mob guys after they saved my life," said Damone. "I liked hanging out with them; they were nice guys, you know? Once they shook your hand, boy, that was like a contract." Peter Lawford once set up a lunch between Damone and Robert Kennedy, the attorney general, who was investigating organized crime. When

Kennedy quizzed him about the hotel incident, Damone claimed he didn't remember it or know the gangster involved. Kennedy stormed out of the meeting in anger.

Vic Damone was a stand-up guy.

Vegas was a boomtown not just for big-name entertainers, but also for the rank-and-file performers who filled the chorus lines, lounge shows, dance troupes, and hotel orchestras. As a jobs program, Vegas was the entertainment industry's answer to Hoover Dam.

The city, for one thing, was a glorious last stand for big-band music in America. The famous orchestras of Benny Goodman, Tommy Dorsey, Stan Kenton, and others had begun breaking up after the end of World War II, and most were gone by the 1960s. But Vegas provided a welcome landing spot for many of their best players. Each of the major hotels had a house orchestra, with a regular conductor (Antonio Morelli at the Sands and Jack Cathcart at the Riviera were among the longest serving) and sixteen or more full-time musicians. In the most active years there were even two "relief bands," which rotated among the hotels, filling in for the regular bands on their night off. More work could be found in the small jazz groups that often entertained in the lounges. For musicians, it was a godsend.

"The work was steady, the pay great," said Frank Leone, a piano player who moved to Vegas from Philadelphia in 1967 and never left. "It prompted a lot of great players to give up their traveling ways and settle in Vegas." Carl Fontana, the highly regarded trombonist for Woody Herman and Lionel Hampton, moved to Vegas in 1958 and played there for the rest of his career. Buddy Childers, the former lead trumpeter for Stan Kenton's orchestra, was a full-time Vegas player for much of the 1960s. Bill Chase, the former Woody Herman trumpeter who later led an acclaimed jazz-rock fusion group, performed in Vegas lounges during the late sixties and was the musical arranger for one edition of *Vive Les Girls*.

"All the top guys were here, the best in the world," said Pete Barbutti, who first came to Vegas in 1960 with a jazz-and-comedy group called the Millionaires. There was so much work that some musicians did double shifts—playing the main room at 8:00 p.m. and midnight, moving over to the lounge for the 10:00 p.m. and 2:00 a.m. shows. (Trumpet players who did double duty sometimes blew out their lips.) "Scale in those days was $650 a week, so they could make $1,300 a week," said Barbutti. "You couldn't make that in New York or at the Philharmonic."

By the late sixties Las Vegas had at least fourteen hundred working musicians. For seasoned players who were tired of the traveling grind, Vegas was a place to settle down, raise a family, have a career. "It was musical heaven," said Mark Massagli, a bass player who came to Vegas in 1957 and later became head of the Las Vegas chapter of the Musicians Union. There may have been more studio work in Los Angeles or Nashville. "But for someone who wanted to take the horn out every night, this was it."

It was striking—but maybe not surprising, in a town where the Rat Pack were macho role models—that nearly all the musicians, as well as the directors, choreographers, and producers, were men. Vegas was a guy's town. But for female performers, at least those with the right attributes, Vegas also offered a mother lode of opportunities.

The women who filled the chorus lines and production shows in Las Vegas fell into two categories. There were the showgirls—tall, statuesque beauties, typically five feet eight inches or more, whose job was mainly to parade around and look pretty. (Some appeared topless—and usually got paid extra for it.) Then there were the dancers, who could be shorter (often called ponies) and who had enough training to do the steps that a Ron Lewis or Jerry Jackson might throw at them. They came from all kinds of backgrounds, with all kinds of skill sets: sophisticated young women from Britain and South Africa, brought over from Paris by Madame Bluebell; wannabe Broadway dancers who moved to Vegas to find steadier work; starry-eyed teenagers from the Midwest headed for Hollywood who stopped off in Vegas and never left; fading burlesque queens who could still parade their assets, as long as the assets held up.

The talented ones could have long careers. Maria Pogee, a pixieish, five-foot-four-inch dancer from Argentina (where her uncle served as a minister in Juan Perón's government), first came to Vegas in the spring of 1960, at age eighteen, with an Argentinian troupe called the Lobato Dancers. After an appearance on Dinah Shore's TV show, they arrived in Las Vegas by train for an engagement at El Rancho Vegas—on the very day the hotel burned down. Stranded without work, they were given temporary lodging in the hotel bungalows, while a local Catholic church and the stage workers' union brought them food to tide them over, before they landed another gig in Lake Tahoe.

Two weeks later they were back in Las Vegas, opening for Dean Martin at the Sands Hotel. Pogee was rarely out of work after that. She performed in lounge shows with the Maldonado Dancers; starred in a revue called *Bonjour Paris* for director Barry Ashton (who changed her stage name from Maria Victoria to Marie Pohji, because it sounded more French); and danced with stars like Juliet Prowse, Shirley MacLaine, and Sammy Davis Jr., before moving into choreography. "For a dancer," she said, "Las Vegas was *the* place."

For a showgirl, it could be the place to fall on your face. Dance moves might not be required, but balance, poise, and strength were.

The feathered headdresses could be six feet high; strapped underneath the chin, they came close to strangling some girls. (Costume designers and choreographers were often at odds: it was hard to do a Ron Lewis head roll with a six-foot headdress.) "You had to learn how to walk," said Sonia Kara, who joined the Lido in Paris when she was eighteen, started out in Vegas in the chorus line at the Sahara, and later worked in Donn Arden's *Pzazz '69.* "Not just forward but sideways. And you had to know how to hold those feathers. Because back then the headpieces were thirty pounds and the backpack was like fifty. And the stairs—you could be up thirty-some feet, and you could never look down. You had to walk with feet pointing out, in at least three-inch heels. I've gone flying." The saying in Vegas was that you weren't a true showgirl until you fell down the stairs.

But the work was glamorous and well paying. Claire Fitzpatrick Plummer had some dance training back in New York and even one Broadway credit—in the chorus for a revival of *Pal Joey*—when she came out to Vegas with her two roommates in 1958. Her first job was as a Texas Copa Girl at the Sands. (She hailed from Long Island, but was told to call out "Corpus Christi" when the girls went down the line identifying their hometowns.) "Vegas was a great place to work," she said. "When I came here I made $150 a week. I was only getting $125 on Broadway." She went on to dance in the chorus line behind stars like Ginger Rogers and Mickey Rooney; flew in from the ceiling for Donn Arden's *Hello, America!*; and turned down a Barry Ashton show because she didn't want to work topless.

Kathy McKee did. She came to Las Vegas from Detroit in 1965, at age fifteen, and got work in a Watusi show at the downtown Mint Hotel. Her first paycheck was $240—more than her father was making after twenty years at the Ford Motor plant. She moved on to Minsky's burlesque show, where most of the girls were "typical mob types, bleached blond, silicone breasted, hard-nosed—they hated me." Then she landed a spot in Ron Lewis's classier topless show at the Dunes, *Vive Les Girls*. But she had to overcome a handicap that few other dancers in Vegas faced. Her father was black, and she got jobs only by passing for white.

"I don't think I would have had any career if I'd said I was mixed," said McKee. "There were no girls of color, no Latinos. There were no blacks in any show. Not even the pit bosses or waitresses in the casinos. The only black people you saw were in the bathroom or cleaning the rooms." Indeed, the first black person she ever saw gambling in a casino was Sammy Davis Jr.'s father. They struck up a conversation, and he took her to meet Sammy—who later hired her as a dancer in his stage show. (She toured with him for years and also became his on-the-road girlfriend.)

A showgirl's job didn't necessarily end when the show was over. At most of the hotels they were also expected to hang around in the casino afterward, serving as decoration to lure gamblers to the tables. "You had no choice—it was called mixing," said Lisa Medford, who came to Vegas in 1957, where she made her first appearance topless as part of a Harry Belafonte show. "People would come up to you and ask for autographs and want to buy you a drink. Famous people would want you to stand at the table with them because you're a showgirl." Sometimes the casino bosses would stake them with gambling money. "They'd give us a hundred dollars, real silver dollars, and we'd play," said Claire Plummer. "We'd always end up pocketing some of it. Guys would come over, win a couple of hands, and throw me a hundred. We made a lot of money that way. I was sending money home to my family all the time."

Any additional mixing was optional. "It didn't have to go any further if the girls didn't want to," said Plummer. But for some, undoubtedly, it did.

For Elvis, the women were the main attraction. Vegas gave him a chance to relax, to party all night, and to see favorite lounge entertainers like Della Reese, the Four Aces, and Fats Domino. (Elvis was dismayed when he went to say hello to Fats in between sets in the Flamingo lounge, and the old rocker, down on his luck, tried to sell him his diamond cuff links.) But mostly Elvis loved Vegas for its banquet of beauties.

"Each show opened with fourteen to twenty magnificent showgirls. We were determined to meet every one," said Joe Esposito, Elvis's former Army buddy and frequent companion in Vegas. "In those days, the dancers were required to stay in the hotel lounges between shows to mingle with guests and ensure that gamblers didn't defect to other casinos. We used that to our advantage. 'See those five girls over there,' we'd say to the maître d'. 'Ask them if they'd like to join us for a drink after the show.'"

Esposito was struck by one dancer wearing a poodle costume in Dean Martin's show, made a point of meeting her afterward, and wound up marrying her. Elvis preferred to keep his options open. He picked up showgirls, had girlfriends meet him in Vegas, and dated the occasional star. When he was in Vegas for two weeks in January of 1964, he saw a lot of singer Phyllis McGuire, despite warnings from his pals that she was mobster Sam Giancana's girlfriend. (When Elvis visited her in her suite at the Desert Inn, he noticed a gun sticking out of her purse. She told him Giancana had given it to her for protection. "Yeah," Elvis said, "well, tell him I carry two of 'em.")

But Las Vegas couldn't relieve Elvis's growing frustration over his stalled career. After *Viva Las Vegas*—which, despite its success at the box office, Colonel Parker thought cost too much—the movies got even dumber and more demeaning. Yet the Colonel kept signing new studio contracts, keeping Elvis on a schedule of three movies a year, with accompanying soundtrack albums that were no longer producing hit singles. Shuttling back and forth between his Graceland home in Memphis and two leased California residences, in Beverly Hills and Palm Springs, Elvis looked to Vegas for distraction and escape. But he needed more.

In the spring of 1964 Elvis got a new hairdresser, Larry Geller, a twenty-four-year-old stylist at Jay Sebring's fashionable LA salon. While he was cutting Elvis's hair, Geller began talking about his spiritual studies, and Elvis responded with interest. Geller brought him books to read—including *The Impersonal Life*, a guide to self-realization written in 1917, and *Autobiography of a Yogi*—and soon they were inseparable, talking long into the night about God, the self, and the meaning of life.

Geller found Elvis to be intelligent, curious, and absolutely sincere in his spiritual seeking. Elvis's Memphis pals mostly found Geller to be a pain in the ass. Elvis, their formerly fun-loving companion, was suddenly serious, buried in books, and spending all his time with his new guru, whom they dubbed the Swami. "We were having fun and now all of a sudden Elvis is outside looking at the stars all night or reading these books," said Joe Esposito. "We used to sit and watch football games. All that stuff was gone."

Worse, their meal ticket was being threatened. One day, when Elvis and the entourage were driving through the Arizona desert to California, Elvis suddenly looked up into the sky and saw Joseph Stalin's face in the clouds. He stopped the van and ran into the desert in ecstasy, dragging Geller with him. "The face of Stalin turned right into the face of Jesus, and he smiled at me, and every fiber of my being felt it!" Elvis cried. "For the first time in my life, God and Christ are a living reality!"

When they got to LA, Elvis told Geller he wanted to quit show business and go into a monastery. Geller told him to get some sleep. "Remember, you're Elvis Presley," he said. "You have a responsibility to the world."

Elvis's spiritual quest continued in earnest for the next couple of years. He dabbled in meditation and experimented with LSD. He spent hours with Sister Daya Mata, the leader of a spiritual group called the Self-Realization Fellowship, with headquarters outside Pasadena. The trips to Las Vegas were less frequent now: no more two-week binges, just a few days here or there, in between his movie shoots.

In March of 1967, Colonel Parker put his foot down. After a health scare, when Elvis suffered a concussion following a mysterious fall in the middle of the night (probably drug related), the Colonel banished Geller from the group, made some other cutbacks in the bloated entourage, and moved to reassert control over all of Elvis's affairs. Among the first things on his agenda was Elvis's wedding.

Though he had promised to marry Priscilla ever since she moved to Memphis in 1963, Elvis was clearly ambivalent about marriage. Yet, just before Christmas in 1966, he surprised her with a three-and-a-half-carat diamond ring and a formal proposal. No one was exactly sure what prompted this. Some suspected Priscilla's father had demanded that Elvis finally make good on his promise, now that Priscilla was twenty-one. Others figured it was the Colonel, who felt Elvis needed to legitimize the relationship or risk damaging his image. Most likely it was a combination of both. In any event, Colonel Parker set about making arrangements for the wedding. It would take place on May 1, 1967—in Las Vegas, at his friend Milton Prell's new hotel, the Aladdin.

News of the impending wedding was kept under wraps, and planning was done in strict secrecy while Elvis was in LA shooting the movie *Clambake.* The day before the wedding, he and Priscilla drove to Palm Springs, to throw reporters off the scent. (Gossip columnist Rona Barrett got wind of the plans and reported that a wedding was imminent, but mistakenly said that it would take place in Palm Springs.) Then, in the middle of the night, they flew to Las Vegas aboard Frank Sinatra's Learjet, got a marriage license at the Clark County courthouse at 7:00 a.m., and showed up at Prell's private suite at the Aladdin at 9:40 a.m. for the wedding.

Elvis was dressed in a satin tuxedo, and Priscilla in a white organza dress she had purchased at a Westwood bridal shop a few days before. Nevada Supreme Court justice David Zenoff had a private chat with the couple before conducting the vows. "I was simply amazed at the boy's modesty," the judge recalled. "He was low-key, handsome as a picture, very respectful and very intense . . . and so nervous he was almost bawling." After the eight-minute ceremony, the couple were whisked into a press conference that had been arranged by the Colonel. "Well, I guess it was about time," Elvis said, when asked why he took the plunge. Then everyone adjourned to a banquet room for a brunch reception, where a hundred guests picked from a buffet offering ham and eggs, southern-fried chicken, and roast suckling pig. By the evening, Elvis and Priscilla were back in Palm Springs.

The rushed wedding left some hurt feelings. The Colonel wanted to keep the event small, and only fourteen people were at the ceremony— Priscilla's family, two best men (Joe Esposito and Marty Lacker, the "co-foremen" of Elvis's entourage), along with George Klein, an old friend from Memphis, and Harry Levitch, Elvis's jeweler. Some of his friends (including Larry Geller) learned of the wedding only later, when they read about it in the newspaper. Red West, Elvis's old high school friend and sometime bodyguard, had flown to Vegas for the event, only to learn at the last minute that he was not invited to the ceremony, just the reception. He flew into a rage, got a flight back to Los Angeles, and quit his job with Elvis. (He returned a few years later, but the resentment may have lingered; West was one of the authors of *Elvis: What Happened?*, the 1977 book that first revealed the extent of Elvis's drug use.)

"Elvis and I followed the colonel's plan," Priscilla wrote in her memoir, "but as we raced through the day we both thought that if we had it to do over again, we would have given ourselves more time." It might not have mattered, for the marriage was probably doomed from the start. Priscilla became pregnant instantly (their daughter, Lisa Marie, was born on February 1, 1968, nine months to the day after the wedding). When Priscilla was in her seventh month, Elvis suggested that they "take a little time off, like a trial separation." They stayed together, but after their daughter's birth Elvis no longer wanted to have sex. (He was never sexually attracted to women who had given birth.) He and Priscilla remained a couple, at least officially, until their 1973 divorce, and Elvis was a doting father. But that hardly stopped him from returning to his outside dalliances—or, once she realized the situation, Priscilla from starting her own.

A bad marriage certainly didn't help Elvis's state of mind as he sank deeper into his career funk. But the glimmers of an escape route were starting to appear, and it would run through Las Vegas.

Five

CHANGES
(Elvis Rising)

By the late 1960s, Vegas was beginning to lose its juice. Beatlemania was hardly the passing fad that Vegas thought—hoped—it might be. The rock 'n' roll craze of the 1950s had been easier for Vegas to ignore; it appealed mostly to teenagers, not the adult gamblers who constituted the bulk of Vegas' audience. But the second rock revolution, sparked by the arrival of the Beatles, was of a different order. It was part of a much broader cultural and social upheaval, encompassing not only music, but also politics, fashion, sexual mores, and a whole antiestablishment ethos. And it was embraced by far more than just kids.

Yet Las Vegas, in almost every way, represented the old guard. The boozing, macho Rat Pack still embodied Vegas' ideal of cool. The music in Vegas showrooms was still dominated by pop standards and Broadway show tunes, along with a few of the mellower contemporary hits. Yet the city was falling out of step with the fast-changing times. The old stars were starting to look dated, and younger audiences, plugged into the new rock sounds and shunning the bourgeois values that Vegas seemed to embody, were staying away in droves.

Behind the scenes, meanwhile, Las Vegas was undergoing its own transformation. The era of the free-spending, mob-run hotels was coming to an end, and a new set of players was moving in.

In the early morning hours of November 27, 1966, a van pulled up to a rear entrance of the Desert Inn Hotel. In the darkness, a frail man in blue pajamas was carried on a stretcher into a service elevator and whisked up to the ninth-floor penthouse. The suite there had already been outfitted with an array of electronic and medical equipment, and the windows sealed and blacked out, for its finicky new resident.

Howard Hughes's stealth arrival in Las Vegas marked the start of a new chapter for the entertainment capital. Hughes, the famous aviation pioneer, Hollywood mogul, and business titan (ranked by *Fortune* magazine in 1968 as the richest man in America), had recently sold his majority stake in Trans World Airlines for a profit of $547 million and was looking for something to do with his money. Hughes had been a frequent visitor to Las Vegas since the 1940s, often seen in the casinos and lounges around town doling out $100 tips to musicians who would play the songs he requested. By the time he moved to Vegas in 1966, however, he was deteriorating both mentally and physically.

Suffering from obsessive-compulsive disorder, hooked on codeine and Valium, Hughes refused to cut his hair or fingernails and stored his urine in mason jars, while surrounded by mounds of trash in a room that was rarely cleaned. His dietary demands were exacting and bizarre. He obsessed over the size of his peas and the shape of his slices of chocolate cake. When he learned that Baskin-Robbins was about to discontinue his favorite flavor of ice cream, banana nut, he had the Desert Inn kitchen order 350 gallons of it. Then he switched to French vanilla, and the kitchen was stuck with the stockpile. Paranoid and depressed, Hughes never went out of his room, communicating with his top aide, former CIA operative Robert Maheu, by telephone or handwritten memos scrawled on yellow legal pads.

A couple of weeks after Hughes's arrival, Desert Inn owner Moe Dalitz ordered the reclusive new guest to vacate: the hotel needed the top-floor VIP suites for its high-rolling customers expected to descend on the hotel during the Christmas holidays. But Hughes refused to leave—and offered to buy the hotel instead. Following several weeks of negotiations, a $13.2 million deal was struck, and on April 1, 1967, Hughes became owner of the Desert Inn.

It was a measure of the weirdness of Las Vegas that the arrival of a nutty billionaire who kept his pee in mason jars was seen as a step up in respectability. With growing federal scrutiny of Vegas' links to organized crime—Dalitz had been indicted on tax charges, and the FBI was investigating illegal skimming in Nevada casinos—Hughes was "greeted with messianic enthusiasm," as one journalist put it, "by Las Vegas desperately waiting to be redeemed from the stigma of Bugsy Siegel and his heirs." Hughes's application for a casino license was approved swiftly, with the state Gaming Control Board waving even the usual requirement that the applicant make a personal appearance. "This is the best way to improve the image of gambling in Nevada by licensing an industrialist of his stature," said Clark County district attorney George Franklin. "It will be an asset and a blessing." (Hughes, a shrewd political manipulator, cultivated state officials like Nevada governor Paul Laxalt and didn't hurt his cause by pledging to donate up to $300,000 a year to support the University of Nevada Medical Center.)

Hughes's purchase of the Desert Inn was just the first strike in what would be the greatest buying spree in Las Vegas history. In August 1967 he acquired the Sands Hotel from the mob interests that ran it. Next he bought the Frontier, the smaller Castaways, and the Silver Slipper casino, as well as the unfinished Landmark Hotel, a circular high-rise in the Convention Center area that was mired in bankruptcy. "Did you hear that Hughes just bought the Sahara?" went a joke going around town. "Not the hotel, the desert." Only when he made a move to add the Stardust Hotel to his portfolio did the Justice Department's antitrust division raise red flags, objecting to a deal that would have put more than 20 percent of the city's economic activity in the hands of one man.

Though blocked from buying more hotels, Hughes continued to gobble up everything else in Las Vegas he could get his hands on. He purchased TV station KLAS (which he ordered to program his favorite old movies all night long), the North Las Vegas Airport, and hundreds of acres of vacant land in prime areas along the Strip. He announced plans for a vast expansion of the Sands, to create a four-thousand-room mega-resort, with one floor of retail stores open twenty-four hours a day and another devoted to family recreation, including a bowling alley, ice-skating rink, movie theater, and computerized indoor golf course— "a resort so carefully planned and magnificently designed that any guest will simply have to make a supreme effort if he wants to be bored," wrote Hughes. The project never got off the ground, but Hughes antic- ipated Vegas' theme-park future more clearly than he probably realized.

Hughes wanted to clean up Vegas, to push out the mob elements that controlled most of the hotels, to make the town "as trustworthy and respectable as the New York Stock Exchange." He arrived at the right time, both for civic leaders eager to improve Vegas' image, and for the mob owners themselves, who were feeling the heat and saw in Hughes an opportune exit strategy. "The increased governmental scrutiny may be becoming too much of a headache for some who would rather sell out now than have it forced upon them," noted *Variety* in March 1967.

Some Vegas historians have pointed out that, even after Hughes's buying spree, the mob bosses remained in the picture, continuing to manage his operations and secretly siphoning off money for years. (The Sands and the Desert Inn both lost money after Hughes took over.) "Dalitz and other members of his Las Vegas clique saw Hughes' arrival for what it was," wrote one journalist, "an opportunity to take an unbelievably wealthy mark to the cleaner's."

Still, Hughes began to supplant the old mob bosses and opened the door to a new era of corporate ownership in Las Vegas. In 1967 the Nevada legislature made a significant revision in the rules that governed the granting of casino licenses. Previously, corporations were effectively barred from owning casinos because of the requirement that every prospective owner—which, in the case of a corporation, meant each individual stockholder—be vetted by the state authorities. Once that onerous requirement was removed, corporate owners—from Kirk Kerkorian, the LA mogul who would soon challenge Hughes's supremacy in Vegas, to national hotel chains like Hilton and Holiday Inn—had a clear path to invest in Las Vegas.

Most immediately, Hughes changed the way Las Vegas hotels were run. He installed new managers, many of them from his circle of Mormon advisers, who instituted a more corporate, bottom-line approach—a major change for the high-flying, free-spending Vegas hotels. Big-name showroom entertainment, for example, had always been treated as a loss leader. The lofty salaries for top stars (combined with low cover charges and minimums in the showrooms) were hard to justify on the ledger books. But they drew customers into the casinos, which in turn provided the gambling revenue that supported the high-priced entertainment.

Under Hughes's regime, however, each element of the operation—showroom, restaurant, hotel rooms—was expected to pay for itself.

That led to a kind of belt-tightening Vegas had never before experienced. The chorus lines of glamorous showgirls, for example, were now seen as expensive frills, and the hotels started to drop them. The lounges, where top comedians and singers could be seen for the price of a Coke, were not moneymakers either, and they began to close down. Hughes tried to hold the line on star salaries and also put a clamp on many of the perks and fringe benefits that the entertainers had grown accustomed to.

To veterans of the Vegas entertainment scene, all this was heresy, the beginning of the end of the golden age. "When the bean counters in the suits came in, all of a sudden everything had to go by the book," said Lorraine Hunt-Bono, a onetime lounge singer whose family owned a popular Vegas restaurant for years. "They knew nothing about hospitality or running a bar or a restaurant or gaming. But Howard Hughes knew they'd watch everything." "It was the new bureaucratic regime," said Paul Anka, "where you had all these rules and lists, and functionaries were running around with clipboards, all obeying the great eye in the sky over there at the Desert Inn. A cold, new impersonal wind was blowing."

Hughes had his defenders in the entertainment community. "Howard Hughes maintained the quality," said Vera Goulet, who managed the career of her husband, Robert, for many years. "He lifted the Desert Inn up. He lifted the standard of class and elegance. What he did was positive." Hughes was a champion of some performers—among them Vegas superstar Wayne Newton—and a behind-the-scenes fan of many others. Bob Newhart recalled an encounter with Hughes's aide Robert Maheu during an engagement at the Landmark. "Mr. Hughes is very happy with the business you're doing," Maheu told him. "He sees the reports every night." Impressionist Rich Little got a compliment one night from Hughes's entertainment director, Walter Kane: "The old man thought you were great tonight." Little looked confused, then realized Kane was talking about Hughes. "He had the shows piped up to his room every night," said Little, "and I guess he must have watched a lot of them."

Hughes did plenty of things to alienate people in Vegas. He was virulently anti-union, in a town where unions had a lot of power. He was a footdragger on civil rights, opposing efforts to end racial discrimination in hiring, which was rampant in Las Vegas throughout the sixties. "I can summarize my attitude about employing more Negroes very simply," Hughes wrote in a memo to Maheu. "I think it is a wonderful idea for somebody else, somewhere else."

But what rankled the show-business community most was the strict, impersonal corporate approach that Hughes brought to Vegas. Abel Green, *Variety*'s editor and a longtime observer of the Vegas scene, lamented in 1969, "In a community of brigand beginnings, which long yearned for and, even the most grudging diehards will concede, eventually earned respectability, there is something about the Hughesian and concomitant corporate brand of businesslike operation that has taken away a lot of the glamour." The old mob managers may have been thieves and thugs, but they loved being part of the showbiz world. They catered to the entertainers, made them feel respected and protected. "When the so-called gangsters were in there, you could leave anything in your room," said Florence Henderson. "I left jewelry and nothing was ever stolen. When Hughes took over, I had things stolen."

"Hughes had all these little crew-cut idiots come in from all over the country," Eydie Gormé griped in a 1976 interview. "One was a water commissioner in Buffalo, and another guy was a plumber someplace else, and they came in to run the casinos. These were the assholes of the world." One night, when she was appearing at the Sands with her husband, Steve Lawrence, Gormé asked for a $200 marker in the

casino—credit to gamble with, routinely given to the hotel's stars. The
pit boss asked to see her identification first. "I'm Eydie Gormé!" she
cried. "I'm appearing here at your hotel!" No matter, he said; he still
needed to see ID. A furious Gormé complained the next day to hotel
boss Jack Entratter and refused to do her show that night until he ad-
vanced her $25,000 in chips. She said she kept them in her purse for
the rest of her stay.

At least Entratter was still there. The Sands' longtime entertainment
chief, a friend to Sinatra and so many of the hotel's top stars, was given
a five-year contract to remain with the Sands when Hughes took over.
But even Entratter couldn't prevent the inevitable clash between the
hotel's new management and the Sands' most valuable asset.

Frank Sinatra and Howard Hughes had crossed paths before in
Hollywood and once competed for the affections of Ava Gardner. But
the mogul's acquisition in 1967 of the hotel where Sinatra had reigned
for fourteen years was not something the king of Las Vegas could easily
swallow. It came at a vexing time in Sinatra's life and career. Now past
fifty, with the rock revolution in full swing and his classic pop style
decidedly out of favor, Sinatra was hitting both a career slump and a
midlife crisis. In 1965 he began dating Mia Farrow, a child of Hollywood twenty-nine years his junior. After keeping the gossip columnists
busy for months, the couple got married on July 19, 1966, in Entratter's
suite at the Sands—in a ceremony just as secretive, perfunctory, and
devoid of romance as Elvis and Priscilla's vows at the Aladdin would
be a year later.

The marriage was stormy from the start—Sinatra quickly grew jealous of his bride's budding film career—and only seemed to exacerbate

Sinatra's volatile moods and sense of dislocation. In November 1966 he appeared at the Sands for the first time since his marriage. Mia was in the audience, and the two gazed lovingly at each other as he opened the show with "Strangers in the Night," his latest hit single. "Yeah, I sure got married," Frank said after introducing Mia from the stage. "I had to—I finally found a broad I can cheat on." The crowd gasped, Mia hung her head in embarrassment, and Sinatra knew he had made a faux pas: "I guess I'd better sing. I'm in a lot of trouble."

His troubles only seemed to mount. "During this period Sinatra seemed to be constantly angry and frequently flew into rages," Paul Anka recalled. "The problem was that Sinatra was no longer the god he had once been." There were ugly incidents. In June 1966 Sinatra was having dinner at the Polo Lounge in Beverly Hills with some friends to celebrate Dean Martin's birthday. The group got loud, and two businessmen seated nearby asked them to tone down their language. Tempers flared, and one of the men, Hunt's Food president Fred Weisman, wound up in a bloody pool on the floor—clubbed by a house telephone, wielded either (accounts vary) by Sinatra or by his pal Jilly Rizzo. Weisman was rushed to the hospital and lingered in critical condition for days, before recovering. He declined to press charges.

Jackie Mason was another alleged target of Sinatra's anger. One night at the Aladdin Hotel, with Sinatra in the audience, the acerbic comedian made several jokes about the singer's May-September romance ("Frank soaks his dentures, and Mia brushes her braces"), and Sinatra didn't appreciate them. Afterward, the comedian got a threatening phone call, and a few days later three gunshots were fired into his hotel room. The police found no evidence linking Sinatra to the attack, but Mason remained convinced the singer was behind it. "I don't think he actually shot the gun, but there is no doubt that someone was mad about the incident," Mason said years later. "He was heckling me and interrupting my act; I abused him back from the stage. He was mad that I fought back. I don't think other comedians at the time dared to do that."

All this was mere prelude, however, to Sinatra's infamous blowup at the Sands.

He was opening there for a four-week engagement on Labor Day weekend in 1967, just a few weeks after Hughes's acquisition of the hotel. Opening night was a relatively good-humored affair: Sinatra made some mild jokes about the mogul ("You're wondering why I don't have a drink in my hand? Howard Hughes bought it") and gave a playful twist to the lyrics of his song "Young at Heart":

> *Fairy tales can come true,*
> *It can happen to you,*
> *If you're Howard Hughes.*

But Sinatra wasn't laughing the following weekend, when he ran smack into the new hard-line policies of the Hughes regime at the Sands.

Sinatra had long enjoyed privileged status at the Sands. He was always given unlimited credit in the casino; he rarely paid off his losses and typically kept his winnings. After Hughes took charge, however, a new edict was handed down: Sinatra was to be given no more credit until he paid back what he owed the hotel.

On Friday night, September 8, Sinatra was at a baccarat table with six Apollo astronauts, who had come to see his show. When he asked for a marker, Sinatra got the bad news: no more credit. With guests present, he swallowed the insult, but it gnawed at him all night. Sometime near dawn, angry and drunk, Sinatra was driving a golf cart back to his hotel suite, with Farrow in the passenger seat, when he suddenly swerved the cart around, headed back to the casino, and smashed it into a plate-glass window. Neither he nor Farrow was injured, but Sinatra wasn't finished. "He was already out of the cart and striding into the casino as I trotted after him, clutching my little beaded evening purse," Farrow recalled in her memoir. "He threw some chairs into a heap and with his golden lighter he tried to set them on fire. I watched the rising commotion as people gathered around and casino guards rushed over. When he couldn't get a fire started, he took my hand and we walked out of the building."

Sinatra canceled the rest of his Sands engagement and left for Los Angeles the next day. But that night, still fuming over the incident, he abruptly flew back to Vegas (without Farrow this time) and stormed into the Sands at five in the morning, demanding to see casino boss Carl Cohen. "He threatened to kill anyone who got in his way, used vile language, and said he would beat up the telephone operators if they did not connect him with Cohen," Maheu reported to Hughes later. Cohen was roused from his bed, grudgingly got dressed, and strode into the Sands Garden Room to meet with Sinatra. There the aggrieved star launched into a torrent of abuse—culminating, in some accounts, with a Jewish slur. Cohen, a formidable 250-pounder, but a well-liked boss not known for his temper, threw a punch that knocked out the caps on Sinatra's two front teeth.

The fracas was headline news. "Singer Tony Bennett left his heart in San Francisco, and Frank Sinatra left his teeth—at least two of them—in Las Vegas," began the *Review-Journal*'s story. Much of the town secretly cheered that Sinatra, whose high-handed antics had been tolerated for years, had gotten his comeuppance.

Jack Entratter was angry the next morning that no one had awakened him. (His DO NOT DISTURB sign was on for the night—but it didn't apply when Sinatra was in town.) Yet it's doubtful even Sinatra's old friend and patron could have averted the disaster. "Frank picked a fight,"

said Corinne Entratter. "He wanted an excuse to leave." Two days later
Sinatra announced that he was ending his fourteen-year relationship
with the Sands. He was going to Caesars Palace.

For all that Howard Hughes did to transform Las Vegas, he was only
a buyer, not a builder. The most important new addition to the Las
Vegas Strip in the 1960s came a few months before his arrival, with the
opening of Caesars Palace in August 1966. It was the first entirely new
hotel to open on the Strip in eight years (the other major newcomer,
the Aladdin, was an expansion of the defunct Tally Ho), and the one
that launched the city's modern era—Las Vegas' first "themed" resort.

Caesars Palace was the brainchild of Jay Sarno, a builder from St.
Joseph, Missouri, who thought Vegas hotels needed a fresh approach.
Rather than copying the desert-resort style so prevalent on the Strip,
Sarno conceived of a hotel that would have the opulent decor and luxury
accoutrements of ancient Rome. Architecturally, it broke with Vegas
tradition in a number of ways. The hotel was set far back from the
street, with a palatial entryway lined with fountains and Roman statuary. The egg-shaped casino was a grand space with a high domed ceiling
and a crystal chandelier in the center, in sharp contrast to the densely
packed, low-ceilinged casinos in other hotels. The Roman motif was
carried throughout the hotel, from the swimming pool shaped like a
centurion's shield to the Bacchanal restaurant, where beautiful servers
fed patrons grapes and gave them back rubs. The hotel cost a record
$25 million (mostly financed by loans from the Teamsters Union pen-
sion fund), had twenty-five thousand square feet of meeting space for
conventioneers, and boasted a lavish eleven-hundred-seat showroom,
the Circus Maximus.

The hotel's entertainment aimed for the wow factor too. Dave Victorson came over from the Thunderbird as entertainment chief, and he opened the checkbook for big names. Some were familiar Vegas stars like Andy Williams (the hotel's opening headliner), Tony Bennett, and Harry Belafonte. Others were newcomers to Vegas, among them Broadway star Anthony Newley, comedian Woody Allen, TV favorite Andy Griffith, and even the campy, falsetto-voiced phenom Tiny Tim. Victorson brought in Broadway shows, like *Sweet Charity* and *Fiddler on the Roof*; filled the hotel's 250-seat Nero's Nook lounge with top names like Eartha Kitt and Sarah Vaughan; and even scored with a popular afternoon girlie show, *Bottoms Up*. Landing Sinatra—as well as his Rat Pack pal Sammy Davis Jr., who followed Sinatra to Caesars Palace a little later—sealed the deal: Caesars Palace would quickly become the premier star showcase in Las Vegas.

The arrival of a deep-pocketed new hotel on the Strip—along with fresh competition from arenas around the country, which were paying big bucks for concert performers—helped ratchet up the Vegas salary wars once again, after a period of relative stability. Sinatra got a record $100,000 a week to jump from the Sands to Caesars Palace. Dean Martin finished out his contract at the Sands and then moved to the Riviera, also for $100,000, plus a 10 percent share of the hotel and the title of entertainment consultant. (Riviera shows would henceforth be advertised as "Dean Martin presents.") The Frontier even offered $100,000 to an act that had never played Vegas, Herb Alpert and the Tijuana Brass, but they turned it down, figuring they could make more money doing one-nighters.

When Sinatra finally made his debut at Caesars Palace on November 27, 1968, more than a year had passed since his departure from the Sands, and it seemed like a new era was at hand. He agreed to do only one show a night, except on the weekends, and the $12.50 minimum was the highest yet for a Vegas show. His opening acts—no fewer than four of them—included José Feliciano, singing "Light My Fire," and the pop-soul group the 5th Dimension. Sinatra ditched his usual tuxedo for a trendy white turtleneck and medallion underneath a dark suit. He sang old standards like "I've Got the World on a String," but also new numbers that reflected a more sober mood of middle-aged reflection, such as "That's Life" and "It Was a Very Good Year." Some thought his Caesars shows lacked the electricity of his appearances in the more intimate Sands Copa Room. But the critics were glad to have him back. "A virtuoso display of Sinatra at the top of his form," wrote the *Los Angeles Times'* Charles Champlin, "the kind of evening which comes along only now and then. It was very now, but also splendidly then."

Just a few weeks after his Caesars opening, Sinatra was in a Los Angeles studio, recording a new song written for him by Paul Anka. It was inspired by a conversation the two had had months earlier in Miami Beach, in which Sinatra told Anka he was thinking of retiring. The younger star, who worshipped Sinatra and had long wanted to write a song for him, was so upset at the notion that he spent a sleepless night writing new lyrics to a French song called "Comme d'habitude," for which he had bought the US publishing rights. When he finished a final draft of the song, he brought it out to Sinatra in Las Vegas. A few weeks later, on December 30, 1968, Frank recorded it, and "My Way" went on to become his signature late-career hit—his anthem of survival in a town where he still ruled in name, if no longer in spirit.

Las Vegas never knew quite what to do with rock 'n' roll. In the early years, when even Elvis Presley couldn't excite a staid audience at the New Frontier, the music was either dismissed as kids' stuff or treated as comedy material. Nat King Cole, the revered jazz singer and balladeer who appeared regularly at the Sands, had a number in his act around 1960 called "Mr. Cole Won't Rock 'n' Roll," in which he poked fun at the trendy new music—

> One o'clock, two o'clock, three o'clock rock
> You gotta sing rock or you go in hock

—and went on to do rock 'n' roll parody versions of some of his best-known songs, like "Mona Lisa." When the Twist dance craze was sweeping the country in the early sixties, Vegas made merry. Dick Shawn introduced his own Twist-like dance called the Cockamamie. Gogi Grant sang "When They Begin to Twist the Beguine." Peter Lawford joined Jimmy Durante at the Desert Inn in what *Variety* described as "a beatnik Twister routine." (Chubby Checker, who recorded the song that launched the craze, made it to Vegas himself in 1964, when the fad was largely spent.)

Several of the early rock 'n' roll singers—the clean-cut white ones—showed up on the Vegas Strip in the late fifties and early sixties. But far from trying to change Vegas, they wanted to *be* Vegas. Frankie Avalon, the pretty-boy teen idol who had a No. 1 hit with "Venus," made his Vegas debut at the Sands in 1961 as Joey Bishop's opening act, singing classics like "Ol' Man River" and "Blow, Gabriel, Blow." Connie Francis, perhaps the leading girl singer of the early rock era ("Who's Sorry Now?," "Lipstick on Your Collar"), was a popular headliner at the Sahara for much of the 1960s. She would sing her *American Bandstand* hits during the week, when ordinary folks—"the hayshakers"—made up most of the audience, but sprinkle in Italian love songs and "Hava Nagila" on the weekends, for the high rollers.

Brenda Lee, a four-foot-nine-inch sprite from Georgia who

became a teenage hit machine with songs like "I'm Sorry" and "Break It to Me Gently," made her debut at the Sahara in 1961, at age sixteen, in a conscious effort to remake her image. "My manager's vision was to coif me over gently, from my rockabilly/rock roots, into a more adult audience and situation, for longevity," said Lee. A lover of big-band music, she hired conductor-arranger Peter Matz to do orchestrations and choreographer Richard Barstow (who had worked with Judy Garland on *A Star Is Born*) to stage her show, which included tributes to Sophie Tucker and Jimmy Durante. "It's too early to know just how a teenage femme chirp whose records sell mainly to teenagers will affect the population of a casino," said *Variety*, "but Brenda Lee had the adults in her opening night audience on her side from the first song."

Paul Anka made his Vegas debut at the Sahara in 1959 as Sophie Tucker's opening act and got such a raucous reception on opening night that the old vaudevillian asked him to close the show for the rest of the engagement. But Anka didn't want to remain merely a teen sensation. "A lot of us had a good run as teen singers in the '50s, but we weren't going to be teenagers forever," said Anka. "Those of us who wanted to survive knew we had to do something else to prove ourselves." Within a couple of years Anka was palling around with Sinatra, recording an album of standards, and headlining at the Sands.

The arrival of the Beatles, and the British invasion that followed, was initially viewed in Vegas with a mixture of amusement and disdain. "If the rock 'n' roll craze ever ends," Paul Anka quipped of the Beatles in 1964, "they'll be stuck with four lousy haircuts." When the Rolling Stones appeared on the *Hollywood Palace* TV show in 1964, guest host Dean Martin could hardly have been more dismissive. "They're going to leave right after the show for London," he cracked. "They're challenging the Beatles to a hair-pulling contest." Frank Sinatra found the

Beatles only slightly less objectionable than he had Elvis Presley. "At least they're white," he would joke to friends.

Elvis Presley liked the Beatles, especially their hard-rocking early songs, which reminded him so much of his own music in the early, groundbreaking years. But as their popularity skyrocketed, he felt threatened by them—the hot new phenoms who were making teenage girls scream the way he used to, while he drifted further into irrelevance as a force in the rock world.

They met one time. John Lennon and his bandmates idolized Elvis, acknowledged his profound influence on their music, and wanted to meet him. After some delicate negotiations, their manager, Brian Epstein, and Colonel Parker worked out a plan to bring them together during the group's second US tour in 1965. The Beatles, paying deference to the former king, agreed to meet Elvis on his turf. Following their concert at the Hollywood Bowl on August 27, 1965, the foursome scheduled a drop-in at Elvis's Bel Air home for a strictly private (no photographers, no reporters) get-together.

Most of Elvis's entourage, along with wives and girlfriends (including Priscilla), were on hand when the Beatles arrived in their limousine, a little after 10:00 p.m.; despite elaborate security precautions, hundreds of fans were crowding the gates of Elvis's Bel Air home. When the four were shown inside, Elvis was sitting on the living-room couch, watching TV with the sound turned down. (Paul was impressed; it was the first time he had ever seen color TV.) There were several minutes of strained chitchat and awkward silences. Then Ringo adjourned to play pool with some of Elvis's pals, George went off to smoke dope, and John and Paul finally got Elvis to pick up a guitar and join them in a jam session.

For the Beatles, the evening was something of a letdown. "To be honest, I'd describe Elvis on that showing as a boring old fart," their press agent said later. But when three of Elvis's friends paid a reciprocal visit to the Beatles a few days later, at their rented house in Benedict Canyon, John made a point of telling them how much the meeting with Elvis had meant. "If it hadn't been for him," John said, "I would have been nothing."

Elvis was pleased to hear it, but he couldn't disguise a certain wistful envy. "There's four of them," he said. "But there's only one of me."

As the culture began to shift, concerns grew that Vegas entertainment was not keeping pace, or doing enough to attract younger audiences. Many of the top headliners who had dominated the town for years— Danny Thomas, Red Skelton, Jack Benny, George Burns—were getting old and waning in popularity. Where were the younger stars who would replace them? Virtually none of the hard-rock bands or singer-songwriters who were transforming popular music in the late sixties would come anywhere near Las Vegas. "The hotels didn't want them, and the acts didn't want to play Vegas," said one agent. "If you played Vegas, you were selling out." Lamented *Variety* in early 1968, "Only a handful of new acts and groups are making the transition by having that 'older appeal.'"

A few of the younger pop singers did become Vegas regulars during these years, including such hitmakers as Petula Clark ("Downtown"), Trini Lopez ("If I Had a Hammer"), and Roger Miller ("King of the Road"). And for the most part, they were happy to be there. "At that time Vegas was the thing to do," said Lopez, the Texas-born Latino singer who made his Las Vegas debut in 1965. "It was prestigious. If you were doing Vegas, you were doing well." The Supremes were a popular act at the Flamingo during the late sixties, adding Cole Porter songs to their familiar repertoire of Motown hits. Playing Vegas was "huge for us," said Mary Wilson, one of the group's founding members. But the Supremes had a commercial sheen that made them well suited to nightclubs—and an artist-development team behind them at Motown that groomed them for Vegas. "We were not an R and B act," said Wilson. "We were doing standards before we were doing Motown. We were known as a classy kind of act, so it was a perfect match."

But Vegas was also trying to look hip, in an effort to attract the tie-dyed, peace-and-love generation—what *Variety* liked to call the "juve market." The lounges featured trendy dance shows like *Watusi Stampede* and *Mad Mod World*, and young music groups with a more contemporary vibe, like the Brooklyn Bridge and the Mod Squad (fronted by future country star Lee Greenwood). "Las Vegas, the bastion of adult-appealing entertainment, is going contemporary," reported *Billboard* in 1967, "reaching out for the sounds and sights of the 'now' generation." The older, more traditional lounge acts had to "get out or get groovy," as Mike Weatherford put it in *Cult Vegas*. Freddie Bell, the lounge-show rock 'n' roller from the fifties, came out of retirement to try to catch the new wave, returning to Vegas with a band called Action Faction. "I wore the bells, I wore all the outfits, trying to be what was happening at that time," Bell recalled. "But for me it didn't work."

One younger performer for whom it *did* work was Ann-Margret. The sexy musical star had first appeared in Las Vegas in 1960, as George Burns's hot-wired opening act at the Sahara. ("George Burns has a gold mine in Ann-Margret," raved *Variety*.) After a stretch in Hollywood, including her costarring role with Elvis in *Viva Las Vegas*, she came back to Vegas in July 1967 as a headliner at the Riviera, with a flashy show choreographed by David Winters, who had staged her dances in *Viva Las Vegas* (and had also choreographed three other Elvis films). Winters had barely even seen a Vegas show before. "I wanted to bring a Broadway mentality to Vegas," he said. "I wanted to blow everyone away."

And he did. Ann-Margret's show at the Riviera had a mod-sixties-psychedelic opening, with multiple film projections on a giant screen, flashing strobe lights, and pounding electronic music, as the star and eight male dancers raced out on motorcycles and Ann made a full costume change onstage, hidden by the strobes. The fast-paced show also featured a salute to the miniskirt, with Ann in go-go boots inside a gilded cage, and a tribute to old-time Broadway, with Ann tap-dancing like Ruby Keeler in *42nd Street*. "It's not often that a different kind of show hits the Strip like the Ann-Margret show," said *Variety*. "It's avant-garde, it's old-fashioned, and it's modern . . . with brilliant gimmicks never before seen in a nitery, which are certain to be copied by wise producers." "Avant-garde" might have been stretching it, but Ann-Margret's Riviera show was a landmark for Vegas, the first big show to capture the vibe and visual energy of the new "youth culture."

Contemporary rock and R&B artists were hardly unknown in Vegas during these years. Gladys Knight and the Pips, Ike and Tina Turner, the Temptations, the Righteous Brothers, Little Anthony and the Imperials—all of them played Vegas lounges during the mid- and late 1960s. Wayne Cochran, the pompadour-haired soul screamer, shook up the Flamingo lounge in August 1968 with "possibly the highest decibel count on the Strip," *Variety* reported. The flamboyant early rocker Little Richard did surprisingly strong business at the Aladdin Hotel in the spring of 1968—"the sleeper of the year," according to *Variety*. Even the godfather of soul, James Brown, headlined a show at the Flamingo, easing the crowd into his act with Vegas-friendly numbers like "I Wanna Be Around" and "That's Life." "The lewd stuff will come later," he announced. "This is Dr. Jekyll—stand by for Mr. Hyde."

Las Vegas also spawned at least one standout R&B group of its

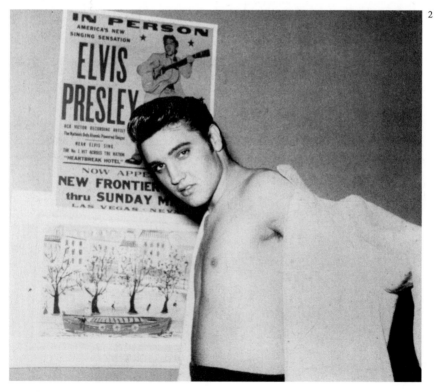

Las Vegas was still being built when Elvis Presley debuted there in 1956 at the New Frontier Hotel, which had opened a year earlier with a famous no-show.

The hip-shaking rock 'n' roller was the "extra added attraction" on a bill with Freddy Martin's orchestra and comedian Shecky Greene.

Teenage girls were screaming for him around the country, but Elvis's act baffled most of the middle-aged Vegas crowd.

Liberace, one of Vegas' most popular stars, helped out with some publicity shots—and a little advice about showmanship.

Classic Vegas:
Frank Sinatra climbed
out of a career slump
and became a fixture
at the Sands Hotel
during the 1950s.

Louis Prima and
Keely Smith electrified
the Sahara lounge
with an act dubbed
simply the Wildest.

While shooting *Ocean's 11*, the Rat Pack would gather each night in the Sands' Copa Room for the show that launched the 1960s golden age.

From left, Lawford, Sinatra, Martin, Davis, and Bishop, along with (second from right) their patron and Vegas' leading impresario, Jack Entratter.

9

Sinatra hated rock 'n' roll, but when Elvis returned from the Army, Frank gave him a welcome-home party on his ABC-TV special.

10

Davis, Martin, and Sinatra, the pared-down Rat Pack, reunited often in Vegas, the boozing, broad-chasing embodiment of Vegas cool.

Elvis had no thought of performing in Las Vegas (or anywhere else) for most of the 1960s, but the city became his favorite getaway.

Celebrating his twenty-seventh birthday in January 1962 with the Colonel's friend Sahara Hotel owner Milton Prell.

Elvis was back in Vegas in the summer of 1963 to shoot *Viva Las Vegas*—with a costar who came close to outshining him, Ann-Margret.

The two were a hot couple offscreen as well: "We both felt a current," she said. "It would become a force we couldn't control."

For virtually every pop singer of the 1960s, Vegas was an essential stop; Eddie Fisher was one of the big crowd-pleasers.

Shecky Greene, who helped introduce Elvis to Las Vegas in 1956, was an improvisational force of nature in the lounges—and offstage as well.

21

Elvis signing the contract for his comeback show (with hotel boss Alex Shoofey and booker Bill Miller) at the still-under-construction International Hotel.

22

His '69 show, which followed Barbra Streisand's in the International's two-thousand-seat showroom, set a new record for Vegas hype.

"His own resurrection," said *Rolling Stone*: Elvis on opening night, July 31, 1969.

At a midnight press conference after his opening, Elvis basked in the acclaim.

For four weeks—two shows a night without a single night off—he played to sell-out crowds in Las Vegas' largest showroom.

Twice a year the International Hotel—later the Hilton—was turned into an Elvis Presley fun zone.

Colonel Parker (with Sammy Davis Jr. and Robert Goulet) was a constant presence, orchestrating his greatest carnival show ever.

28

Elvis was still at the top of his game in 1970; after that, the white suits grew more garish and the shows more bombastic.

29

Elvis appeared in 636 shows over seven years. But he never left the building, his legacy in Vegas kept alive by "Elvis tribute artists" forever.

Elvis brought a broader, Middle America audience to Las Vegas, auguring a new era of splashy, family-oriented entertainment.

And Elvis was the model for a new generation of pop stars signing on for Vegas "residencies," from Céline Dion to (here in 2018) Lady Gaga.

own in the 1960s. The Checkmates were a mixed-race group (three blacks and two whites), headed by honey-voiced lead singer Sonny Charles. They came to Vegas in 1964 to work at the Pussycat A-Go-Go and developed a high-energy act strongly influenced by the Treniers, the popular fifties Vegas lounge group, which featured covers of R&B hits, spiced with comedy antics. They would don cowboy hats and ride stick horses, say, or put on boxing trunks and gloves for a spoof of the Sonny Liston–Cassius Clay heavyweight bout. After Sinatra invited them to entertain at his New Year's Eve party at the Sands, they were booked into the Sands' lounge. From there they moved to Caesars Palace, recorded with Nancy Wilson, and made several national TV appearances, even before they had a hit record. (They made the charts in 1969 with "Black Pearl," produced by Phil Spector.)

The Checkmates were one of the most popular Vegas lounge acts of the sixties, proof that R&B in a relatively undiluted form could work in Vegas if it was showcased with enough razzle-dazzle. "We were such an oddity because we were doing straight-out rhythm and blues," said Charles. "The Temptations, Four Tops, Gladys Knight, and all those people would come to town, and their Vegas act would be a bunch of show tunes. The Temptations came to see us and they went, 'They're doing our songs and packing the place, and we're doing "42nd Street." We should be doing *our* show!'" The outsiders taught the Checkmates some lessons too. When Sly Stone was booked into the Pussycat A-Go-Go, he refused to appear after discovering that blacks in the audience were segregated and relegated to a side section. "He'd come from San Francisco, and they didn't do that there," said Charles. "After that we looked at it and go, 'You know, Sly's right.'" They insisted that the club end the practice and got their way.

The changing musical winds were reflected in the shows of more mainstream Vegas singers as well. Vic Damone sang "MacArthur

Park" and "For Once in My Life." Everyone from Wayne Newton to the Lennon Sisters ("no relation") was covering Lennon and McCartney's "Yesterday." Yet there were perils for a performer who tried to update his act and image too drastically. The major cautionary tale was Bobby Darin.

He was born in East Harlem in 1936, a sickly child raised by his maternal grandmother and an older sister—who he discovered in later years was actually his mother. He worked his way into the Brill Building group of pop songwriters and wrote and recorded such early hits as "Splish Splash" and "Queen of the Hop." But Darin slid into a more sophisticated jazz groove with his swinging 1959 take on Kurt Weill's "Mack the Knife." George Burns brought Darin to Las Vegas in May 1959 as his opening act at the Sahara. "Self-assured, almost cocky in manner, young Bobby Darin cradled a sophisticated house in the palm of his hand," said *Downbeat*, "and made his bid as leading contender to the title, Young Sinatra."

Darin became a popular headliner at the Flamingo (recording an excellent live album there in 1963, unreleased until after his death) and proved to be one of Vegas' most versatile and dynamic young performers. He specialized in jazzy, up-tempo versions of old songs like "Beyond the Sea" and "Artificial Flowers" and also dabbled in folk, country, and gospel. He even did impressions. For a while he seemed the frontrunner to inherit Sinatra's mantle as the swinging, swaggering king of Vegas—with an ego to match.

But he left Las Vegas for three years in 1963 and returned as a more serious, politically committed performer, adding folk and social-protest numbers to his act. He worked on Robert F. Kennedy's 1968 campaign for president; then, after Kennedy's assassination (Darin was with him at the Ambassador Hotel in Los Angeles on June 6, the night he was shot), he retreated to a cabin in Big Sur and rethought his career.

When he returned to Vegas in 1969, he dumped the tuxedo in favor of jeans and a denim jacket, replaced his orchestra with a rhythm quartet, and insisted on being billed as Bob (not Bobby) Darin.

The makeover did not sit well with the Vegas audience. Darin filled his set with socially conscious message songs, including his own composition, "A Simple Song of Freedom." When someone in the audience called out for "Artificial Flowers," Darin shot back, "That was yesterday!" His appearance at the Sahara Hotel in December 1969 was something of a disaster. "Bobby sat on a stool for forty-five minutes and bored everyone to death," recalled his agent, Don Gregory. "Everyone came out in shock." Darin's friend Dick Clark tried to knock some sense into him: "Go back and put on the tuxedo and go to work. Do what the people expect of you."

Darin eventually compromised, restoring some of his old hits to the act, and when he appeared at the Landmark Hotel a few months later, his two-week engagement was extended to six weeks. His career had a mild uptick after that—he returned several more times to Vegas and got his own NBC variety show in 1972—until his premature death in 1973, from a congenital heart ailment, at age thirty-seven.

The cultural upheavals of the sixties were felt especially acutely by the younger generation of stand-up comics influenced by Lenny Bruce, the rebel-satirist who died of a drug overdose in August 1966 (and was one of the few major comedians of the era who never played Vegas). Richard Pryor made his Las Vegas debut that same month, opening for Bobby Darin at the Flamingo, and got a warm welcome: "The young comedian scored consistently with first-nighters," said *Variety*, "through the Bill Cosby school of reminiscing and identifiable storytelling." But Pryor was moving into rougher, more overtly racial material, and when he appeared at the Aladdin Hotel a year later, he was fired after ignoring warnings about his explicit language. Pryor described his last performance there as a kind of drug-fueled epiphany, triggered when he saw Dean Martin staring at him from the audience.

"I imagined what I looked like and got disgusted," he wrote in his memoir, *Pryor Convictions*. "I grasped for clarity as if it were oxygen. The fog rolled in. And in a burst of inspiration I finally spoke to the sold-out crowd: 'What the fuck am I doing here?' Then I turned and walked off the stage." Marty Beck, the Las Vegas–based agent for GAC (General Artists Corporation), who represented Pryor and many other performers in Vegas, remembered a somewhat more colorful walk-off: Pryor singing new lyrics to the *Mickey Mouse Club* theme song—"F-U-C-K-E-Y, M-O-U-S-E"—crying "Fuck you!" to Aladdin owner Milton Prell, and storming out. The entertainment booker for the hotel, sitting at a table with Beck, turned to him and said, "You just cost me my job."

George Carlin was another young comic who was experimenting with more provocative material and testing the boundaries of Vegas acceptability. At the Frontier Hotel in 1969 he did a routine about his small ass: "When I was in the Air Force, black guys used to look at me in the shower and say, 'Hey, man, you ain't got no ass.'" Some conventioneers in the audience complained, and the hotel cut his engagement short. Comedians like Buddy Hackett were getting away with much stronger language on the Strip, but the long-haired Carlin seemed a different, more dangerous kettle of fish. A few months later he was back at the Frontier to fill out his contractual obligation and got into more trouble with a routine about the word *shit*: "Buddy Hackett says 'shit' right down the street. Redd Foxx says 'shit' on the other side of the street. I don't say 'shit.' I'll *smoke* a little of it. . . ." This time he was fired for good.

Even as the sixties revolution was challenging old taboos and freeing up artists of all kinds, Vegas was still a conservative place. Its mostly middle-aged, Middle American audiences didn't want to be provoked or lectured to or unsettled in any way. They wanted warm, comfortable, reassuring entertainment; they wanted to feel the love. They wanted Wayne Newton.

He was the quintessential Vegas entertainer of the post–Rat Pack years: a corny, crowd-pleasing avatar of an earlier show business era. He wasn't cool and edgy like Sinatra and his Rat Pack cohorts, but old-fashioned, sentimental, eager to please—more like Al Jolson or Eddie Cantor, or that old Vegas schmaltzmeister Liberace. He was Vegas' greatest homegrown star: a performer who came of age in Las Vegas, who spent virtually his entire career there, and who never approached the same level of success anywhere else.

Carson Wayne Newton was born in Norfolk, Virginia, on April 3, 1942, one of two sons of half–Native American parents. He began playing the piano at age four, and by six was singing regularly on a local radio show. His chronic allergies forced the family to move to Phoenix when Wayne was ten. While still in high school, he and his older brother, Jerry, appeared on a local TV variety show and caught the attention of a booker for the Fremont Hotel in Las Vegas. He brought them up for an audition and hired them for two weeks in the hotel's lounge. Wayne was only sixteen, not old enough to step into the casino.

Their two-week gig was extended, and the Newton brothers spent the next five years in the downtown Fremont lounge—Wayne singing, Jerry making jokes and accompanying him on guitar. They made their national TV debut on Jackie Gleason's CBS variety show, and Bobby Darin signed them to a recording contract, handing Wayne the song that would become his first big hit, "Danke Schoen." In 1965, after a couple of years touring with Jack Benny, they were big enough to headline their own show in the main room at the Flamingo Hotel.

They were still a brother act, but Wayne was clearly the star: a pudgy, cherub-faced singer with a velvety, androgynous soprano. He could swing on oldies like "Swanee" or "Won't You Come Home Bill Bailey," or belt out a Broadway showstopper like "What Kind of Fool Am I?"; he ranged easily from country ("Your Cheatin' Heart") to contemporary ("Goin' Out of My Head") and often closed the show with a roof-raising "When the Saints Go Marching In." While Wayne did the singing, his brother provided a kind of Greek chorus of acerbic commentary. "I want to do something that we've never tried before," Wayne might announce, and Jerry would quip, "Who are you kidding? We do the same bloody thing every night." Jerry would taunt him with nicknames like "Fig" Newton, or "Hey, you with the pompadour hairdo and shoulder pads." The show would always include a segment in which Wayne would show off his musical versatility by playing five or six instruments in a row—guitar, banjo, violin, trumpet—and Jerry would crack, "I'd take off my coat, but I'm afraid he'd play that too."

Newton nuzzled up to the audience, teased it, flattered it by promising to entertain until the cows came home: "We got no place to go— I'd just as soon stay here with you, is that all right?" He was hammy and sentimental. For one closing number, he donned clown makeup and had a conversation with himself in a mirror, lamenting all the friends who didn't come to his birthday party, before closing with "You're Nobody Till Somebody Loves You." In another maudlin bit, Wayne would sing "Danny Boy" while his brother read a letter written by a slain serviceman to his mother. "When he sings 'Dreams of the Everyday Housewife,' women in the audience do everything but fetch him cookies and milk right there in the nightclub," *Time* said in a 1970 profile.

"Wayne is square and he knows it. . . . American mothers get precious little filial devotion these days, and Wayne represents an age when boys loved their mamma and weren't afraid to show it."

Vegas audiences went wild for him. "The Flamingo is charged with a near revivalist hysteria as Wayne Newton exhorts his flock of glory-be's into pandemonium and standing ovations," said *Variety* in a 1968 review. The Frontier Hotel hired him away from the Flamingo for $52,000 a week, and he became one of Howard Hughes's favorite stars—the kind of wholesome, all-American entertainer that Hughes thought Vegas needed more of. Walter Kane, Hughes's veteran entertainment director, became such a close friend and benefactor that Wayne referred to him as Grandfather. Newton never saw Hughes (nobody did), but he felt like a favored son. "Many nights there would come a knock on the door," Newton wrote in his autobiography, "and a guy would appear in my dressing room and say to me, 'Mr. Hughes wants you to know he knows what you're doing and he's proud of the kind of entertainment you're representing. He's happy that you're a member of his family.'" (Newton, a lifelong Republican, was the one performer James Watt, President Reagan's interior secretary, picked to entertain at the July 4, 1983, celebration on the Capitol Mall, after he banned rock groups for promoting drug use.)

Newton was a longtime Las Vegas resident and booster, buying a forty-acre ranch he called Casa de Shenandoah, where he raised Arabian horses. His weight ballooned (up to 275 pounds at one point, before he began working out with Hollywood muscleman Steve Reeves), and so did his shows, which often ran two hours or more, flouting the hotels' customary time limits. Ron Rosenbaum, who profiled Newton for *Esquire* in 1982, saw this as the key to his popularity: his ability to create the illusion that every show was a unique personal gift to the audience: "Everyone leaves The Show feeling totally satisfied, thinking how hip, how simpatico, how special the whole evening was, how they've been present at one of those rare moments when the rules went by the board; how Wayne drove himself past his own limits, knocking himself out just for them."

Not everyone in Las Vegas was in love with Wayne Newton. He seemed to collect enemies. Paul Anka, Totie Fields, and comedian Jan Murray were among the performers he had feuds with. He hated Jack Entratter because the Sands chief supposedly once told his manager, "Get that fag out of here." When Johnny Carson began making gay jokes about Newton on the *Tonight* show (the girlish voice always raised eyebrows—though Newton was married twice and had two daughters), Newton stormed into Carson's NBC office and threatened him if he didn't stop. Many Vegas musicians found Newton arrogant and difficult to work with and hated doing his extralong shows. "The one show I found I had to drink to get through was Wayne Newton," recalled one player. "It was like giving a pint of blood."

Newton and his brother had an acrimonious split in 1971. Jerry was clearly overshadowed by his brother, and Wayne later admitted he had grown resentful of Jerry's constant mockery. "It got to the point in the late '60s where, no matter what I was doing onstage, he would either interrupt or make jokes about it," Newton said. "It was driving me crazy." Newton claimed the settlement left him $3 million in debt, and the two didn't speak for ten years. (Jerry Newton was later convicted of bank fraud, in a case unrelated to his brother, and sentenced to six years in prison.) Most notoriously, Wayne Newton filed a much-publicized libel suit against NBC, over a story that linked him to mob figures, stemming from his purchase of the Aladdin Hotel in 1980. (Newton won a $19.3 million verdict from a federal jury in Las Vegas, but it was overturned on appeal.) None of which seemed to matter to Newton's fanatically loyal fans, who continued to flock to his Vegas shows. By the mid-1990s he had made more than twenty-five thousand Vegas appearances, a record that will probably never be broken.

"Vegas is unto itself," Stan Irwin, the Sahara Hotel's entertainment director, liked to say. "In those days it set no precedent and followed no precedent. It just was." Wayne Newton might have been Exhibit A. He was, if nothing else, an original: he seemed to inhabit his own musical world, an imitator of no one who came before, a model for no one who came after. But Vegas in the late sixties was also opening its doors to singers who reflected more of the changes taking place in contemporary music. One was Tom Jones.

He was born Thomas John Woodward, in the coal-mining country of South Wales. He dropped out of high school at age sixteen to marry his pregnant girlfriend and by his early twenties was fronting a local rock band, Tommy Scott and the Senators. A London manager and songwriter named Gordon Mills discovered him, changed his name to Tom Jones, and guided him to overnight stardom in 1965 with his first hit, "It's Not Unusual." Jones had a husky, raspy baritone, redolent of the fifties rock 'n' roll and blues singers that he listened to growing up. (Elvis Presley, like many others hearing Jones for the first time, assumed he was black.) Onstage he was a galvanic, openly sexual performer—his shirt unbuttoned to the navel, hips gyrating in his skintight pants. "I'm trying to get across to the audience that I'm alive," he told an interviewer. "All of it, the emotion and the sex and the power, the heartbeat and the bloodstream, are all theirs for the asking."

By 1968, after several hit singles and TV guest appearances, he came to Las Vegas. "There was a strong sense at the time that playing Vegas was something you earned the right to do—that it was something you had to qualify for," Jones said in his memoir, *Over the Top and Back.* Not everyone in Vegas was ready for him. Jack Entratter turned down a chance to book him at the Sands. "Entratter could no more relate to Tom Jones than he could to Mötley Crüe," recalled GAC agent Marty Beck, who represented Jones in Las Vegas. "He said, 'I don't want this kind of act in my hotel.'"

Jones wound up at the Flamingo, which gave him a big promotional push, touting the engagement as "Tom Jones Fever" (partly to distinguish it from *Tom Jones*, a bawdy musical-comedy show based on Henry Fielding's novel, which was doing good business at the Desert Inn). His debut in March 1968 drew sellout crowds and stirred up a kind of frenzy that Vegas had never before seen. *Variety* found him "different in both sound and delivery; he puts both voice and body into each song, the anatomical animation giving tablers an interesting visual treat." Observed John Scott in the *Los Angeles Times,* "The tall, ruggedly handsome young man from Britain held first-nighters in the palm of his hand with a dynamic, temperature-raising performance. As he bounced and wriggled his way around the Flamingo's theater-restaurant stage, Jones had mink-clad matrons and mini-skirted maids screaming with excitement." When he played the Copa in New York, women in the audience threw their panties onstage. In Vegas they started throwing room keys.

Much of that electricity onstage is captured in an album he recorded at the Flamingo in 1969, *Tom Jones: Live in Las Vegas.* ("That album is steaming, if I say so myself," Jones said.) He holds back nothing with his angsty, tonsil-straining performances of "I Can't Stop Loving You" and "I'll Never Fall in Love Again"; pushes the Beatles' "Yesterday" further over the top than anyone thought possible; and does a version of the Irish ballad "Danny Boy" so bombastic it could frighten small children. The soft-spoken, Welsh-accented lilt of his stage patter only accentuates his fevered, breath-defying performances. You almost sweat while listening to him.

Tom Jones was a belter for a new Vegas era. And the person who would come to embody that new era was paying attention. Indeed, if there was one entertainer who laid the groundwork for Elvis Presley's comeback in Las Vegas, it was Tom Jones.

The two had first met on the Paramount lot in 1965, where Elvis was finishing up the filming of *Paradise, Hawaiian Style*, and the young Welsh singer, in Los Angeles for a TV appearance, stopped by for a visit. Tom was flattered when Elvis greeted him by singing "With These Hands," one of the songs on Tom's new album. Three years later Elvis drove up from Los Angeles with Priscilla to see Tom's debut at the Flamingo and went backstage afterward to congratulate him. He wanted to see Tom's show, Elvis said, because he was thinking of returning to live performing himself.

They met again a couple of months later in Hawaii, where Elvis was vacationing and Tom was appearing at the Ilikai Hotel. The two spent a long afternoon together at Elvis's rented beach house, jamming to fifties rock 'n' roll songs, talking about the Beatles and Tom's childhood in Wales, and comparing stage moves on the lawn.

Jones's influence on Elvis's Vegas show was obvious to many of those who saw them both. "What Elvis got from Tom was the trick of working the Vegas stage," said the International Hotel's publicity director Nick Naff. "Tom showed him you have to be sensual in a way that gets through to the overthirties. Tom gave Elvis the freeze poses at the end of songs, the trick of wiping the sweat with a cloth and then throwing it out in the house." Jones was the kind of magnetic stage performer that Elvis used to be and longed to be again.

He had not done any live performing since a benefit concert in Hawaii in March 1961—an entire decade had essentially passed him by.

Colonel Parker was the main culprit, keeping him on a nonstop movie treadmill, while steering him to the bland pop songs that Elvis's publishing company, Hill & Range, owned the rights to. But Elvis's own inertia was also to blame. "The Colonel behind the scenes controlled a lot," said Jerry Schilling, Elvis's Memphis friend and sometime employee. "But Elvis was really in charge of his career. If he had wanted to tour, he could have. But most of the time he was doing three movies a year. And the music business had changed drastically. He didn't have a hit for seven years. When you're not having hit records, when nine or ten months of the year you're on a movie set, and you've got to record for those films— I don't think he had time to really think about it that much."

By the end of 1967, however, Elvis was nearly at the breaking point. And the Colonel, too, was finally ready for a change. He had little choice. Elvis's last few films had barely made enough money to cover their costs, and when his current contract with MGM was fulfilled, it was doubtful that any major studio would sign Elvis for more films—at least, not for the money Colonel Parker thought his star deserved. So the Colonel switched gears and went to NBC in December 1967 with a proposal that Elvis star in his first-ever television special, to air the following December. A deal was quickly made; Singer sewing machines was lined up as sole sponsor; and taping was set to begin in June.

The Colonel's original idea was for a conventional Christmas special—Elvis singing holiday songs, like Andy Williams or Bing Crosby. But NBC hired a hip young director named Steve Binder, who had a more ambitious idea. Binder—who had directed NBC's rock-music show *Hullabaloo*, as well as a critically acclaimed Petula Clark special—wanted to showcase the full range of Elvis's talents, to reintroduce the viewing audience to the "real" Elvis Presley. The Colonel balked, but Binder won Elvis's confidence and essentially got free rein to put together the show he wanted.

Binder junked the Christmas idea and came up with a concept for the show that revolved around the Jerry Reed song "Guitar Man," with Elvis playing a small-town guitar player who tries to make it in the big city. But after watching Elvis jamming with friends in his dressing room, Binder came up with the idea of trying to re-create one of those jam sessions for the show: just Elvis and a few musicians onstage, casual and unrehearsed, on a small boxing-ring-style stage, surrounded by a couple of hundred spectators. Elvis was excited by the idea, but also petrified. When the segment was preparing to tape in late June, he was so nervous that Binder practically had to push him onstage.

Singer Presents Elvis aired on December 3, 1968. The show had some fairly standard, TV-variety-show elements, including the long, choreographed "Guitar Man" sequence. But it was Elvis's amazingly fresh and dynamic vocal performance—both in solo, concert-style segments and in the unrehearsed jam session, joined by Scotty Moore and D. J. Fontana, his original guitarist and drummer—that was a revelation. Looking trim and gorgeous in a black leather suit with a high Edwardian collar (designed by Bill Belew, who would later design all of his Vegas outfits), Elvis blasted away the cobwebs on old hits like "All Shook Up" and "Heartbreak Hotel," seemed reanimated on rock numbers he hadn't done in years, like "Tryin' to Get to You" and "Love Me," and showed a softer side with new songs like the sentimental "Memories," which he introduced on the show. (And, to placate the Colonel, one holiday number: "Blue Christmas.")

For the closing number, the show offered a taste of things to come. Binder had asked arranger Earl Brown to write a new song to end the show, something that would connect Elvis with the social and political idealism of the times. Brown came up with "If I Can Dream"—a heartfelt, if generalized, plea for tolerance and understanding. Dressed in a white double-breasted suit, with ELVIS in giant, red-bulb-lit block letters behind him (which would become his omnipresent logo in Vegas), Elvis delivered the song with passion and power. Released as a single in November, before the show aired, "If I Can Dream" was his biggest-selling record in four years.

The Elvis comeback special, often referred to as the Singer special, drew 42 percent of the viewing audience, NBC's highest-rated show of the season. More important, it gave notice, to fans and critics alike, that Elvis Presley was relevant once again as a rock artist. "There is something magical about watching a man who has lost himself find his way back home," wrote critic Jon Landau. "He sang with the kind of power people no longer expect from a rock 'n' roll singer." "It was like nothing I had ever seen on television before," recalled Elvis biographer Peter Guralnick, "both a revelation *and* a vindication."

Elvis and everyone around him recognized the show as a breakthrough and turning point. "He could have done it so much earlier," said Billy Smith, his cousin and longtime member of the entourage. "But he had to be shoved into a corner and almost kicked before he would bite." In his dressing room after the taping in June, Elvis was excited in a way he hadn't been in years. "I want to tour again," he told the Colonel. "I want to go out and work with a live audience."

Las Vegas, meanwhile, was getting ready for him.

Like Howard Hughes, the man he would soon challenge for supremacy in Las Vegas, Kirk Kerkorian began his career as an airplane pilot. During World War II he ferried transport planes across the Atlantic for the British Royal Air Force, and after the war he built a successful air-service company that leased and chartered planes. He often stopped over in Las Vegas, where he was a big gambler, and began buying up property there in the early 1960s, including the land on which Caesars Palace was later built. In 1967 he acquired the Flamingo Hotel, along with an eighty-two-acre parcel of land off the Strip, near the Convention Center. There he made plans to build Vegas' biggest hotel yet.

The $60 million International Hotel was a perfect symbol of Las Vegas' corporate transformation. It had no architectural distinction or theme-park gimmicks; it was simply a massive, thirty-story tower with three wings, 1,512 rooms, and the largest casino in the world. Kerkorian, a self-effacing mogul almost as shy of the press as Hughes (but without the psychoses), used the Flamingo as a training ground for the staff that would eventually move over to the International for its opening in July 1969. To run both hotels he hired Alex Shoofey, longtime vice president at the Sahara, who was known as one of the shrewdest hotel operators and toughest bean counters in town. ("He knew where every goddamn penny was spent," said one Vegas PR man. "He counted the rolls of toilet paper.") Shoofey, in turn, coaxed Bill Miller to come out of retirement to be his director of entertainment.

Miller—who had come to Vegas in the mid-1950s and booked entertainment for the Sahara and later the Dunes Hotel—was in his sixties now, but he was a crafty booker, willing to take chances. He hired Tom Jones at the Flamingo when Jack Entratter wanted nothing to do with him. He rescued Sonny and Cher from a career slump, booking them into the Flamingo's main room, where they developed the bantering, bickering act that led to their popular CBS variety series. To open the International, he wanted a star who was big enough to fill the huge two-thousand-seat showroom and would set the hotel above and apart from its many Vegas competitors. His choice was Elvis Presley.

It probably seemed like a long shot at first, since Colonel Parker had for years turned down all offers for Elvis to perform in concert. After the NBC comeback special, however, the Colonel was looking for a suitably high-profile follow-up. Lamar Fike, a longtime member of Elvis's Memphis Mafia, recalled a conversation with Colonel Parker in a limousine as they were driving into Las Vegas, not long after the taping of the NBC special. "The Colonel was in the front seat of the limo with his driver, and I was in the back with Elvis," said Fike. "The Colonel turned around with his cigar and said, 'You know, we can take that show you just did and put it in Vegas and make a lot of money.' Elvis looked at me, shrugged his shoulders and said, 'Sounds like we're playing Vegas.' "

A couple of weeks after the NBC special had aired, to big ratings and much acclaim, Colonel Parker struck a deal with the International. Elvis would get $100,000 a week—matching Sinatra and Dean Martin at the top of Vegas' salary scale—for a four-week engagement at the hotel. There was only one sticking point: Colonel Parker did not want Elvis to open the hotel. It was too risky, he argued, for his boy to launch a new showroom in a new hotel before all the technical kinks—the sound system, the lighting—had been worked out. Get someone else to be the guinea pig, Colonel Parker said; Elvis will come in second. So Bill Miller went after his backup choice, Barbra Streisand, and signed her (for the same $100,000 salary) to open the hotel on July 2, 1969. Elvis Presley would arrive four weeks later.

Before he could start planning for Las Vegas, however, Elvis had a couple of other obligations. One was dutiful and dreary: in the spring of 1969 he shot his thirty-first and last movie, *Change of Habit*, costarring Mary Tyler Moore as a nun helping out Elvis (as a doctor!) in an inner-city health clinic—a film Colonel Parker had convinced NBC to finance as part of the deal for the TV special. The other project was considerably more rewarding: in January and February Elvis went into a Memphis studio for one of the most important recording sessions of his career.

Elvis had been doing most of his recent recording at RCA's studios in Nashville—routine sessions of mostly mediocre songs, with Elvis increasingly bored and disengaged. He was scheduled to go back to Nashville in January of 1969, but two of his Memphis friends, George Klein and Marty Lacker, told him he ought to try recording at Chips Moman's American Sound Studio, right there in Memphis. Moman's studio was getting a lot of buzz, having turned out a string of hits for singers like Wilson Pickett, Dionne Warwick, and the Box Tops. Elvis didn't need much convincing. Moman was eager to work with him and postponed a Neil Diamond session so that Elvis could begin recording there on January 13.

Moman, a savvy producer who had been one of the founders of Memphis's Stax Records, told Elvis he wanted to find some first-rate new material for him. That meant reaching out to new songwriters and picking songs that Elvis's own company might not have the publishing rights to. Elvis said he cared more about hits than publishing rights, and he gave Moman the OK. The result was a bounty of quality songs, among them "Suspicious Minds" (written by Memphis songwriter Mark James, who had recorded it himself the year before), Eddie Rabbitt's "Kentucky Rain," and Jerry Butler's "Only the Strong Survive"— all songs that suited Elvis's big voice and flair for dramatics, songs that would form the core of his repertoire for years to come.

The most controversial number of the Memphis sessions, however, was an overt piece of social commentary called "In the Ghetto." It was written by a young Atlanta songwriter named Mac Davis—who had also composed "A Little Less Conversation" for Elvis's 1968 movie *Live a Little, Love a Little*, as well as "Memories," which Elvis had introduced on the NBC special. "In the Ghetto" was a message song, about the vicious circle of poverty and crime facing inner-city children. (Davis had initially called it "Vicious Circle," and he assumed it would be recorded by an African American singer. He even went to Lake Tahoe to show it to Sammy Davis Jr., who turned it down.) Elvis and others in his camp weren't sure whether he should record it, worried that the song was too political. But when Moman said he would give it to another of his artists instead, Elvis changed his mind, and he performed it with a quiet intensity that buried all doubts. "In the Ghetto" was the first single on the album to be released, in April 1969. By June it was No. 3 on *Billboard*'s Hot 100 chart, the best performance for any Elvis song since 1965.

Mac Davis, who went on to a substantial career as a country-music singer himself, remained one of Elvis's favorite songwriters. (The Colonel liked him too. When they first met, after "A Little Less Conversation" was recorded, Colonel Parker told Davis to bend over so he could rub his curly head. "Now you go tell everybody that the Colonel rubbed your head," said the old carny. "You're gonna be a star.") Davis's work—particularly "In the Ghetto," "Memories," and another of his numbers that Elvis recorded in Memphis, "Don't Cry Daddy"— satisfied Elvis's craving for songs of more substance, emotion, and not a little sentimentality. "Elvis was really trying to find his way out of that vicious circle too," said Davis. "He wanted to get back to being the performer that he was."

And soon he would.

Six

COMEBACK
(Elvis Reborn)

What was going through Elvis Presley's mind in the early summer of 1969, as he prepared for his first live stage appearance in eight years, at the International Hotel in Las Vegas?

It has been a rough decade for him, in many ways a disastrous one. His two-year hitch in the Army, from 1958 to 1960, had effectively bisected his career: ending the skyrocketing-to-fame early phase, during which he virtually revolutionized American popular music. He returned from the Army a much-changed, much-diluted performer. After one awkward "welcome home" TV special (forced to play second fiddle to Frank Sinatra), he largely retreated to Hollywood and abandoned live performing—along with much of the hard-driving rock 'n' roll that had launched his career, in favor of mostly bland, disposable pop songs. Amid the radical changes that were taking place in music, and the rest of the culture, during the 1960s—the arrival of the Beatles, the ascension of the singer-songwriter, the embrace of social and political protest, and the quest for spiritual enlightenment, often aided by drugs—the founding father of rock 'n' roll was looking increasingly out of touch, over-the-hill.

"You have to remember how the counterculture hated him," said rock critic Richard Goldstein. "By then he was doing music that we considered plastic. The talent was always there, but it was encrusted with this horrible veneer of stylization and commercialization, an utter inability to be authentic—that 'good boy of the South' image. He was led in the wrong direction."

Yet, against all odds, now there was some hope. His comeback special on NBC in December 1968 had reintroduced a still-vital performer to a public that had largely written him off. Emboldened by the reception, and at the end of his rope in Hollywood, Elvis was now determined to return to live performing. It was Colonel Parker's idea, not his, to make that return in Las Vegas, but from a promotional point of view, it made sense. Elvis would be headlining in the biggest showroom, in the biggest hotel, in the biggest entertainment center in the nation, guaranteeing maximum attention. But it was a make-or-break gamble, the most daunting challenge of his career. Could Elvis Presley, at age thirty-four, resurrect his career in Las Vegas?

Nearly everyone was rooting for him. For all the weirdness of Elvis's world—the reclusive star, the entourage of sycophants, the cornpone Svengali pulling strings behind the scenes, the private eccentricities and drug problems that became widely known only later—people liked Elvis Presley. Those who met him or worked with him or became part of his circle in these years were struck by his modesty, his gracious Southern manners, his genuineness. He was still, in many ways, an overgrown country boy. He never got over the loss of his beloved mother (who died at age forty-six, of heart failure brought on by acute hepatitis, in August 1958, just as Elvis was getting ready to go overseas for his Army service) and kept his father, Vernon, close by to manage his finances. Elvis spent money wildly, often irrationally, but was unfailingly generous—buying cars and houses for friends, giving out gold watches (ordered in quantity from his Memphis jeweler) to dozens of people he crossed paths with. He grew up in a churchgoing family and retained a strong religious faith; singing gospel music was his favorite form of relaxation.

He was insecure, and his ego needed to be fed constantly. He had what Jerry Schilling called "the worst temper I ever saw." But he was not pretentious or phony. He was curious about people, a good listener, and an avid reader. Even after his spiritual guru, Larry Geller, was banished from his inner circle, Elvis's room was always piled high with books of spiritual and religious seeking. He had a high school kid's playfulness and irreverence, with a penchant for juvenile pranks and jokes. "I liked him a lot," said Mac Davis, the singer-songwriter who composed several hits for him and became a casual friend. "He was an easy laugh. He was kind of a poster boy for arrested development, you know—he was nineteen forever. But he was a pretty amazing guy, really. It was the circus that went on around him, that was the thing."

The circus consisted of an entourage of longtime friends and employees—a constantly evolving group that included old high school pals, family members, former Army buddies, and assorted hangers-on. In some ways they were good for him: they kept him grounded, connected to his roots, and provided an outlet for his frustrations and bad moods. Yet they also coddled and flattered him shamelessly and kept him insulated from honest criticism. Priscilla Presley describes in her memoir a telling incident during her first trip to the United States to visit him. After returning from a recording session, Elvis played for her some of the songs he was working on and asked her opinion. She made the mistake of telling him what she really thought: she loved his singing, but wished he would do more old-style rock 'n' roll songs, like "Jailhouse Rock." Elvis flew into a rage—"God damn it, I didn't ask for your opinion on what style I should sing; I asked if you liked the songs!"—and stormed out of the room. Priscilla, still in the first flush of her romance, was shocked to find herself the target of a temper she had seen but not yet experienced. She learned to tread carefully after that. So did everyone else.

Colonel Parker usually bears the brunt of blame for Elvis's career stagnation in the 1960s. The Colonel went for the surefire payday in Hollywood, over and over, even as Elvis's confidence and creative spirit were withering. In the mid-1960s the Colonel negotiated an exploitive deal with Elvis, his only client, which gave him 50 percent of the profits from all Elvis enterprises, on top of his usual 25 percent management fee. He pushed away talented people who won Elvis's confidence and threatened the Colonel's sway over his star—among them Steve Binder, director of the 1968 comeback special on NBC, and Chips Moman, the producer who oversaw the 1969 Memphis recording sessions that were Elvis's most productive in years, neither of whom ever worked with Elvis again. The Colonel never allowed Elvis to travel overseas, for what would surely have been lucrative and rejuvenating foreign tours, owing to the shady circumstances surrounding his own illegal immigration to the United States from Holland in 1929. Colonel Parker, it seems, didn't have a passport.

Yet Tom Parker also deserves much of the credit for orchestrating Elvis's spectacular rise to fame, as well as for staying out of the way creatively; once Elvis stepped inside the recording studio, the Colonel's role ended. Nor was Elvis himself entirely blameless for the rut his career fell into. "The Colonel did not make any deals that Elvis didn't approve in advance," said Loanne Miller Parker, who was working at the International Hotel when Colonel Parker hired her as an assistant (and who would become his second wife). "In fact, if I ever saw him a little nervous, it was when he was going to meet with Elvis and hoped that Elvis would or would not do whatever he was going to present to him." Joe Esposito, Elvis's longtime road manager, felt that Elvis often used the Colonel as a buffer. "The Colonel was forced to speak for Elvis many times because Elvis hated interviews, so it often appeared that the Colonel exercised more control than he actually did," Esposito said. "Despite his complaints, Elvis always reserved the final decision. If he followed the Colonel's advice more often than he should have, it was because he preferred that someone else take responsibility in case a decision turned out to be wrong."

By 1969, however, they were in agreement on one decision: it was time for Elvis to return to the concert stage. His movies were no longer doing much business, and live concerts were becoming a more lucrative option; top rock groups and solo superstars like Barbra Streisand were getting up to $100,000 for one-nighters. Tom Diskin, Colonel Parker's assistant, acknowledged to the press that Elvis's movie income was declining and that "for the time that goes into it, it's more profitable for him to appear in public." Elvis had been away for a long time, and there was no assurance he could draw crowds like he used to. But the Colonel's plan was to test the waters and light the promotional spark in Las Vegas, setting the stage for Elvis's return to national touring.

The timing was good, for it came in the midst of a revival of interest in vintage rock 'n' roll. Pioneering rockers from the 1950s like Chuck Berry, Little Richard, Fats Domino, and the Everly Brothers, out of the limelight for years, were back doing concerts—some even playing Las Vegas. Radio stations around the country were revisiting rock's classic era with "oldies" formats. At the Woodstock rock festival in August 1969—which came smack in the middle of Elvis's comeback engagement in Las Vegas—one of the more unlikely hit acts was a greased-up sextet doing tongue-in-cheek versions of old doo-wop numbers, called Sha Na Na. "Teenagers seem to be tiring of bloodless electronic experimentation and intellectualism," said *Time* magazine in August 1969, "and may be ready to discover for themselves the simplistic, hard-driving Big Beat."

But Elvis had no intention of becoming a nostalgia act. Nor did he want to do a conventional Vegas show. The Colonel's initial idea was to put Elvis onstage with showgirls and glitzy production numbers, maybe something like the dancing jailbirds in his movie *Jailhouse Rock*. But Elvis had a dream one night in which he saw himself on a Vegas stage filled with a huge collection of musicians: a rhythm band, two backup singing groups, and the biggest orchestra Vegas had ever seen. When he called Colonel Parker in the morning to tell him his vision, the Colonel balked and said plans were already underway for something much different. Elvis insisted that he would do the show he wanted or not at all. It was the first time, he told friends, that he actually hung up on the Colonel.

Then Elvis set out to do it his way.

News that Elvis would make his return to live performing in Las Vegas broke in mid-December 1968, as soon as his deal with the International Hotel was completed. On February 26, after finishing his Memphis recording sessions, Elvis flew to Vegas to pose for publicity photos, signing the contract with the International's Alex Shoofey and Bill Miller on the construction site of the still-unfinished hotel. (Elvis is the only one of the three not wearing a construction hat.) From there he went on to Hollywood to shoot his final movie, *Change of Habit*, took a two-week vacation in Hawaii, then returned to Memphis for most of May and June. There he made an effort to be more visible—spending many evenings in front of his Graceland home, greeting fans and signing autographs. The Colonel, who was usually careful to keep Elvis under wraps, wasn't happy with his sudden gregariousness, but felt it was probably good for Elvis to "get used to the crowds again."

Meanwhile, Elvis was beginning to plan for his Las Vegas opening, set for July 31, 1969. And he was doing it largely on his own. For his big comeback show in Las Vegas, Elvis had no director, no producer with any hands-on involvement, not even a music-industry guru or Vegas veteran whom he could rely on for advice in shaping and staging the show. To help choose songs and put together his set, he depended mostly on his frequent jamming partner, Charlie Hodge, an affable, wisecracking guitar player from Memphis whom Elvis had gotten to know in the Army. But for this pivotal moment in his career, his first stage appearance in eight years, in a city that had not been kind to him the first time around, Elvis was guided mainly by his own instincts. "Not many people told Elvis what to do regarding music," said Jerry Schilling. "If you want to know who put together that show, it was Elvis Presley."

First he needed to assemble a backup band. He approached the musicians at Chips Moman's studio in Memphis, who had worked so well with him in the recording sessions that winter, about joining him in Vegas, but they had too much studio work to take the time off. He made an overture to Scotty Moore and D. J. Fontana—his original backup guitarist and drummer from the fifties, who had rejoined him for the NBC special—but they turned down the $500 a week apiece that Colonel Parker offered them, reasoning that they could make more money doing session work in Memphis, where Moore now had his own studio. (Scotty Moore, whose relations with Colonel Parker had been strained for years, felt the salary was lowballed because "management wanted new personnel.")

So Elvis began casting about for a new group, asking everyone he knew for the best session musicians available. For lead guitarist, the two names that came up most often were Glen Campbell and James Burton. But Campbell's own singing career was taking off (he had just gotten his own TV variety show). So Elvis called up Burton, a lean, low-key Louisiana native who had created the memorable guitar licks for Dale Hawkins's 1957 single "Susie Q" and spent years as the lead guitarist in Ricky Nelson's band on the TV sitcom *Ozzie and Harriet*. Since playing in the house band on ABC's mid-1960s rock 'n' roll series *Shindig!*, Burton had become one of the busiest session players in Los Angeles, working with everyone from Dean Martin to Merle Haggard.

Elvis and James had never met, but when Elvis phoned, he told Burton he used to watch *Ozzie and Harriet* just to see him play. They talked for a couple of hours, found they had a lot in common musically, and by the end of the conversation Burton had agreed to be Elvis's lead guitarist and help put together the rest of the band. Elvis told Burton he wanted musicians who were versatile, able to play a broad range of music, from rock and country to operatic ballads. "Elvis wanted me to find players that could play different styles and could improvise," Burton recalled. "He believed in me and respected my opinion and I wasn't gonna let him down."

On keyboards, Burton's first choice was Glen D. Hardin, a talented pianist and songwriter who had been part of the *Shindig!* band. But Hardin had too many other commitments, so Burton instead recruited Larry Muhoberac, a Memphis musician and producer who had worked on several Elvis albums and had been music director for two charity concerts Elvis gave in Memphis in early 1961. On rhythm guitar, Burton picked John Wilkinson, a mustachioed folk-singer-guitarist from

Springfield, Missouri, who had just signed an RCA recording contract and whose work Elvis also knew and admired.

Hiring a bassist took a bit more convincing. Burton called up Jerry Scheff, another fellow *Shindig!* alum, to come in for an audition. But Scheff, a red-haired California native who was into jazz and black rhythm and blues, initially wasn't much interested in the job. "I didn't like Elvis Presley's music. I thought he was just some southern white guy trying to sound black," Scheff recalled in his memoir, *Way Down*. "I had definite opinions about what was cool and what wasn't. Elvis wasn't." But Scheff told his wife he would go to the audition anyway, simply out of curiosity.

He was immediately impressed by Elvis's charisma and obvious commitment to his craft. "When Elvis started singing, I couldn't believe how natural he sounded," said Scheff. "His phrasing wasn't mechanical, as it can be with a lot of white singers (and even some black singers). No matter what style of music we played, he always focused on the story of the song. It was like the words and melody went through his brain, then to his heart, and then came out of his mouth." When the audition was over, Scheff was offered the job, and to his own surprise he accepted it—the only Yankee in a band full of Southerners.

The drummer spot proved to be the most complicated to fill. Burton offered the job first to Richie Frost, who had played with him in Ricky Nelson's band, but Frost declined, saying he didn't want the hassle of a live gig. Several more drummers auditioned, none of whom satisfied Elvis. Time was running short when Larry Muhoberac called a drummer he knew from Texas, Ronnie Tutt, who was thinking of making a move to LA, and told him if he could get on a plane and be at an audition the next night, he might have a shot at the job.

Tutt, a bearded, bearlike Dallas native, was not a particular Elvis Presley fan. They had crossed paths once before, at a country jamboree in Fort Worth in 1955, when Tutt was playing with a Western swing band and Elvis, touring the South with Scotty Moore and bassist Bill Black, appeared on the same bill. In the middle of his set, Elvis, chunking away on his guitar, broke the strings and on the spur of the moment grabbed another guitar from a member of Tutt's band—then trashed it, too, without so much as an "I'm sorry." Tutt also wasn't thrilled that his girlfriend thought Elvis was cute.

Still, fourteen years later, the chance to work with Elvis Presley was enough to get Tutt on a flight to Los Angeles, lugging his drum set with him, in time for the Saturday-night audition. Once there, he had to wait quietly while another candidate, Gene Pello, a well-respected Motown session drummer, auditioned first—even commandeering Tutt's drum set—and seemed to win over everyone in the room. The musicians were all but packing up to go home when Muhoberac reminded them that Tutt had flown in from Texas for the audition, and Elvis agreed to hear him out.

They did a number together, and then a couple more, and Elvis felt a connection: Tutt seemed to pick up on every move Elvis made. "We had this great eye communication," Tutt recalled. "We could kind of read each other. They had me stay over an extra day so Elvis could make up his mind. And that's basically what he said: 'I wanted you because you watched me like a hawk; you anticipated what I was doing.'" Elvis told friends he needed "at least one guy onstage with my temperament." So he passed over some of the top session players in Los Angeles and hired Tutt, a virtual unknown, to fill out the group. Rehearsals started the next day; Tutt didn't even have time to return home for a change of clothes.

Elvis wanted two backup singing groups—one female and one male—and they were just as important to him as the band. "I wanted voices behind me," he said, "to help add to the fullness of the sound and dynamics of the show." He liked the popular girl group the Blossoms (who had appeared in his 1968 NBC special), but they were working with Tom Jones, so instead he hired the Sweet Inspirations, a group he had never met but who had done fine work with Aretha Franklin and had recorded a hit single of their own, "Sweet Inspiration." (The quartet's lead singer at the time was Cissy Houston, Whitney's mother.) The Jordanaires were the natural first choice for a male backup group, having worked with Elvis regularly ever since the mid-1950s. But they turned down the job—a decision they later regretted—because it would have meant giving up too much session work in Nashville. So Elvis opted instead for the Imperials, a gospel quartet that had sung with him on his 1967 album, *How Great Thou Art*.

"I think Elvis was more influenced by his gospel roots than people realize," said Terry Blackwood, who joined the group in 1967, and whose father had been part of the Blackwood Brothers, a gospel quartet Elvis had often heard in church while growing up in Memphis. "We were power singers. And Elvis liked that. He didn't want to just croon a song. He wanted to sing a song with power and with everything that's within him. He learned that from watching gospel quartets."

The final piece in the musical conglomeration was a full Vegas orchestra, which would be conducted by the International's new music director, Bobby Morris. A widely respected drummer, who had played for years with Louis Prima and Keely Smith, Morris was originally hired as music director of the new hotel's lounge, but was asked to take over the main showroom as well when bandleader Harry James backed out. Morris had never led an orchestra before and actually took conducting classes at the University of Nevada, Las Vegas, to prepare for the job. Colonel Parker put him on the payroll and flew him out to Los Angeles to meet with Elvis, help pick songs, and work on the orchestrations. Morris put together an exceptionally large group of more than forty musicians, including two dozen string players. Kirk Kerkorian even told Morris to have the hotel's tailor make him a new tuxedo for the show. This was going to be a big deal.

Too big, in some ways, for Colonel Parker, who wasn't happy with the huge array of musicians and singers Elvis had assembled, since all of their salaries (save for the hotel orchestra) would come out of Elvis's pocket—a total payroll of $80,000 for the four-week engagement. The Colonel took out his displeasure on the band members by ignoring them as much as possible, to make sure they didn't get the idea that they were indispensable. "Most of us in the band had very little to do with Colonel Parker," said Ronnie Tutt. "He wanted as little association to be seen between him and us—because it made us less valuable, dollar-wise."

Yet the Colonel gave Elvis no pushback; for his big return to the concert stage, Elvis would have all the company he wanted. The musicians onstage represented a grand coming together of all the music Elvis loved and that had shaped him as a singer: rock 'n' roll, country, gospel, rhythm and blues—plus the symphonic sound of a full orchestra, for the Memphis kid whose favorite singers growing up had included opera star Mario Lanza. "For the first time, Elvis could have everything that influenced him on the stage," said Jerry Schilling. "This was the deprived musician, who had not been able to control his music, either in the recording studio or the movies. And now he was going to satisfy all his musical desires on that stage."

Rehearsals began on July 18, two weeks before the scheduled opening, at the RCA studios in Los Angeles. Colonel Parker gave each member of the rhythm band a suitcase filled with every album Elvis had recorded, so they could be familiar with the songs. But Elvis made it clear that he didn't want them simply to duplicate the old recordings. "I asked if Elvis wanted me to play the songs as he had recorded them," said Ronnie Tutt. "And he said, 'No, man, that's the reason you're here. I want you to play what you play, what you hear.' And that's the way our relationship was the whole time. I don't think I can even count on one hand the times he said I need this or I need that."

The rehearsals, by all accounts, went smoothly, in a relaxed and collaborative atmosphere. "Elvis always wanted to know what the band felt. He wanted the band to be as happy as he was," said James Burton. "But it was always his decision." Jerry Scheff described the typical working process: "When we started working on a new song, we would start by listening to it on tape. Sometimes it would be a studio version. We'd listen to the song a few times and then start discussing how we were going to turn it into our own version. Someone would make a suggestion; someone else would throw their two cents in. We talked about the tempo and the feeling; we tore the song apart and put it back together again." For Larry Muhoberac, the rehearsals were "fun but pressurized. We wanted it to work for him so badly."

Burton estimated that the group learned about one hundred and fifty songs, though the final playlist was whittled down to fifty or so, only about thirty of which were actually performed in the show. Elvis and Charlie Hodge worked together to fine-tune the set list as the week of LA rehearsals progressed. Songs like "Memphis" and "The Green, Green Grass of Home" (a current hit for Tom Jones) were included early on, but later discarded, replaced by a mix of vintage Elvis hits and contemporary numbers reflecting his new, more ballad-oriented style.

After a week in Los Angeles, the rehearsals moved to Las Vegas, where the two vocal groups were added to the mix; the orchestra joined for the final two days of rehearsals in the Showroom Internationale.

The Sweet Inspirations met Elvis for the first time, and they were won over instantly. "He was so gorgeous," said Myrna Smith, one of the singers and the group's informal business manager. "He showed up, introduced himself, 'Hi, I'm Elvis,' and gave each of us a kiss on the lips. Cissy was so excited she fell off her stool." The group picked up quickly on what Elvis wanted and needed. "He didn't give us much musical input except if he didn't like what we were doing," said Smith. "Then he'd wait until we had finished the song and tell us, 'I don't want you to sing there.' He did it in such a nice way where it wasn't like he was chastising you." The Imperials, his gospel backup group, were in less familiar musical territory, but they, too, found Elvis supportive and easy to work with. "Very seldom would he say, 'No, don't sing there,'" said Terry Blackwood. "Because we kinda had like minds about where the vocals should go, even though it was music we weren't used to singing."

Anticipation and spirits were high. "Elvis was in a great mood," said Scheff, "and as he heard the energy build, day after day, song after song, he became even more buoyant. He was wonderful to be around at that time—kidding around, singing naughty lyrics to songs, laughing all the while." Elvis looked as good as he had in years—trim and energetic, his weight down to around 165 pounds. He wore weights on his wrists and ankles during rehearsals to build up his strength and stamina. Bill Belew, who had designed Elvis's black leather outfit for the NBC special, came up with several two-piece karate-style outfits for him to wear in Las Vegas, made of stretch gabardine (manufactured by the same company that made costumes for the Ice Capades) that would allow him to move as freely as possible. Elvis fretted over what to do with his hair—which was longer than in the old days, dyed black, with big, bushy sideburns—and he got testy about it one day when Priscilla suggested that he take a look at Ricky Nelson's new hairstyle, which she had seen on a billboard on Sunset Boulevard. Elvis snapped at her, angry that she would suggest he copy one of the many young rock 'n' rollers who for years imitated *him*.

Colonel Parker for the most part stayed away from the rehearsals and focused instead on what he did best: building the hype. "This town has never seen a promoter like me," he told columnist Earl Wilson. And soon he proved it. Loanne Miller Parker, then working in the publicity department at the International Hotel, recalled the first meeting in May between Colonel Parker's team (including representatives of RCA Records) and the hotel's publicity staff, in Kirk Kerkorian's cottage behind the hotel. "Colonel did not ask how to publicize the Elvis show," she said. "He guided and directed the publicity always. The hotel's publicity and advertising department followed his direction."

Working from a suite on the hotel's fourth floor, Colonel Parker orchestrated a publicity campaign unlike any Las Vegas had ever seen. He bought up nearly every available billboard in town and plastered them with Elvis's name. Signs touting Elvis's show popped up on taxicabs and bus-stop benches across the city. Ads for the show blanketed local radio, some of them simply repeating "Elvis! Elvis! Elvis!" before a final message giving the time and place of the show. (The hotel's publicity director, Nick Naff, thought they were "schlocky as all hell.") The Colonel ordered thousands of photo albums, posters, banners, and other souvenirs, which were stored at the hotel, to be hauled out for sale in the lobby as soon as the engagement began.

"If you don't do any business, don't ever blame me," Colonel Parker told Elvis. "Because even the gophers in the desert know you're here."

Parker was confident, but still nervous. Elvis had been away from the stage for years and was unproven as a Vegas attraction. Some were skeptical that he could bring in the crowds. "They didn't know whether Elvis would be able to fill that room consistently," said Loanne Miller Parker. "Coming to Vegas was not an inexpensive trip for people. And most of Elvis's fans were blue-collar workers. They didn't have the income to do this." Yet four weeks before the opening, his shows were 80 percent sold-out—"the cafe box-office surprise of the season," said *Variety*, an advance sale matched only by that of Vegas superstars like Frank Sinatra and Dean Martin. Soon Elvis would surpass them. Requests came in from overseas—France, Germany, Japan—some fans wanting tickets for a whole week of performances. "We got calls from all over the world," Alex Shoofey marveled. "We couldn't accept all the reservations."

And still, the old carnival promoter didn't let up. "The Colonel's philosophy was, once the show sells out, double the advertising," said Jim McKusick, whose father was hired to place the billboard and other "out of home" advertising. You couldn't turn a corner in Vegas and not know that Elvis Presley was going to be there. "The way Colonel Parker did promotion, he changed the dynamics of how the hotels marketed their headliners," said Ron Garrett, a longtime Vegas publicist, producer, and radio host. "After Elvis it was a whole different ball game."

The summer of 1969 was an eventful, often traumatic one for a nation coming to the end of a turbulent decade. In July 1969, Neil Armstrong became the first man to walk on the moon. In the early-morning hours of August 9, actress Sharon Tate and four others were murdered in her rented Los Angeles home by members of the Charles Manson family. A week later, thousands of rock fans gathered on a muddy farm in upstate New York for the Woodstock music festival. A new president, Richard Nixon, was in office, promising to bring US troops home from Vietnam, even as protests against the war were mounting and divisions in the country worsening.

And Las Vegas was trying to adapt to the social, cultural, and musical changes that were sweeping the country—changes that were making Vegas entertainment look increasingly dated and out of step.

Most of the city's longtime stars were still riding high, but they were looking more and more like relics of a fading show-business era. Sinatra was drawing sellout crowds at his new home, Caesars Palace. Dean Martin had made a successful transfer from the Sands to the Riviera's newly enlarged Versailles Room. Dinah Shore, Donald O'Connor, and Danny Thomas were among the old favorites headlining on the Strip the same week Elvis Presley opened at the International. Vegas' notion of a new-generation star was Wayne Newton, the wildly popular headliner at the Frontier Hotel, who covered hits by the Beatles and Glen Campbell and dubbed himself Mr. Excitement.

To be sure, a few more contemporary, rocklike (if not quite rock) acts were trickling into Vegas. Tom Jones, the Welsh dynamo, returned in June for another packed engagement at the Flamingo Hotel. Elvis went to see him at least twice, studying his moves and even hiring Jones's opening act, comedian Sammy Shore, to open his own show. (Shore, a journeyman from Chicago who had been working in Vegas for a couple of years—he would later open LA's famous comedy club the Comedy Store with his wife, Mitzi—couldn't believe his good fortune when Parker visited him backstage, said he was "a funny guy," and offered him the biggest job of his career.) Another new pop phenom from Britain, Engelbert Humperdinck (née Arnold Dorsey), made his Las Vegas debut in June and was immediately signed to a three-year contract at the Riviera. Caesars Palace, in a bid for the hip crowd, even brought in a road production of *Boys in the Band*, the landmark gay play that had opened off-Broadway the year before. (The show did poor business and was soon cut back from two performances a night to one.)

Behind the scenes, Las Vegas' two leading hotel moguls were in a battle for bragging rights. Kirk Kerkorian was racing to finish construction on the International, billed as the largest resort hotel in the world, in time for its July 2 opening. Howard Hughes, miffed that his supremacy in Las Vegas was being challenged, was trying to steal some of Kerkorian's thunder with his own new megahotel, the Space Needle–like Landmark, just down the street from the International. Hughes had rescued the unfinished hotel from bankruptcy the year before and doubled its size to thirty-one stories—one more than the International, so that he could call it the tallest hotel in Vegas. (The International was actually still taller: 365 feet, to the Landmark's 346.) Hughes succeeded in opening the Landmark one day before Kerkorian's hotel—on July 1, with Danny Thomas starring in the showroom—but only after a chaotic few days, as Hughes had to resolve some last-minute financial issues and refused to OK a guest list or send out invitations until a day before the opening.

The International's opening the following night was a more conventionally well-managed Vegas affair—though the last-minute construction work meant that nearly as many workmen were on the premises as guests. Cary Grant, Rudolf Nureyev, Andy Williams, and Rita Hayworth were among the stars on hand, along with celebrity impersonators who stepped out of limousines dressed as absent bigwigs like Queen Elizabeth. Amid all the hoopla, the press-shy Kerkorian slipped by all but unnoticed—exiting the front door of the hotel, walking to valet parking, and driving off before anyone in the press recognized him.

All eyes were on the opening headliner, Barbra Streisand, who began a four-week engagement that night. Entertainment director Bill Miller had turned to her only after Elvis had demurred, but she was still a big catch: one of the top concert stars in America, just coming off her Academy Award for Best Actress in *Funny Girl*.

Yet Streisand, who hadn't appeared in Vegas since her rocky stint as Liberace's opening act in 1963, seemed out of her element. She came in with a bare-bones show more suited to New York cabarets than a big Vegas showroom: no opening act, little production, none of the usual gushy star patter. Dressed in denim overalls (which she changed for a chiffon gown midway through the show), Streisand simply walked onstage, sat on a stool, and sang. Her first number, "I Got Plenty of Nothin'," was perhaps meant as a joke, but nobody got it. She followed that with the lugubrious "My Funny Valentine" and four or five other numbers before she even spoke to the crowd. And then it was to grumble about the unfinished hotel. "Welcome to the almost-ready International Hotel," she quipped. "Just shows what some people can do with a GI loan." It was just the sort of thing Colonel Parker had feared when he turned down Miller's offer to have Elvis open the new room.

"She's a sweet girl, but she had that New York mentality," said Bobby Morris, the hotel's music director, who saw trouble ahead even in rehearsals and tried to warn her manager, to no avail. "Certain things work in New York and don't work in Las Vegas. There was too much wisecracking. She seemed above it all."

The reviewers mostly agreed. "The jokes she cracked at the unfinished condition of the hotel, rather than making the audience laugh, alienated them," wrote columnist May Mann. "They settled into a cold, resentful disgust." *Variety* said Streisand "seemed ill at ease before the huge crowd" and compared her unfavorably with the singer who was appearing in the hotel's lounge at the same time, Peggy Lee. Charles Champlin of the *Los Angeles Times* came in for the opening and was uncharacteristically brutal: "Even allowing for the opening night tension, Miss Streisand's appearance was a curious, cold, and intensely disappointing 80 minutes worth.... It was a performance which originated in a cool intellect rather than a warm heart; it was a handout, not a sharing."

Streisand cried in her dressing room after the show. "I felt hostility come up on the stage in waves," she would later say. "I worked, but it was total fear time. Of course it showed. They thought I was a snob, but I was really just scared." Then she gathered herself and tried to salvage the show. The next night she changed her opening number to the more upbeat "Don't Rain on My Parade," following it with more of her big hits, like "People." She got a much better reception, and as the engagement went on, Streisand grew more comfortable; some local columnists came back and found the show much improved. Champlin re-reviewed the show near the end of Streisand's four-week run and called it a "scintillating display of her gifts. . . . More than that, she seemed to be having a ball, relaxed, amiable and in charge." Still, Streisand did only middling business, with plenty of empty seats for the weeknight shows.

Elvis, in the middle of rehearsals for his own opening, came to see Streisand on her next-to-last night. The first thing that struck him was how big the stage was, and how poorly her stripped-down show seemed to fill it. He was also put off by her wisecracking Jewish New Yorker shtick. Midway through the show he turned to one of his Memphis pals and muttered, "She sucks."

As a courtesy to the hotel and its opening headliner, Colonel Parker waited until Streisand finished her last show on her last night before turning the International into an Elvis Presley fun zone. By the next morning, seemingly every wall in the hotel was plastered with Elvis photos, banners, and posters. A souvenir stand in the lobby suddenly materialized, hawking Elvis merchandise—photos, pennants, Elvis records, miniature teddy bears. Dealers in the casino were given Elvis straw hats; the waitresses wore Elvis buttons (ELVIS NOW and ELVIS IN

PERSON, they read). "It looked like a political convention, like 'Elvis for President,'" said Terry Blackwood. The giant marquee in front of the hotel now broadcast the name ELVIS in ten-foot-high block letters (with BILL MILLER PRESENTS above them), so big that they had to be put up in sixteen different pieces and wired down, rather than clipped as normally, so they wouldn't blow off in the desert wind.

There was a full dress rehearsal in the afternoon. An eighteen-year-old Elvis fan named Ian Fraser-Thomson, who had come all the way from Britain to see the show and managed to sneak into the balcony to watch some of the rehearsals, reported that Elvis was "dressed in black pants and puffed-sleeve green shirt" and sat on a barstool through most of the session, calling out numbers for the run-through. "Sometimes they'd run through an entire song, other times they'd work on an intro or work on the ending of a song. There was a lot of fine-tuning going on," Thomson observed—before one of Elvis's people spotted him and chased him out of the room.

Elvis was as ready as he could ever be: well rehearsed, backed by first-rate musicians, and heralded by the biggest publicity campaign in Vegas history. Yet his show still had something of a homemade, seat-of-the-pants quality. Elvis hadn't been on a concert stage in years and knew little about modern sound systems and other technical matters. "We went in there in '69 not knowing a damn thing," said Lamar Fike. "He didn't even have an act, much less a Vegas act. We literally designed that show from scratch—made it up as we went along." Fike, who had spent some time as road manager for Brenda Lee, was in charge of the lighting. Charlie Hodge not only helped Elvis put together his set, but was kind of an adjunct member of the band—playing a guitar (which wasn't hooked up to an amplifier) and joining in the backup vocals, but onstage mainly to hand Elvis water and scarves, and generally to make him feel comfortable.

Elvis was scheduled to do two shows a night—a dinner show at 8:00 p.m. and a late show at midnight. (The minimum charge for each was fifteen dollars, top of the Vegas scale at the time.) But for the opening night on Thursday, July 31, there would be only one show, at 8:00 p.m. The audience was filled mostly with invited guests: Hollywood celebrities, other Vegas entertainers, assorted high rollers and local VIPs, along with the many rock critics and entertainment reporters from around the country that Colonel Parker had invited (many of them flown in from New York City on Kerkorian's private jet). Even in a town used to star-studded opening nights, the array of celebrities— Cary Grant, Sammy Davis Jr., Tom Jones, Ann-Margret, George Hamilton, Paul Anka, Carol Channing, Juliet Prowse, Henry Mancini, Dionne Warwick—was impressive.

Backstage before the show, in his smoke-filled dressing room, Elvis was a nervous wreck. "I can remember Elvis sitting on a couch," Jerry Scheff recalled, "his knee going up and down like a piston, his hands dancing like butterflies." "He was pacing back and forth, back and forth," said Joe Esposito; "you could see the sweat just pouring out of him before he went onstage. He was always nervous before a show, but he was never nervous like that again." Everybody tried to keep him calm. "If you get lost, just turn around and we'll start playing louder," John Wilkinson reassured him. "Don't worry about it, your friends are here." Elvis had someone fetch his Memphis friend Sonny West—Red West's cousin— who was sitting in the audience with his wife. When Sonny came backstage, Elvis asked him to stand in the wings during the show; it would make him feel safer. (Elvis later asked Sonny to serve as his chief of security for the rest of the engagement.) "He was scared to death," said James Burton. "Just before we went onstage, Elvis walked up to me backstage, and he said, 'James, I'm so nervous, I don't know if I can do this.' I said, 'Elvis, don't worry, all you gotta do is walk out there.'"

The Showroom Internationale was filling up, anticipation building. The room was immense, twice as large as any other showroom in Vegas (and the first one with a balcony), with room for fifteen hundred people at the dinner show, two thousand for the late show. The expansive stage was sixty feet wide, with a ten-thousand-pound, Austrian-made gold-lamé curtain. The ornate decor featured crystal chandeliers and figurines of angels hanging from the ceiling and a hodgepodge of ancient Greek, Roman, and Louis XIV–era paintings and statuary arrayed around the room. A setting fit for a returning king.

The Sweet Inspirations opened the show at 8:15 p.m. They kept their set short, just three or four numbers—pop songs and show tunes like "Born Free" and "The Impossible Dream," along with their own hit, "Sweet Inspiration." "The audience was very good to us," Myrna Smith recalled. "We knew that they were there for Elvis, and we knew they wanted us to get off the stage as fast as possible."

The same went for Sammy Shore, the comedian who came next. Shore was facing the toughest assignment imaginable for a stand-up comic: trying to keep an audience desperate for Elvis Presley from hooting him off the stage. It got even tougher when Sammy took the microphone, began talking, and nothing came out.

"The microphone was dead. No sound. I panicked," Shore recalled. He vamped for a couple of minutes—doing some Shakespearean gibberish, shouting at the top of his lungs, "They spend fifty-three million bucks to build this hotel, and fourteen dollars for a microphone!" Then, when a new microphone was finally handed to him, he began mouthing his words, pretending that the new mike was dead too. That got him a big laugh and eased the way into his twenty-minute routine, with jokes on everything from gambling to bullfighting (the Colonel liked Sammy because he worked clean), and closing with his showcase "Brother Sam" bit, in which Sammy impersonated a Southern evangelical preacher, beating a tambourine and imploring people in the balcony to jump out and "be saved."

Backstage, the band was listening for another of Sammy's bits, the one about eating lobster in a restaurant. Whenever he had to pick a live lobster out of the tank for his dinner, Sammy would say he felt all-powerful, like "God among the lobsters." That line was the band's cue to start setting up. It would become a running joke among them; whenever they had to start setting up for an Elvis show, it was "God among the lobsters" time.

As he finished his routine and walked offstage, Sammy ran into Elvis and shook his hand; it was cold and clammy. "I saw in his face the look of terror," Sammy said. Usually in Vegas the headliner would be announced by a disembodied voice—"Ladies and gentlemen, direct from the bar—Dean Martin!" But as the band started its rocking intro music and the curtain rose, Elvis simply walked out to center stage, an acoustic guitar slung over his shoulder, grabbed the microphone in his right hand—which was visibly trembling—paused for a moment, then launched into the familiar lyrics: "Well, it's one for the money, / Two for the show, / Three to get ready / Now go, cat, go . . ."

As he sang "Blue Suede Shoes," the crowd erupted. It was the old Elvis, rocking as hard as ever on one of his classic hits, a song they hadn't heard him sing in over a decade. He was wearing one of Bill Belew's two-piece karate outfits, dark blue, with flared pants and a sashlike belt that whipped around as Elvis moved. His high-collared shirt was unbuttoned nearly to his navel, with a scarf loosely knotted around his neck. (Larry Geller claimed that Elvis wore high collars to imitate the spiritual masters in David Anrias's book *Through the Eyes of the Masters*. Priscilla said it was because Elvis thought his neck was too long and always wanted it covered.)

Even for a non-Elvis fan in the audience—Margot Hentoff, writing about the show in *Harper's Magazine*—he was a sight to behold:

Elvis comes onstage wearing a midnight-blue karate tunic and trousers. His hair is black and Indian-straight. He is skinny as a knife and looking very good. It is perhaps the first time I have ever seen him look good. He has lost the look they loved—that old sensual quality of being "grease," a truck driver from Memphis who could shake that thing. The oily wavy hair is gone and the pouty baby-round face. There are planes on this face, creases in his cheeks, and he has been a superstar for so long that he glows just standing there. . . . I wish for a moment that he had been one of *my* heroes, envy the delicious shiver of the sense of time gone, the awareness of what time can do which is sweeping over those who screamed for him as schoolchildren and are now grown up, sitting at a ringside table with the grown-ups in Las Vegas.

The frenzied reaction from the crowd startled the performers on-stage. "They wouldn't shut up," John Wilkinson recalled; "all through the first song they kept shouting and cheering, they couldn't get enough of him." As he finished his opening number (in a brisk minute and a half), Elvis let the cheers and applause wash over him, then turned around to face the musicians behind him and sort of shrugged his shoulders—as if to say, "Maybe this isn't going to be so bad."

Then he roared on, doing a hard-driving version of Ray Charles's "I Got a Woman," followed by a string of his biggest fifties hits: "All Shook Up," "Jailhouse Rock," "Don't Be Cruel," "Heartbreak Hotel"— and "Love Me Tender," during which Elvis planted kisses on as many female fans in the front row as he could reach. He did the up-tempo songs faster than in the old days—with a certain distance, almost self-parody, as if he were trying to get through them as quickly as possible. "I think he did them because people expected those songs," said drummer Ronnie Tutt. "You could tell he just wanted to rush through them. He wasn't necessarily thrilled with who he was in the fifties. Because he had become a different man." When he got to "Hound Dog" (a song he didn't like anymore), he prefaced it with a long, tongue-in-cheek buildup, telling the audience he wanted to do a "special song" for the evening, a song that "says something," a song just right for a "tender, touching moment"—before the sudden explosion: *YOU AIN'T NOTHIN' . . ."* He raced through that one so fast it was almost disrespectful.

After the trip down memory lane, Elvis changed the pace with several numbers that showcased his more mature, emotional, ballad-driven style: "Memories," the sentimental Mac Davis song that he had introduced on his 1968 special; "In the Ghetto," the Davis number that had given him his biggest hit in years; the angsty ballad "I Can't Stop Loving You"; and in a nod to the Beatles, a medley of "Yesterday" and "Hey Jude." The set reached a climax with Elvis's feverish, seven-minute, no-holds-barred performance of a song almost no one in the audience had heard before (the single would be released during his Vegas run), "Suspicious Minds," which nearly brought the house down.

In the last part of the show, Elvis circled back to the 1950s, with an energetic cover of Chuck Berry's "Johnny B. Goode," and one of his early Sun releases, "Mystery Train" (that favorite of all Elvis classicists), which slid neatly into "Tiger Man," featuring the same rhythm line. Then he revved up the jets for the old Ray Charles rouser "What'd I Say," before closing the show (as he would nearly every live show for the rest of his career) with "Can't Help Falling in Love," his ballad from the 1961 film *Blue Hawaii*—the only one of his sixties movie songs that Elvis would regularly perform in Las Vegas.

The show lasted an hour and fifteen minutes, and Elvis worked himself to a frazzle: pacing the stage like a panther, crouching, lunging, leaping, doing karate kicks and punches. He was audibly huffing and puffing after just a few minutes. He gulped water and Gatorade and mopped his sweat with towels handed to him by Charlie Hodge, or handkerchiefs and napkins tossed onstage by women in the audience. "He was like a wild man," recalled Felton Jarvis, his RCA record producer. "He was all over that stage. I mean, he almost hurt himself—he was doing flips and cartwheels and all kinds of stuff; on 'Suspicious Minds' he'd be down on one knee and do a flip across stage and just roll." The cartwheels may have been an exaggeration, but no one could doubt that Elvis was giving it everything he had. In one show later in the run, he actually split his pants doing one of his kick moves and had to retreat offstage, where his entourage formed a protective ring around him while he changed quickly into a new pair. (This prompted Bill Belew to switch to the one-piece jumpsuits—more forgiving in the crotch—that Elvis wore for his later Vegas shows.)

He talked to the audience in between numbers—nervously, self-consciously, with a few awkward jokes. He noted that this was "my first live appearance in nine years. Appeared *dead* a few times. . . ." He joked about the garish showroom—"Welcome to the big, freaky International Hotel, with those weirdo dolls on the walls and those funky angels on the ceiling"—and its owner, Kirk Kerkorian, whose name he pretended to have trouble pronouncing. "I'd like to get him and Howard Hughes in a crap game," he quipped. The same lines would be repeated almost every night, but the evening had a loose, spontaneous quality too. On opening night Elvis saw entertainment columnist Rex Reed at one of the front tables and exclaimed, "I saw you on TV the other night!"

The awkwardness and spontaneity were refreshing. This was no slick Vegas headliner, with polished stage patter, well-crafted jokes, and fake effusions of love for the audience. Elvis was still the overgrown, overawed kid from Memphis, as anxious about talking (as opposed to singing) to an audience as the audience was eager to make him feel welcome. But musically, he was a revelation, not least to the musicians onstage. "Elvis surprised us with his range and his stamina," said Joe Moscheo, of the Imperials. "We were blown away by how good he was." When the show was over, Elvis got a standing ovation—"one of the rare occasions," Myram Borders reported in the *Nevada State Journal*, "when a Las Vegas standing salute was sincere rather than rigged with a few cronies of an entertainer planted down front to stamp and scream approval." The show was a clear triumph.

"Good God! You are something!" cried Sonny West, the first to greet Elvis as he walked offstage. Elvis responded with a grin, "It felt good." Surrounded by his entourage, he went downstairs to his dressing room, where the mood was ebullient. Colonel Parker got there a little late and had to wait while Elvis was changing clothes. When he emerged, the two embraced, for one of the only times anyone could remember. "We did it!" the Colonel said. Some claimed they saw tears in his eyes.

Friends and fellow performers streamed into Elvis's dressing room to congratulate him. Sammy Davis Jr., who had led the cheers from a ringside table, gave him a big Sammy Davis Jr. hug. Cary Grant told Elvis he'd never seen a show to match it. Pat Boone—who first met Elvis in 1955, when they appeared on the same bill at a Cleveland sock hop—brought along his twelve-year-old daughter, Debby, who used to climb all over Elvis when he came to visit at their Bel Air home. Carol Channing laughed when Elvis greeted her with a joke: "Ain't you in show business?" Bobby Vinton, the silky-voiced young crooner of "Blue Velvet" and other sixties hits, came by with his agent, who asked if Elvis would pose for a photo with Bobby. The Colonel, who frowned on that sort of thing, was a little annoyed, but Elvis happily obliged.

Everyone knew they had witnessed something extraordinary, possibly historic. "It was absolutely spectacular, totally electric from beginning to end," said Terry Blackwood. "This was a new venue and a whole new image for him, but it all worked." "Musically and energy level, there was nobody to compare to him," said Bobby Morris, who spent sixty years in Las Vegas and worked with practically everybody. "There was nothing to match that particular evening and that engagement at the International." It was the first time Priscilla Presley had ever seen her husband perform live on a concert stage, and she was knocked out: "I got it. He owned that stage."

"I never saw anything like it in my life," said Mac Davis, who was in the audience, flattered when Elvis gave him a shout-out—"Hiya, Mac"—before singing "In the Ghetto." "It was unbelievable. He was physically beautiful at that age, just a specimen. You couldn't take your eyes off the guy. It was just crazy. Women rushing the stage, people clamoring over each other. I couldn't wipe the grin off my face the entire time." Ann Moses, editor of the teen magazine *Tiger Beat*, said, "I saw the Beatles at the Hollywood Bowl, and the Rolling Stones at the Cow Palace in San Francisco. But there was something about that night that was so special. The overall excitement in the room was overwhelming. Every aspect of his performance was dead-on. Everyone was dumbstruck and didn't want the night to end. It was one of the greatest shows I've ever seen."

Steve Binder, director of the 1968 NBC special that resuscitated Elvis's career, was there too. Though he had nothing to do with the Vegas show, he was thrilled to see Elvis fulfilling the promise of his

TV comeback. "I thought he was fantastic, every bit as good as I had seen and worked with him in '68," said Binder. "I had been in Vegas for other projects, but I never saw that kind of energy in the air. And he delivered." But when Binder tried to go backstage to congratulate Elvis, the guards turned him away, saying his name wasn't on the guest list. He suspected it was the handiwork of Colonel Parker, who had essentially made him persona non grata after the '68 special. Years later, Joe Esposito apologized to Binder, saying Elvis didn't know he was there.

Typically, for big Vegas openings, members of the press would be invited backstage after the show for interviews with the star. But so many reporters and critics were on hand that the Colonel arranged for a press conference—the only one Elvis would ever do in Las Vegas. Some two hundred people gathered in a hotel ballroom a little after midnight, and when Elvis walked in, wearing a new Bill Belew outfit, black with a bright red scarf, they gave him another standing ovation.

Elvis stood behind the head table, flanked by his father, Vernon, and Joe Esposito, his road manager. The Colonel stood by, dressed in a cheesy white smock with ELVIS INTERNATIONAL IN PERSON stenciled all over it. Elvis was relaxed and in high spirits, standing the whole time, often cocking one leg up to rest a foot on the table as he answered questions.

Elvis was candid when asked why it had taken so long for him to return to live performing: "We had to finish up the movie commitments before I could start on this. I really missed it. I love the live contact with an audience. It was getting harder and harder to perform to a movie camera all day long. The inspiration wasn't there. I'm tired of playing a guy singing to the guy he's beating up."

Was he nervous during the show? a reporter asked. Yes, Elvis said, for the first three or four songs—"before I loosened up. Then I thought, 'What the heck. Get with it, man, or you might be out of a job tomorrow.'" Did he dye his hair? "Sure, because I've always done it for the movies." (Why? "Because it's gray.") Asked to name some of the singers who influenced him, Elvis pointed out one of them sitting right there in the room—Fats Domino, who was appearing in a lounge show on the Strip. Someone from England announced that he'd been authorized to offer Elvis "one million pounds sterling to make two appearances at the Wembley Empire Stadium." Elvis referred the question to Colonel Parker. "Just put down the deposit," said the Colonel. "Cash, not pounds."

Colonel Parker ended the questioning after about twenty minutes and handed out press packets to the visiting reporters. Elvis stuck around for a few more minutes, talking and signing autographs, then retreated with his entourage to his suite on the hotel's twenty-ninth floor (temporary quarters, while the thirtieth-floor suite—where he would spend all of his future Vegas engagements—was being finished). There the celebration continued for the rest of the night.

The reviews rolled in over the next several days. A few of the locals were blasé or outright skeptical. *Las Vegas Sun* columnist Ralph Pearl found "the glamorous rock and roll movie hero really cashing in on his reputation and not truly earning the enormous standing ovation. . . . There was a pounding, ear-aching sameness to many of Presley's songs." But nearly everyone else was bowled over. "It was not the Elvis with the rough edges of the middle 1950s, on stage Thursday," said *Billboard*, in a review headlined "Elvis Retains Touch in Return to Stage." "It was a polished, confident, and talented artist, knowing exactly what he was going to do and when." *Variety* found him "very much in command of the entire scene as he went on to prove himself as one of the more potent Vegas lures." Mike Jahn, recently hired by the *New York Times* as its first reporter assigned to the rock beat, wrote, "With his stature, it is fairly logical to expect him to go the Vegas route, that is, live out the rest of his life singing soft ballads in the style of Dean Martin or Paul Anka.... But with the opening song on his first night, it was clear that Elvis Presley still knows how to sing rock 'n' roll. He seems, in fact, to have lost nothing in the past decade."

The nation's top rock critics soon weighed in, with nearly universal praise. "Presley came on and immediately shook up all my expectations and preconceived categories," wrote Ellen Willis in the *New Yorker*. "There was a new man out there." Seeing Elvis onstage, wrote Richard Goldstein in the Sunday *New York Times*, "felt like getting hit in the face with a bucket of melted ice. He looked so timeless up there, so constant.... He was still the boy who makes little girls weep. Still the man of the people, even though the people had moved to the suburbs. And still the jailhouse rocker." *Rolling Stone* put its imprimatur on Elvis's comeback with a long, adulatory piece by David Dalton the following February, which began, "Elvis was supernatural, his own resurrection, at the Showroom Internationale in Las Vegas last August."

Elvis's comeback in Vegas was soon the talk of the rock world. Ray Connolly, who covered the show for London's *Evening Standard*, was in the office of Bob Dylan's manager, Albert Grossman, a few days later, trying to set up an interview. Unexpectedly, Grossman put Dylan on the phone, and Connolly mentioned that he had just come from seeing Elvis in Vegas. Dylan immediately began quizzing the journalist: "What did he do? Did he do the Sun stuff? Did he do 'Mystery Train'? Who's in the band?" A couple of days later Connolly was back in London, talking to John Lennon. Again he mentioned Elvis's Vegas show, and Lennon peppered him with almost exactly the same questions. Everybody was a fan again.

Once past the pressure-filled opening night, Elvis got more comfortable and confident onstage. "The first night I thought it was good," recalled Larry Muhoberac, "but I knew it was a handpicked audience. It was the next night when it was so amazing, so exciting, and the audience were hard-core fans who had paid money to see their star." The set list remained fairly consistent throughout the run, though there were several additions, including Del Shannon's "Runaway," the Jimmy Reed blues song "Baby What You Want Me to Do," and the sentimental oldie "Are You Lonesome Tonight?" (which Elvis had recorded in 1960—reputedly the only song Colonel Parker ever asked him to record, because it was his wife's favorite). Elvis tinkered with the selections and the order from night to night, depending on his mood and his sense of the crowd. "If he felt a certain audience, a certain arrangement, was not going to do as well, he would change gears," said Bobby Morris. "He was absolutely wonderful when it came to reading an audience. He had that instinct." The band members had to be constantly on their toes. "He might do the first three songs, then he would jump all over the place," said James Burton. "Elvis was an entertainer who could judge by the audience. He always seemed to have the right mood. Every show was different."

There is no film or video of any of Elvis's 1969 Las Vegas shows. But RCA recorded several of his performances, beginning on August 21 (cuts from those shows were released on a live album in October of that year and can be heard on various other compilation albums released since), which give at least a sense of the excitement Elvis created onstage. He is in superb voice—that rich, heaving baritone, emanating from deep in the chest cavity, a voice that seems to come with its own echo chamber. In the old days he had a youthful, rockabilly twang; his more robust, mature sound gives the early songs more body and weight, without losing the rocking energy. "Mystery Train" has more mystery; "Heartbreak Hotel" (a song inspired by a man's suicide note that read,

"I walk a lonely street") more heartbreak. Elvis seems especially energized by the songs that are newer to his repertoire, such as "Baby What You Want Me to Do." Like his very first release for Sun Records, "That's All Right, Mama," it's a near-inarticulate cry of sexual helplessness ("Goin' up, down / Down, up / Any way you want it"), only now he's a hardened veteran of the love battlefield. Elvis pays his respects to Jimmy Reed's loping blues original, while giving it his own defiant rock exclamation point. (It's also one number where Elvis is able to show off his frequently underrated rhythm-guitar playing.)

Vegas also gave him a chance to demonstrate his flair for emotional dramatics. "In Vegas Elvis discovered that he was extremely good at melodrama," wrote Dylan Jones in *Elvis Has Left the Building*, "and actually developed the acting skills that had eluded him for over a decade. He was a much better actor on stage in Vegas than he had been in any of his films." Most white singers would sound phony doing "In the Ghetto" (and that over-articulated *t* in *ghetto* is easy to make fun of), but Elvis puts it across with the sheer intensity of his attack and the beauty of his vocals. A big, steamy ballad like "I Can't Stop Loving You" is right in his wheelhouse, but he can also take an unlikely number, like the Bee Gees' somewhat drippy "Words," and give it real passion and splendor. He turns "Suspicious Minds" into a seven-minute symphony of anguished love—with its four-minute-long, almost incantatory coda, in which the first three lines ("I'm caught in a trap / I can't walk out / Because I love you too much, baby") are repeated nearly twenty times, with a series of diminuendos and crescendos that tease the audience, as the song builds to a furious, almost orgasmic climax and Elvis seems ready to keel over from exhaustion.

The big assemblage of musicians and backup singers aren't simply Vegas overkill; they seem to *complete* the songs, to unleash their full power. The soulful embellishments of the Sweet Inspirations fill up the house beautifully, and the James Burton–led rhythm group is always tight and on the money. ("Play it, James," Elvis would say, introducing Burton's slick but never showy solo turns.) Only the orchestra seems a little underused. Frank Leone, who played piano in the Bobby Morris–led outfit, felt it was handicapped by Elvis's lack of any conventional charts, or arrangements. "Elvis came in with no music; he was very naive as to charts," said Leone. "The rhythm section was like gold—they were great musicians. But the [house] band would just sit there. It was a shame. It was a wasted orchestra."

As the engagement went on, Elvis's patter between songs got wackier and more freewheeling, with stream-of-consciousness ramblings that are often silly, disjointed, and sometimes nearly incomprehensible. He mumbles and meanders, constantly interrupts himself, makes self-referential asides, laughs at jokes he seems to be the only one in on ("Whassat? Whassat? Oh, it's me, it's me").When he clears his throat, he jokes about clearing his throat. When he asks for water, he calls it "wa-wa"—then makes fun of himself for using the baby word. There are nervous, self-deprecating interjections: "They're watchin' me, folks, they're gonna put me away, I know it!" But nobody was watching him more closely than Elvis himself—who always felt like an outsider, never quite comfortable with the success that he feared could vanish any minute.

Midway through the show, Elvis delivered his most extended monologue, a somewhat rambling recap of his life and career: the early Memphis years, *The Ed Sullivan Show*, the Army, Hollywood—"my side of the story," as he put it. It was as self-revealing as Elvis would ever get onstage, if you could navigate through all the digressions, fits and starts, bad jokes, and country-boy cuteness:

> I was just out of high school, I was driving a truck, and I was train-ing to be an electrician. And I got wired the wrong way, baby. One

day on my lunch break I went into a . . . hot-dog stand! No, a record company. To make a record for my own use, you know. I really
wasn't trying to get into the business. The guy put the record out
about a year and a half later. So just overnight in my hometown,
it started to get a lot of reaction. People were saying, "Who is he?"
"What is he?" "Is he, is he?" I don't know, I'm saying, "Am I? Am I?"
I had sideburns and all. Fourteen years ago it was weird, you know.
You think it's weird now, fourteen years ago I couldn't walk down
the street, man—"Get him! Get him! He's a squirrel, man!" So I
was goin', "Hmmpfh hmmpfh!" Shaking. In fact, that's how I get into
this business was shakin'. May be how I get out of it too. So anyway,
the guy put the record out, and it became pretty big in my home
town, Memphis, and in certain parts of the country it got to be
pretty big, pretty well-known. But nobody really knew who I was.
So I was workin' little nightclubs, little football fields, little alleys,
you know, weird-looking rooms with little things crawling around
the ceiling lookin' at you, you know. And I did it for like a year and
a half. And in 1956 I met Colonel Sanders—Parker!

Elvis was always at his worst talking onstage, trying to sound casual and unscripted; as a stand-up comedian he was hopeless. "He was
so undisciplined it was a joke," said Joe Guercio, who became Elvis's
orchestra leader a year later. "I don't think he was ever really at ease
onstage. Every time he felt an insecure moment, he would turn around
and do a ha-ha to somebody, go to Charlie for a minute or somebody
else." Elvis never used four-letter words onstage, but he began to get a
little loose with the racy double entendres. (Talking about his time in
the Army, Elvis joked that the men must have been awfully lonely because they kept calling each other "mother.") Midway through the run,
Colonel Parker wrote Elvis a note cautioning him to watch himself,

especially during dinner shows, when families could be in the audience. "The pressure is getting a little heavy regarding the off-color material," the Colonel wrote, warning him not to "undo all the good that we have created during the first part of our engagement."

In rehearsals Elvis would often play around by slipping jokey or off-color lyrics into familiar songs, just to amuse himself and loosen up the room. He mostly restrained himself from that kind of thing in his first Vegas engagement, with one notorious exception. At the midnight show on August 26, Elvis was in the middle of "Are You Lonesome Tonight?" when he mischievously changed the lyrics and created a blooper reel for the ages. The lines he usually sang were:

Do the chairs in your parlor seem empty and bare?
Do you gaze at your doorstep and picture me there?"

At this performance, he sang instead:

Do the chairs in your parlor seem empty and bare?
Do you gaze at your bald head and wish you had hair?

The altered lyrics were clearly planned in advance, and he delivered them so deftly that some in the audience might not even have realized the switch. But the stunt so cracked him up that he burst into a laughing jag that he simply couldn't stop. He kept trying to resume the song, only to dissolve back into guffaws—right through the sober talking interlude ("I wonder if you're lonesome tonight . . ."), even as Cissy Houston continued her florid soprano accompaniment, untethered to the absent lead singer. That seemed to crack up Elvis even more.

"That's it, man. Fourteen years, right down the drain," Elvis said when he finally, breathlessly, reached the end. It was an unprofessional, really inexcusable lapse—yet one of the most disarming and delight-fully genuine moments of his career.

He performed for four solid weeks, two shows a night, without a single night off. Elvis claimed he didn't mind the grueling schedule. "I'd go stark raving mad if I had to sit around one night, just twiddling my thumbs," he told friends. But the punishing pace almost surely contrib-uted to his mounting drug use—pills to keep him alert, more pills to get himself to sleep. "Do you realize what kind of hell four weeks is?" said Lamar Fike. "That's a marathon—nearly sixty performances. And Elvis had such a high-energy act that when he would do an honest hour and fifteen minutes twice a night, he was so tired he was cross-eyed. That's why he took all that stuff to keep him going."

But no one was paying much attention to that now, least of all Elvis, who seemed fully in control and rejuvenated by the triumph in Vegas. "He was like a newborn child," said Jerry Schilling. "He was smiling, he was in a great mood, he was untiring. He wanted to see everybody. He wanted to talk about the show. It was a great time professionally and personally. I would say, outside of the birth of his child, that was the happiest I ever saw him. And he was not just happy for himself; he was happy for the whole group. He was happy for the audience."

"It gave me a new life," Elvis told Frank Lieberman of the *Los An-geles Herald-Examiner*. "I was human again. There was hope for the future."

Every night after finishing his midnight show, Elvis would hold court in his suite at the top of the International Hotel, with its pan-oramic view of the city he had just conquered. Often he would jam with members of the band or get the Imperials to join him in a late-night round of gospel songs. The singers enjoyed the time with him—but were just as happy when the call didn't come and they could retreat to their own rooms, at a motel three blocks away. "I had never even been to Vegas," said Terry Blackwood. "The whole Vegas scene was not one that I was really that comfortable with. So I basically did the show and went to my room. My parents were very devout Christians, and they didn't want me there. But I had a lot of prayer offered for me, to protect me, keep me from messing up, being caught up in that. And I didn't."

Elvis was feeling some of the same conflict, between his deep religious roots and the bacchanalia surrounding him in Vegas. Pat Boone, the former teen idol well-known for his clean-cut image and Christian family values, visited the suite one night and was surprised when Elvis took him into a walk-in closet to talk about religion. "I wish I could go to church like you," Elvis told him. Boone asked what was stopping him. "I think I'd make too much of a scene," Elvis said. "It would distract from the preacher." Then he asked if Boone could help him get in touch with Oral Roberts, the Oklahoma televangelist. Though amused that Elvis thought he needed an intermediary, Boone did make the connection with Roberts, who later met with Elvis in Los Angeles. Boone felt that Elvis was "spiritually starved. He had been to church as a boy with his folks, and he was missing that experience." Other performers who met with Elvis in Las Vegas were similarly struck by his eagerness to talk about his religious faith. Even Sammy Shore—who only *played* a preacher in his comedy act—would sometimes get visits in his dressing room from Elvis, who would read him Bible verses.

Elvis always had some ambivalence about the sins of Sin City. He loved the shows, the women, and the all-night action. (He would generally sleep until late afternoon, then get up for a 5:00 p.m. breakfast that usually included a Spanish omelet and a pound of bacon.) But he gambled only occasionally, and never with much enthusiasm. He would drink, but not to excess, and he had little patience for those who did. Comedian Rich Little was impressed when he met Elvis for the first time after one of his '69 shows: "He was very nice, very courteous, very interested in what you were doing. He poured drinks for you." But when a TV actor who was visiting got rip-roaring drunk, Elvis simply walked out of the room. "He didn't like that, and he left. Didn't say goodbye or anything. Just left."

Old friends and colleagues from Memphis descended on Vegas to see his show and share in his triumph. Elvis told George Klein and Marty Lacker—the two Memphis friends who had convinced him to record at Chips Moman's studio—to skip the opening and come out for the second night instead, so they could give him a better appraisal of his performance. ("The reception Elvis is getting here is incredible," they told the *Memphis Press-Scimitar*. "You've got to see it to believe it.") Mark James, the Memphis songwriter who had written "Suspicious Minds," came out to see how Elvis had transformed the song into the galvanizing high point of his Vegas act. Dr. George Nichopoulos, the Memphis doctor who supplied Elvis with his prescription drugs, came to see the show, and so did Ed Parker, Elvis's karate instructor, who used the opportunity to talk up the marketing plans for his new Kenpo karate system. Sam Phillips, his old patron at Sun Records, drove out for the opening in a limo that Elvis sent for him. They had talked during rehearsals, and Phillips had one piece of advice: never mind the big orchestra, he said; just get yourself the best rhythm section around and make sure they are right behind you, "kicking you in the ass." Phillips was happy to see the result. "I never heard a better rhythm section in my life," he told Elvis. He had only one complaint: "That song 'Memories' has got to go!"

Nearly every entertainer appearing in Las Vegas at the time made it over to the International to see Elvis, and they too were won over. "I wasn't a fan of his until then," said Lainie Kazan, the sexy young singer who was about to open at the Flamingo (and was drawing protests for some racy publicity photos that showed too much of her breasts). "But he was fantastic. I was enchanted, and I was moved." Petula Clark, the British pop singer who was appearing at Caesars Palace, had heard that Elvis was nervous for the show, and she was nervous for him. "But his performance was much better than I expected," she said. "They have an expression in French. Elvis was a *bête de scène*. That's somebody who was a stage animal, and you could tell that night that's what Elvis was born to do. There was a great animal magnetism in the way he sang, the way he moved, and the way he smiled."

Dave Clark, of the British band the Dave Clark Five, was in town for the show and spent a couple of hours with Elvis, who had been such an important early influence on him. "I went in expecting the impossible because he changed all of our lives," said Clark. "He was as good as I expected him to be and even better. He was magic." Vic Damone, whom Elvis would often come to see in the Riviera lounge (usually requesting the same song: "Over the Rainbow"), thought Elvis was drinking too much water onstage and gave him an old Broadway singer's tip: bite your tongue before you go onstage, to keep your mouth lubricated. Tom Jones came by the suite a couple of times, joining in the jam sessions and comparing notes about the toll their exhausting shows were taking. "Elvis at least knew how to do it, vocally, without wrecking himself," Jones said. "He was better with pacing. He told me, 'You need more singers onstage. That's why I've got the fellas. When I go up at the end, they go up with me. I could virtually pull out, and the note will still be there. I'm covered.'" Jones said he didn't want to be covered—and paid the price for it with voice problems a few years later.

With Priscilla around for much of the engagement, Elvis had to somewhat curtail his romantic adventures. But that didn't mean he wasn't surrounded by beautiful women. During the engagement he met Joyce Bova, a striking, twenty-three-year-old brunette who worked in Washington for the House Armed Services Committee. She was standing in line with a friend to see one of Elvis's shows when a hotel employee picked her out and asked if she would like to meet Elvis. To her amazement, she was brought to see Elvis backstage, where he flirted with her, invited her to dinner in his suite, and tried to convince her to extend her stay in Las Vegas so he could "get to know her better." (She had to return to Washington—where her House committee was investigating the My Lai massacre—but they consummated their relationship a year later, when Elvis came to Washington to get a special Narcotics Bureau badge from President Nixon.)

For many young and aspiring musicians, seeing Elvis in Vegas was a powerful, formative experience. Tony Brown was a twenty-three-year-old piano player with the Stamps Quartet, one of Elvis's favorite gospel groups (they would replace the Imperials as his backup group in 1972), when the group's leader, J. D. Sumner, routed their tour through Las Vegas just so he could catch Elvis's show at the International. Sumner made the rest of the group stay on the bus while he went to see the show, but Brown got to go backstage with him afterward to meet Elvis. "Oh, man, it was like going to see the pope," said Brown, who later played piano backup for Elvis, before becoming a Grammy-winning country-music producer. "He looked like a million bucks. I was just in awe of him. I said, 'Damn, if I looked like him, I could get any chick I want.'"

Terry Mike Jeffrey was a fifteen-year-old high school kid from Kentucky, who had been singing along to Elvis records since age three, when he heard that Elvis would be returning to the stage in Las Vegas. He pleaded with his divorced mother to let him make a trip to Vegas during summer vacation to see the show. She finally agreed and even took out a loan from the bank to pay for the trip.

He flew out to Las Vegas with a family friend as chaperone, and the two had seats for Elvis's dinner show on August 1, his first performance following the invitation-only opening night. After the show, determined to try to meet his idol, Jeffrey sneaked into the backstage area, worked his way through the kitchen and down some stairs, eluding security long enough to catch sight of Elvis emerging from his dressing room with Sonny West. Just then the security guards grabbed him. "The guards had me by the arms and were taking me upstairs," Jeffrey recalled. "And I turned around and said, 'Hey, Elvis!' He looked at me and smiled. And I said, 'I'd just love to shake your hand.' And he called off the guards and said, 'It's OK, he's just a kid.'"

Elvis spent ten minutes talking to his young fan, who couldn't believe his luck. "He was very, very nice to me. Not in a hurry at all. His reaction was 'You came all the way from Kentucky to see this show?' It was a thrill for me, but you could tell it was exciting for him as well, because he had been away from the stage for so long." Elvis even had Charlie Hodge arrange for an extra table to be set up at the front of the balcony so Jeffrey could come to the sold-out midnight show as well. Jeffrey—who later became a country-gospel singer and frequent performer at Elvis tribute shows—ended up seeing thirty-eight Elvis concerts, in and out of Las Vegas, over the next seven years. "But that was probably the best one I ever saw. Simply because he was so excited. It was almost like he was auditioning. It was that new to him."

Elvis's comeback show was a turning point for Las Vegas. It set an all-time record for attendance, drawing 101,500 people over the four weeks. Every show was a sellout, with gross ticket receipts topping $1.5 million. (And that didn't count the $100 tips that patrons shelled out to maître d' Emilio Muscelli for a prime table; he could make thousands a night during an Elvis engagement.) In a town where showroom entertainment was traditionally a loss leader, Elvis's was reputedly the first Vegas show to actually make money, and it helped introduce a new business model. The people who came to see Elvis Presley weren't high rollers—or even, in many cases, gamblers at all. But they came in volume. They were Elvis fans, not necessarily Vegas fans; an estimated 10 percent were members of Elvis fan clubs. They came from all parts of the country and the world, and from all economic strata. (They were diverse in every way except race. Then, as always, Elvis's fan base was overwhelmingly white.) They may not have dropped thousands at the crap tables, but they plunked their quarters into slot machines, filled up the city's hotel rooms, ate in restaurants, and bought souvenirs. When Elvis came to town, all of Las Vegas felt flush.

Alex Shoofey, head man at the International, didn't have to wait for the final figures to realize that the hotel's bet on Elvis was going to pay off big. The night after the opening, he and Colonel Parker met in the hotel's coffee shop and sketched out a long-term contract on a pink tablecloth. According to the deal, Elvis would appear at the hotel for two four-week engagements a year for the next five years. His salary was increased to $125,000 a week (applied retroactively to the current engagement), boosting his annual pay to Colonel Parker's favorite round number: $1 million.

Some Elvis chroniclers claim that Colonel Parker got taken by Shoofey, since the contract didn't provide for any pay increases over the five years (though there would be bonuses, as well as an assurance that the hotel would match the salary of any other entertainer who got paid more during the term of the contract). The Colonel even turned down an offer of stock in the hotel; he never believed in anything but cold, hard cash. Some have speculated that Parker agreed to less than

Elvis could have commanded because the hotel was willing to cover at least some of his hefty gambling losses. Colonel Parker's addiction to the casino action was well-known in Vegas; he spent long hours at the roulette table, where he could lose thousands in a single night. "The Colonel was one of the best customers we had," Shoofey told journalist Alanna Nash. "He was good for a million dollars a year." (Interestingly, there was never any suggestion of connections between Colonel Parker and mob figures in Vegas. And to his credit, he made sure to keep Elvis away from them too—refusing to allow him even to be photographed with known wiseguys.)

But Elvis was hardly thinking about money as he basked in the acclaim for his Vegas comeback. "We didn't decide to come back here for the money, I'll tell you that," he told the British journalist Ray Connolly, who got a rare sit-down interview with him during the engagement. "I've wanted to perform on the stage again for the last nine years, and it's been building inside of me since 1965 until the strain became intolerable. I got all het up about it, and I don't think I could have left it much longer. The time is just right. The money—I have no idea about that. I just don't want to know. You can stuff it."

The Colonel, who was standing by monitoring the interview, interjected with a laugh, "He can flush all his money away if he wants to. I won't care."

When the engagement was finished, Elvis remained in Vegas for several more days; he liked the extra time to unwind, to wait out his fans, and to see some shows with less chance of getting mobbed. He went to the opening night of Nancy Sinatra's show at the International, which followed his in the big showroom (she had trouble filling up the room, which was partially draped off to make it look less obvious), as well as to the party her father threw for her afterward, stocked with Hollywood celebrities like Kirk Douglas, Fred Astaire, and Yul Brynner. Mac

Davis, who was working as a songwriter for Nancy's company, appeared in the show as well and even got a solo spot singing "In the Ghetto," the hit that he had written for Elvis. Davis was so nervous on opening night that he forgot the lyrics; Elvis, watching from the audience, kicked out his legs and held his stomach, he laughed so hard.

"Suspicious Minds" was released as a single near the end of August. The studio version Elvis had recorded in Memphis was overdubbed in Las Vegas with vocal and orchestral backup to match the way Elvis was performing it live. Engineers in the studio even tried to duplicate the diminuendo-crescendo effect of his live performances, by simply turning the recording volume down and then dialing it back up again, for a "false ending" before the big finish. It was a tacky gimmick (Chips Moman, back in Memphis, thought it ruined the recording), but it didn't much matter. "Suspicious Minds" rose to No. 1 on the *Billboard* Hot 100 chart, Elvis's first No. 1 hit since "Good Luck Charm" way back in 1962.

In October 1969, RCA released a live recording of the Vegas show—one disk in a double album, *From Memphis to Vegas / From Vegas to Memphis*, which also included more material from the American studio sessions. Elvis took a vacation in Hawaii with Priscilla and a handful of friends—an all-expenses-paid thank-you gift from the International—followed by another week in the Bahamas. But he returned to Las Vegas at least three more times that fall, revisiting the scene of his conquest and having some fun without Priscilla. Spotted at the blackjack table with two beautiful women at his side, smooching with him in between hands, Elvis quipped, "That's what a bad marriage does for you."

Meanwhile, with the Vegas engagement winning all the hosannas he could have wished for, Colonel Parker set about making plans for Elvis's return to national touring. After a second engagement at the International in January, Elvis did six shows in three days at the massive

Houston Astrodome. Then, just after finishing his third Vegas run in September 1970, he went to Phoenix for the start of a six-city tour, his first time back on the road in a dozen years. Propelled by Las Vegas, Elvis was finally back where he had longed to be, all through those agonizing last few years in Hollywood: in front of his fans again.

Las Vegas, meanwhile, was assessing the impact of Elvis's stupendously successful show.

Most immediately, it gave the new International Hotel instant credibility, as well as a signature star. Elvis became as identified with the International (and later the Hilton, after Kirk Kerkorian sold the hotel in 1971) as Sinatra had been with the Sands. More broadly, Elvis provided a much-needed booster shot for a city that had been trading on its old stars and formats for too long. "The International came along as the first example of Vegas thinking really big," said Vegas entertainment reporter Mike Weatherford. "Vegas needed some help by then. It was certainly losing its luster."

For years Las Vegas had shown little interest in reaching out to younger audiences, for the simple reason that they weren't gamblers. But by the end of the sixties—with the radical changes in popular music, the rise of the "youth culture," and the continuing fade-out of traditional nightclub entertainment—Vegas was realizing it couldn't ignore the younger generation forever. Just a couple of months after Elvis's show, the International brought in a production of the now-generation musical *Hair* (fending off a threat by the local DA to shut it down for indecency because of its controversial nude scene). In December, Caesars Palace, emboldened at least in part by Elvis's rock 'n' roll triumph at the International, booked the jazz-rock band Blood, Sweat & Tears—the only musical act to play both Woodstock and Las Vegas in the same year—into its Circus Maximus showroom for three nights during the Christmas holidays.

"It is something of a test for producer Dave Victorson to determine the solidity of a jazz-rock unit versus name headliner for pulling power," wrote *Variety's* Bill Willard. "If there are sufficient amounts of people inside the showroom, will those under and over 25 who are drawn by the contemporary pop music band play the games in the casino?" The show was the biggest draw on the Strip on its opening night, and the booking was judged a qualified success. "They appeal to the younger, swinging crowds, who will soon be populating Vegas in sufficient numbers to seriously consider their entertainment preferences," Willard wrote. "An entirely different perspective of the pop music milieu is taking place and Vegas moguls will have to view the change in a new, hard business light. The old headliners can't last forever."

Elvis Presley, to be sure, was a cutting-edge rock performer only by Vegas standards. He appealed mostly to the over-twenty-five crowd, who remembered him from his glory years. And his success at the International did not exactly open the floodgates for rock acts in Vegas. None of the major rock groups and singer-songwriters who were setting the agenda in popular music in the late sixties—the Rolling Stones, Led Zeppelin, Bob Dylan, Simon and Garfunkel—wanted anything to do with Las Vegas. The rock critics who praised Elvis's comeback also made clear their disdain for the venue where he chose to make it. "Like the Temptation of Saint Anthony, Las Vegas bristles with absurdities," wrote David Dalton in his otherwise admiring *Rolling Stone* piece; "it reeks of unreality. Its suddenness in the desert is a thirst-demented prospector's hallucination; the neon totems on the Strip pumping liquid light into the brain like pulsating neurons, the endless chrome dispensers of fate in the casinos . . ." And so on.

Still, Elvis showed that Vegas could be more than just a comfortable sinecure for aging rock 'n' rollers at the end of their careers. Though he had been in eclipse for years, Elvis was still a powerful commercial force: releasing chart-topping hits, able to fill up huge arenas. "Before Elvis went back to performing in Vegas there was a stigma," said Jerry Schilling, who later managed the Beach Boys (another group that shunned Vegas). "It meant you weren't an arena artist anymore. The only reason you played Vegas was you couldn't play anywhere else. Elvis changed that." Sonny Charles, lead singer of the Vegas R&B group the Checkmates, was gratified to see the shift in attitude. "Before Elvis, it seemed that all these concert acts and rock acts would think of Vegas as a step down," he said. "You played Vegas at the end of your career. But Elvis came and there was really a whole different mood."

"I think Elvis made it OK to play Vegas," said Tony Brown, who worked in Vegas with Elvis, as well as with other singers, like Johnny Cash. "Up until then, you thought of Vegas as shlock kinda stuff. But now, when an artist reaches the legacy level and doesn't want to do arena tours, they come to Las Vegas. It's an easier gig: you just come down the elevator and go do the show; the production is over-the-top, better than anything you can take on tour. Elvis started that."

The Vegas showroom scene was not entirely comfortable for Elvis and the band. "I always hated the place," said Jerry Scheff. "In my opinion nothing could ever make Vegas hip." Elvis was particularly distracted by the dinner shows—with plates and glasses clanking while he was trying to emote onstage. But for James Burton—who had played Vegas several times before, with such rock performers as Leon Russell—the excitement Elvis created made up for everything. "It was a great place to play," he said. "We had 747s coming in from Japan, two planes a day. We always had great audiences. I enjoyed playing Vegas."

Elvis wasn't greeted warmly by everyone in Vegas. Some of the old-timers saw him as an interloper, a rebuke to the classy, sophisticated Rat Pack era. "Elvis was uncultured, uneducated," said Corinne Entratter, wife of the longtime manager of the Sands (and who later married George Sidney, the director of *Viva Las Vegas*). "He was a complete outsider. He knew nothing about show business. He made the crowd happy, but it was not a sophisticated crowd." Yet Elvis made an effort to be a supportive member of the city's showbiz community. Even after he became Vegas' most celebrated star, he (or more likely Colonel Parker) would always send congratulatory telegrams or flower bouquets to others who were opening in Vegas while Elvis was there. That generated a lot of goodwill. Nelson Sardelli, a lounge singer whom Elvis had never even met, got one of the notes and later went up to thank Elvis when he saw him in the lobby of the Flamingo Hotel. "Elvis looked at me as if we were oldest buddies," Sardelli recalled. "'Nelson, man, nice to see you!'" Trini Lopez was a little insulted when Tom Jones came to see his show, brought an entourage that took up two booths, and told Trini's manager that he wouldn't be able to come backstage after the show, but would hang out in the lounge if Trini wanted to say hello. Elvis, by contrast, came to Lopez's show with just his father and Priscilla, no entourage at all, and asked Trini's manager to alert him before the singer's final number—so Elvis could get backstage before the crowds and congratulate him.

Elvis would often drop in on other lounge shows in Vegas, sometimes even popping up onstage, which always caused a stir. One night, after finishing his show, Elvis was passing by the International's lounge when he heard the Righteous Brothers singing "You've Lost That Lovin' Feeling," which Elvis had begun doing in his own act. He suddenly walked onstage, greeted singer Bill Medley—"Hi, Bill"—then walked off. Word got around of the visit, and a big crowd gathered the next night for the Brothers' show, in hopes of seeing Elvis again. Sure enough, Elvis was passing by at the same time with his entourage, sauntered onstage for another "Hi, Bill," before scooting away like the Lone

Ranger. "OK, I don't know who he is," Medley quipped, "but now he's starting to piss me off."

Elvis's comeback at the International established a new template for the Las Vegas show: no longer an intimate, sophisticated, Sinatra-style nightclub act, but a big rock-concert-like spectacle. "Elvis didn't go in saying, 'I'm doing a show for Vegas,'" said Jerry Schilling. "He did a touring show onstage in Vegas." It was, by Vegas standards, a relatively pared-down spectacle—no chorus line of showgirls, levitating stages, laser-light shows, or much production at all. But for the sheer size of its musical presentation (not one but two backup singing groups, a rhythm band, plus a full orchestra—nearly sixty people onstage), the almost superhuman energy Elvis displayed, and the electricity he created in the showroom, Elvis's show set a new standard for Las Vegas. The star was now his own spectacle.

His show was, most of all, an *event.* In the old days, people would plan their trips to Las Vegas and then book their shows: if Frank or Sammy wasn't in town, there were always plenty of others to choose from, among the many stars who were constantly circulating in and out of Vegas. Now people began to schedule their trips to Vegas around Elvis shows. He was the first major star to establish something like a regular schedule in Las Vegas: two four-week engagements a year, one in the winter, one in the summer—a forerunner of the "residencies" of latter-day Vegas stars like Céline Dion. Elvis fans came from all over the world, and some would get tickets for a whole week of shows. The big gamblers who didn't care for Elvis could plant their wives in the showroom and spend their evening at the crap tables. The International would give complimentary tickets for Elvis's shows to high rollers from other hotels; in return, the Riviera or Caesars would comp the International's guests for *their* headliners. When Elvis was in town, everybody did well.

Elvis hardly enhanced his stature in the rock world by becoming a Las Vegas star. The gaudy setting, the showbiz affectations, the sentimental ballads, the mostly middle-aged, middlebrow audience, the housewives with bouffant hairdos who sat swooning in the front rows—it hardly jibed with the motivating ethos of so many rock performers in the late sixties. They saw their music as an avenue for personal expression, social-political protest, and artistic experimentation. All Elvis wanted to do was sing.

And sing to everybody. Las Vegas wasn't just a creative resurrection for Elvis; it was also his grand statement of inclusiveness. No one was more responsible than Elvis, back in the mid-1950s, for driving the initial stake that split the music audience, and eventually the entire culture, in two: the adults who listened to the pop standards and Hit Parade tunes sung by Frank Sinatra, Perry Como, and Rosemary Clooney; and the kids who embraced a new kind of music called rock 'n' roll. By the end of the sixties, the battle had grown awfully lopsided: rock was becoming mainstream, while the old-style crooners were reduced to a few creaky TV variety shows, a diminishing roster of nightclubs—and Las Vegas.

Elvis wanted to bring everyone back together under one tent. He was a rocker and a child of Memphis blues, but also an unabashed romantic; he loved Mario Lanza as well as Bo Diddley. He could kick ass in "What'd I Say" or go for the tears with "Memories." For Elvis, it was all music. He was a great populist—a uniter, not a divider—and Vegas gave him his greatest platform. He brought his showmanship, his matchless voice, and the urgency of an artist on a mission to redeem himself. Las Vegas brought the crowds. Neither would ever be the same again.

Seven

AFTERMATH
(Elvis Forever)

He got better before he got worse.

When Elvis Presley made his long-awaited return to the concert stage at Las Vegas' International Hotel in August 1969, many people, both inside and outside his circle, assumed it would be a onetime event. But the phenomenal success of his show, and the long-term contract that Colonel Parker drew up with the hotel shortly after the opening, ensured that Las Vegas would become a recurring, twice-yearly stop on Elvis's soon-to-be-resumed touring schedule. And for at least the first two or three of those Vegas appearances, Elvis was still engaged, energized, and musically at the top of his game.

First there were some personnel changes. Larry Muhoberac, the keyboard player in Elvis's backup band, decided to return to session work in Los Angeles rather than continue with Elvis. So James Burton recruited Glen D. Hardin, who had passed on the job the first time

around because he was too busy. An affable West Texas native who had
played with Buddy Holly's backup group, the Crickets, Hardin had a
solid track record as a session player, as well as some experience as an
arranger—a skill that quickly proved valuable. During rehearsals for
his January show in Vegas, Elvis said he wanted to try doing the old
Everly Brothers song "Let It Be Me," but had no arrangement. Hardin
showed up the next morning with one he had written overnight. Elvis
was pleased, the number was incorporated into the show, and Hardin
went on to become Elvis's reliable in-house arranger.

Drummer Ronnie Tutt also opted out of the second Vegas engagement to take a better-paying job with Andy Williams. His replacement,
Bob Lanning, was a competent session player, but Elvis missed Tutt's
hard-charging backup, and he made sure that Colonel Parker paid Tutt
enough to lure him back for the next Vegas gig. Tutt and Hardin, along
with holdovers Jerry Scheff, John Wilkinson, and James Burton, would
remain the core of Elvis's backup band for most of his Vegas years. Elvis
even gave them a name, the TCB (for Taking Care of Business) Band
and cemented the fraternity by giving each member a bracelet and gold
pendant with TCB and a lightning bolt insignia engraved on it.

Elvis opened his second engagement at the International on January
26, 1970, and it proved the first one was no fluke. Reservations poured
in even faster than they had the previous summer. The opening-night
dinner show was packed with 1,780 people, 300 more than at opening
night six months earlier. Elvis wore the first of his flashy, Bill Belew—
designed jumpsuits—most of them white, but also in black and blue,
with plunging necklines and a variety of jeweled designs. Ringo Starr
was in the audience on opening night. Fats Domino came to one show,
and Elvis sang "Blueberry Hill" in his honor. On closing night Dean
Martin was in the audience, and Elvis acknowledged him with a few
bars of "Everybody Loves Somebody Sometime."

Elvis's repertoire was expanding, with several numbers that would remain part of his act for years. He still began the show with a string of his old hits ("All Shook Up" replaced "Blue Suede Shoes" as the opening number), but he added several contemporary selections: two singles from his Memphis recording sessions the previous year, "Kentucky Rain" and "Don't Cry Daddy," as well as several songs associated with other artists, including Neil Diamond's "Sweet Caroline," Creedence Clearwater Revival's "Proud Mary," and Tony Joe White's country-fried dish of swamp rock, "Polk Salad Annie," which gave Elvis a chance to deliver a little opening catechism on Southern customs. RCA released another live album from the show, and the critics were once again enthusiastic. "It was a flawless demonstration of his vocal ability and showmanship," said Robert Hilburn in the *Los Angeles Times*. "Elvis, with the uncanny guidance of Col. Tom Parker, has done what once seemed impossible. He has become king on his own terms."

His third Vegas engagement, in August 1970, brought another key personnel change, as Joe Guercio replaced Bobby Morris as orchestra leader. (According to Morris, the hotel let him go after a dispute unrelated to Elvis: Morris had hired twenty-four string players for Julie Budd, Bill Cosby's opening act, then had to fire them when Cosby switched to another opening act. The union objected, and the hotel blamed it on Morris.) Guercio was a fortuitous addition. He was a well-traveled and well-connected Vegas conductor, who had worked with everyone from Patti Page to Steve and Eydie, and he made his mark almost immediately. "Joe was the first one to really put the band to work," said pianist Frank Leone. Guercio helped flesh out the arrangements, suggested new endings for some numbers, and in general got the orchestra more involved. His most notable contribution, however, came in January 1971, when he introduced a new opening for the show: heralding Elvis's entrance with the dramatic theme from Richard

Strauss's *Thus Spoke Zarathustra*, which Stanley Kubrick had used so memorably in *2001: A Space Odyssey*—a suitably majestic introduction for the new king of Las Vegas.

For his summer show in 1970, Elvis-mania in Las Vegas reached a new peak. The hotel was festooned with pennants announcing THE ELVIS SUMMER FESTIVAL. Colonel Parker shipped in tens of thousands of souvenir postcards, catalogs, photo albums, and ELVIS SUMMER FESTIVAL straw hats, which the waitresses, dealers, and other hotel employees were required to wear during the run. The old carny's promotional ingenuity knew no bounds. Among the souvenirs on sale were expensive framed posters of Elvis, identified as "original Renaldis from Italy." Renaldi was an Italian American employee in the International's carpenter shop.

Colonel Parker also brought in a documentary crew to film several nights of the August 1970 engagement. The Colonel's original idea was to broadcast one of the Las Vegas concerts live for a closed-circuit pay-per-view TV event. But when news of the planned telecast leaked to the press prematurely, the Colonel scrapped the idea and instead made a deal with MGM, the Hollywood studio that Kirk Kerkorian had recently acquired, to produce a feature documentary on the Vegas show. The result, *Elvis: That's the Way It Is*, directed by Oscar-winner Denis Sanders and released in November 1970, is the best record we have of Elvis's power and charisma onstage at the height of his Vegas years.

The film begins with behind-the-scenes footage of rehearsals in Los Angeles; Elvis is loose, in high spirits, and more naturally engaging than in any of his clumsy "ad-lib" patter onstage. But the bulk of the film is simply a record of his Vegas show, shot by acclaimed cinematographer Lucien Ballard (*The Wild Bunch*). In his high-collared white jumpsuit, open in front with giant silver buttons, Elvis is a magnetic presence onstage: in constant motion, pacing the stage, striking karate poses, whirling one arm like a pinwheel or slashing the air to punctuate the chords. He's sweating by the end, yet he seems more comfortable and controlled than in his often out-of-breath performances in 1969.

His rock engine still hums on old numbers like "I Got a Woman" and new ones (for him) like "C. C. Rider," which opens the show. He tears into the big ballads with unabashed emotion and theatricality. He begins the Righteous Brothers' "You've Lost That Lovin' Feeling" with his back turned dramatically to the audience. He gives an impassioned (but not over-the-top) reading to Dusty Springfield's "You Don't Have to Say You Love Me" and Simon and Garfunkel's "Bridge over Troubled Waters." He loves the big finish, often closing songs with a dramatic freeze-frame, in karate warrior pose or with one hand thrust toward the sky. "Nobody could close a song any better than he could," said Mac Davis. "I used to love watching other entertainers try, from Wayne Newton to Céline Dion. But nobody could. It was absolutely Elvis."

He could take the corniest songs and put them across with the sheer force of his musical conviction. Take "The Wonder of You." The song was originally written for Perry Como, who never recorded it, and became a minor hit in 1959 for the sweet-voiced pop crooner Ray Peterson. When Elvis began performing it in Las Vegas in the winter of 1970 (with an arrangement rustled up in one night by Glen D. Hardin), he went to lunch with Peterson and told him he wanted to record the song. "You don't have to ask permission, you're Elvis Presley," Peterson said. "Yes, I do," Elvis replied. "You're Ray Peterson." Elvis's version of "The Wonder of You," recorded live in Las Vegas and released as a single in April 1970, rose to No. 9 in the United States and No. 1 in Great Britain, one of his biggest hits of the seventies.

His performance of the song in *Elvis: That's the Way It Is* is a vivid illustration of Elvis's ability to transform a conventional love song into something grander, more emotional, almost operatic in its intensity. "When no one else can understand me / When everything I do is

wrong," go to the treacly lyrics, "You give me hope and consolation /
You give me strength to carry on." But Elvis leaves no doubt that he
honestly believes them—or at least wants to. He builds the song beautifully, gathering force as the melody ascends the scale, his voice breaking ever so slightly on the word *hope*, his eyes closing as if imagining
the wondrous woman he was never quite able to find (or maybe it's his
mother). During James Burton's twangy guitar bridge ("Play the song,
James"), Elvis joins with the swelling male-female chorus, guiding the
number toward a thrilling climax and release—Elvis grabbing the air
with one hand, fingers outstretched, tensed and almost trembling on
the last chord, before a furious swipe of the air to end the song. It is the
essence of Elvis in Vegas: schmaltz raised to the sublime.

The decline that followed is a sad, familiar story: told many times, psy-
choanalyzed, moralized about, recounted in books by almost everyone
who had even a passing acquaintance with Elvis during his last few
years. Boredom and overwork, combined with drug use that was either
ignored or enabled by his circle of intimates, sapped his energy, sank his
spirits, and essentially drove him crazy. It was both tragic and ludicrous,
a cautionary tale and parable for the age of rock superstardom—one of
the first of many similarly tragic ends for rock stars unable to cope with
the perks and perils of enormous fame.

   Las Vegas usually gets much of the blame, simply because it's where
the decline could be witnessed in real time. In 1969 and '70 Elvis still
looked and sounded great, buoyed by the enthusiastic crowds, critical
acclaim, and renewed self-confidence. But his grueling, twice-yearly appearances in Las Vegas—two shows a night for four weeks, without a
single night off—soon became a grind, and his thirtieth-floor home

at the International, later the Hilton (a palatial, five-thousand-square-foot suite, complete with private swimming pool and rooftop terrace, from which Elvis and his pals would sometimes hit golf balls), a prison. "When he captured Vegas, he was the most dynamic performer in the world," said Jerry Schilling, who worked with him during much of that period. "But what is the challenge, for an artist, after you've done it and done it, over and over again? To have him there twice a year, sixty shows in a row, the same place, never getting out of the hotel for maybe five weeks. In the wintertime we never saw daylight. We would go to bed, close the curtains just about sunrise. And we'd get up for breakfast, it was five o'clock; by the eight o'clock show, it was dark. It was great for two, three engagements. But then, it becomes decadent, if you will."

An early sign of trouble came in August 1970, when the hotel's security office received an anonymous call warning that a man would try to kill Elvis during his Saturday-night show. The FBI was alerted, armed plainclothes officers and members of the Memphis Mafia were stationed around the room for protection, and Elvis carried two pistols in his boots when he took the stage. Tension was high throughout the show. Elvis stood sideways for much of the performance to make himself a smaller target; an ambulance was parked outside just in case. Despite one scary moment, when a man yelled out from the balcony (just requesting a song, it turned out), the threat came to nothing. But it added to Elvis's paranoia and isolation. He grew more obsessed with guns, and more reckless with them, often firing shots in fits of anger or simply for kicks. His use of prescription drugs—increasingly strong sedatives to help him sleep, amphetamines to keep him going—grew worse, and he found a new physician in Las Vegas, Dr. Elias Ghanem, to help keep him supplied. His marriage was falling apart, he was spending money as fast as he could earn it, and his moods were growing increasingly capricious and foul.

His performances first began to be affected, by most accounts, during his August 1971 engagement. Elvis looked puffy and seemed listless onstage. His sets were rarely longer than forty-five minutes, and filled with so many fits and starts and distracting karate displays that some audience members actually walked out. "Those shows in Vegas in August of '71, that's when you saw the first signs that things were starting to fall apart," said Lamar Fike. "Elvis would be so ripped his tongue would be thick, and he'd tell the audience, 'I'm sorry, folks, I just got up. I'm not really awake yet.'" The critics began to notice. "As performances go," wrote Mark Tan in the *Hollywood Reporter*, "Elvis Presley's at the Las Vegas Hilton is sloppy, hurriedly rehearsed, mundanely lit, poorly amplified, occasionally monotonous, often silly, and haphazardly coordinated. Elvis looked drawn, tired, and noticeably heavier—weight-wise, not musically—than in his last Vegas appearance. He wasn't in his strongest voice, his costume of studded white slacks and vest with black satin high collar and scarf was not his sexiest or most flattering. And do you know what? The packed to overcapacity audience—the first 2,000 of the usual 120,000 he'll draw for his monthlong engagement—positively couldn't have cared less."

That was part of the problem. The fans loved him, no matter how he looked or what he did. The adulation seemed to go to his head. The shows became more bombastic; the white suits more garish. Elvis began wearing a jewel-studded cape, spreading it wide and bowing his head dramatically, like some weird cross between Dracula and Jesus. He began performing a medley of patriotic songs—"Dixie," "The Battle Hymn of the Republic" and the spiritual "All My Trials"—that he dubbed "An American Trilogy," delivered with a sober grandiloquence that was a far cry from his splashy but still self-deprecating early performances.

The strange thing was, he could still sing. Live recordings from his

Vegas shows as late as 1974 reveal a vocalist of still formidable power: still hitting the high notes on "It's Now or Never," rocking with just as much authority on old numbers like "Trying to Get to You" or Chuck Berry's "Promised Land." And Elvis was still the toast of Las Vegas. Other performers came to see him, hang out with him, claim him as a friend. Marty Allen, the frizzy-haired half of the comedy team of Allen and Rossi, was flattered when he first met Elvis and the King told him how much he enjoyed Marty on game shows like *Hollywood Squares*. They would trade practical jokes: once, just as he was about to go onstage, Elvis had some of the guys handcuff Marty to Elvis's dressing-room door. After Marty finally got a security guard to free him, he barged in on the show, wearing a scarf and clamoring for a kiss while Elvis was singing "Love Me Tender." Pop singer Vikki Carr, who was appearing at the Tropicana Hotel, came to see his show for the first time with her fiancé, Elias Ghanem—Elvis's own Vegas doctor. When she went with Ghanem backstage after the show, Elvis told her to close her eyes and slipped a pavé diamond star ring on her finger as an engagement gift.

An occasional project could rouse Elvis's interest, like his January 1973 TV special *Aloha from Hawaii*, which was the first music concert ever beamed live around the world by satellite. But a few days after the broadcast he was back in Las Vegas, appearing worn-out and over-weight, and more dependent than ever on drugs, which now included injections of liquid Demerol. Health problems forced him to cancel five midnight shows in February. Then, on the night of February 18, in an-other security scare, four Peruvian men in the audience suddenly rushed the stage. They turned out to be just overeager, overlubricated fans, but a melee ensued as several members of Elvis's entourage jumped onstage to fight off the intruders; Elvis even knocked one back with a karate kick of his own. He was fuming after the incident. "I'm sorry, ladies and gentlemen," he told the crowd. "I'm sorry I didn't break his goddamn neck is what I'm sorry about."

Elvis was still upset after the show, and he insisted that the attack must have been the work of Mike Stone, the karate instructor with whom Priscilla was having an affair. (She and Elvis would be divorced in October.) Elvis startled even his jaded inner circle by demanding that they hire a hit man and have Stone killed. The Memphis Mafia, not exactly relishing the idea of behaving like the real Mafia, made a show of looking into it, before Elvis cooled down and decided to let the matter slide.

His behavior onstage grew more and more erratic. For one show in August 1973 he came out riding Lamar Fike's back, with a toy monkey attached to his neck. He sang "What Now My Love?" while lying on a bed rolled out onstage and interpolated X-rated lyrics into "Love Me Tender." The *Hollywood Reporter* found it "one of the most ill-prepared, unsteady, and most disheartening performances of his Las Vegas career." On the last night of the run, Elvis launched into an off-the-cuff rant in which he criticized the Hilton Hotel for firing a waiter named Mario, who often brought him room service. "He needs the job, and I think the Hiltons are bigger than that," said Elvis. Colonel Parker was furious that Elvis would publicly embarrass the hotel like that and chewed him out after the show. They had a brutal argument that ended with Elvis actually firing the Colonel—only to make up a few days later, after Parker toted up how much money he claimed Elvis owed him, and Elvis and his father decided they couldn't afford the breakup.

In October 1973 Elvis, semicomatose, was rushed to a Memphis emergency room and spent three weeks in the hospital, as doctors attempted to wean him off at least some of his drugs. He took a couple of months to rest, and when he returned to Vegas in January—his engagements now shortened from four weeks to two—some saw an uptick, his best performances since 1970. But soon he was back to his unpredictable behavior onstage. In August 1974, he rambled on endlessly about his passion for karate, his divorce from Priscilla, and his anger at press reports of his drug abuse: "I hear rumors flying around. I got sick in the hospital. In this day and time you can't even get sick; you are . . . strung out! By God, I'll tell you something, friend, I have never been strung out in my life, except on music. . . . If I find or hear an individual that has said that about me, *I'm going to break their goddamn neck, you son of a bitch!*" Priscilla, who was in the audience, was shocked that he would air his grievances so publicly. "It was like watching a different person," she said.

Even the occasional glimmers of hope for a new challenge were quickly snuffed out. Elvis wanted to tour overseas, but the Colonel (hiding his passport problems) always made excuses for rejecting the idea. Barbra Streisand visited Elvis backstage at the Hilton one night and offered him the costarring role in a remake she was planning of the film classic *A Star Is Born.* Elvis, who still had hopes of making a mark in movies, was excited by the prospect. But Colonel Parker, peeved that Streisand made the offer directly to Elvis and not to him (and possibly realizing that Elvis wasn't capable of such a challenging role at this point), made so many demands on the deal that it was soon abandoned. Kris Kristofferson eventually played the role.

Health problems forced more show cancellations in 1975. In August, overweight and ill, Elvis was so weak he couldn't walk from his dressing room to the elevator; at times he had to call for a chair onstage. He cut the engagement short, rested up, and came back in December, when he seemed a bit revived. But live footage of his last Vegas engagement, in December 1976, shows his deterioration with painful clarity. Elvis looks bloated and is nearly immobile onstage—all the dynamic energy of his early Vegas years reduced to a little leg jiggling and half-hearted swaying to the beat. He seems distracted, depleted, simply going through the motions. Even tossing out scarves to his female fans—Charlie Hodge hands them to him, one after another after another—now looks like a mechanical, joyless ritual.

"After sitting through Elvis Presley's closing night performance at the Las Vegas Hilton," wrote the *Memphis Press-Scimitar*, in an eerily prophetic review on December 15, 1976, "one walks away wondering how much longer it can be before the end comes, perhaps suddenly, and why the King of Rock 'n' Roll would subject himself to possible ridicule by going onstage so ill-prepared."

Eight months later at Graceland, on the afternoon of August 16, 1977, after a night in which he visited his dentist, played racquetball at 3:00 a.m., and swallowed three packets of the sleep medication his doctors had prepared for him, his girlfriend, Ginger Alden, found Elvis lying on the bathroom floor, unconscious and not breathing. He was rushed to Baptist Memorial Hospital, and an hour later, at 3:30 p.m. central time, he was declared dead. The cause was officially cardiac arrhythmia, but an autopsy revealed traces of fourteen different drugs in his system, at least five of them in potentially toxic doses.

Elvis's demons were of little concern to Las Vegas, so long as he kept bringing in the crowds. And he did. His fans continued making the pilgrimage to Las Vegas to the bitter end: Elvis did 636 shows in Vegas over seven years, and every one of them, according to the hotel, was sold out. He was the city's undisputed superstar, a shot in the arm for business all over Las Vegas whenever he came to town. Yet Bill Miller, the veteran Vegas booker who signed him for the International Hotel in 1969, predicted that Elvis's show would mean "the end of Vegas":

his record-breaking salary, Miller feared, would make big-star entertainment in Vegas economically unsustainable. Miller was only partly
wrong. Elvis didn't kill Vegas, but he did change it. His triumph in
Las Vegas helped hasten the demise of the old nightclub shows and
sounded the starting gun for a very different era of Las Vegas entertainment.

The 1970s were a difficult decade for Las Vegas. The transition
from the old mob factions that had dominated the casino business to a
new era of corporate owners was gaining steam. On Thanksgiving eve
in 1970, Howard Hughes left town, as suddenly and surreptitiously
as he had arrived four years earlier: spirited out of the Desert Inn on a
stretcher, driven to Nellis Air Force Base, and flown to the Bahamas,
never to return. In 1971 Kirk Kerkorian sold his International Hotel
to the Hilton organization—the first national hotel chain to get a foothold on the Las Vegas Strip—and moved on to an even bigger project. Having just acquired a controlling interest in Hollywood's MGM
film studio, he set out to build a namesake hotel in Vegas: the MGM
Grand. Constructed in a quick eighteen months and opening in December 1973, the $106 million concrete-and-glass behemoth had no
particular architectural distinction except for its size: with 2,084 rooms
(and a building volume as large as that of the Empire State Building), it
was not only the biggest hotel in Las Vegas, but the biggest in the world
at the time.

The MGM Grand would, however, be the last major resort to open
on the Strip for more than a decade—and would be ravaged by a disastrous fire in November 1980 that killed eighty-five people. (The hotel
had not bothered to install a fire sprinkler system in the casino or the
restaurant, where the fire started.) Several of the older Strip hotels built
new high-rise additions during the 1970s; downtown got a major face-
lift; and the city's national profile grew, as TV hosts like Merv Griffin

and Mike Douglas brought their popular daytime talk shows to Las Vegas and Jerry Lewis in 1973 made Vegas the permanent home for his annual Labor Day telethon for muscular dystrophy. Yet Las Vegas, increasingly, seemed to be living off the glory of a fading show-business era.

Many of the stars from the golden age were still around, but they were well past their prime. Frank Sinatra announced his retirement from show business in June 1971, only to return two years later—still a big draw in Las Vegas, but no longer the cultural force he once was. Dean Martin's lazy-hazy drunk act, overexposed for nine seasons on his NBC variety show, was past its sell-by date. Sammy Davis Jr., with his hip Nehru jackets, flashy jewelry, and cool-cat lingo, was verging on self-parody. Their old patron at the Sands, Jack Entratter, was gone too: dead of a cerebral hemorrhage following a bike accident in March 1971. (His former wife Corinne Entratter Sidney always had suspicions about the death, since it followed a trip Entratter made to New York, when the hotel's mob bosses summoned him to explain some alleged financial improprieties.)

Nor did Elvis's comeback in Las Vegas do much to attract a new generation of rock stars, most of whom still shunned the city as a haven for nightclub has-beens. A few younger, middle-of-the-road pop singers, like Olivia Newton-John and Engelbert Humperdinck, became Vegas headliners during these years. Following Elvis's success, Vegas became more receptive to other vintage rockers (like Jerry Lee Lewis, who followed Elvis into the International Hotel's showroom in 1970) as well as to country music: once confined mainly to downtown, country stars like Johnny Cash, Barbara Mandrell, and Willie Nelson now became top attractions on the Strip.

Yet Elvis's white jumpsuits and bombastic stage shows came to symbolize the gaudiness, fakery, and middlebrow bad taste that people identified with Las Vegas. The city in the seventies was "an uncool polyester dump" (*Time*), a "blight to spirit and soul" (*New York Times*), an object of parody—like Bill Murray's unctuous lounge-singer character on *Saturday Night Live*, crooning the theme to *Star Wars* (and Elvis's *Thus Spoke Zarathustra*). "Gradually between 1968 and 1975, Vegas found itself pushed across the generational line that divides cool from laughable," wrote Mike Weatherford in *Cult Vegas*, "Without a new generation of headliner-types to draw from, Vegas became an elephant's graveyard of has-beens or dependable B-teamers."

Arena concerts and tours were the preferred (and more lucrative) route for the major rock stars of the era. Vegas was regarded as a sellout; the hip agents steered their clients away. Mac Davis, who was trying to make the jump from songwriting to performing in the early seventies, recalled his first meeting with music-industry power broker David Geffen. "Why in hell are you playing Las Vegas?" Geffen said. "That's the worst thing you can do!" Even among the more traditional Vegas stars, the city was no longer considered the essential stop that it had been a decade earlier. "There are a lot of performers who don't want to work here," Petula Clark told reporter Mark Tan in 1976. "Ten years ago everybody would kill to get here, and now it's 'Who needs it?' Concerts have really cut into the prestige of Vegas. People feel they can go out in concert and make more money and work less."

The glamour and cachet of the early sixties were long gone; the high rollers and Rat Pack–era hipsters replaced by a new crowd of budget-conscious, Middle American tourists. (The "flood victims," as some of the old-timers referred to them.) Texas columnist Molly Ivins, on her first trip to Las Vegas in 1979, was both amused and appalled: "Genuine Pa Kettles, wearing overalls and straw farmer's hats, stand pouring quarters into slot-machines bookended by characters sent from Central Casting to give Californians a bad name. Shirts open to the navel, razor-cuts, indelible tans, and little gold coke spoons around their necks. They in turn are bookended by blue-rinse perm grandmas in print dresses wearing cat-eye glasses with sequins on the top."

But that, by and large, was Elvis's audience. And it was Elvis's show, in all its glorious excess, that seemed to presage Vegas' new era.

He gave the Vegas show a makeover and pointed it in a new direction. He turned the Vegas show into an event and set the high bar that the next generation of headliners tried to top. After Elvis, everything got bigger: higher salaries, gaudier productions, more musicians onstage, splashier publicity campaigns. For rock and pop singers who had finished their run in the Top 40 but still had creative (and commercial) ambitions, Elvis showed that Las Vegas could be a viable career option: a little nostalgia for the old fans, then a move into fresh territory, a chance to show off new artistic maturity and range—accompanied by the sort of Vegas hoopla that certified the presence of an authentic superstar.

Cher, already a Vegas veteran from her years with Sonny Bono, came back to Caesars Palace as a solo in 1979, with an opulent show in which she modeled twelve different Bob Mackie outfits (from cowgirl chic to Folies-Bergère feathers), rode a mechanical bull, and sang a medley of rock 'n' roll hits starting with Elvis's "Jailhouse Rock." Two years later Dolly Parton got a record $350,000 a week for her massively hyped Vegas debut at the Riviera Hotel, making her entrance across a drawbridge from a fairy-tale castle, and supplementing her country hits with "House of the Rising Sun" and "There's No Business Like Show Business." Wayne Newton, who considered himself Elvis's heir in Vegas, pumped up his own show with a bigger orchestra, more backup singers, and a tribute segment to Elvis. One night at the Hilton Hotel, in the middle of singing "Are You Lonesome Tonight?," Wayne claimed he saw Elvis's ghost watching him from the balcony. (In 1976 Las Vegas got its first arena-sized venue for rock shows, when the Aladdin Hotel opened its seventy-five-hundred-seat, $10 million Theater for the Performing Arts, with Neil Diamond as the opening attraction.)

The broad-based, Middle American audience that Elvis attracted, moreover, was precisely the target audience for Vegas' own reinvention a decade or so later. The modern era began in 1989 with the opening of Steve Wynn's Mirage Hotel. Situated next door to Caesars Palace, the Mirage was the first resort in Vegas to offer not just a theme, but a veritable theme park. Inside the hotel Wynn created a giant rain forest, enclosed in a glass dome, featuring real palm trees and orchids and twenty thousand square feet of fake plants. Behind the registration desk was a twenty-thousand-gallon aquarium filled with sharks and rays. Outside the hotel, visitors gaped at a fake mountain range, with grottoes, waterfalls, and—the spectacular pièce de résistance—a fifty-foot-high volcano that erupted with fiery fake lava every fifteen minutes. "It's what God would've done if he'd had the money," said Wynn.

The Mirage was an instant success, and a spate of other theme park–like hotels quickly followed: the Excalibur, designed to look like a medieval Arthurian castle; the Egyptian-pyramid-shaped Luxor; the kid-friendly Treasure Island, where a sea battle between pirate ships was staged every ninety minutes. And more: hotels re-creating the canals of Venice, the streets of Paris, the skyline of New York City. It was dubbed the Disneyfication of Las Vegas—but there were designer shops and gourmet restaurants for the grown-ups too. Wynn's Bellagio, opened in 1998, featured a re-creation of Italy's Lake Como, with a giant musical fountain display every fifty minutes, plus a $300 million collection of art by Cézanne, van Gogh, and other modern masters. Las Vegas was now a full-service vacation spot, both mass-market and upscale, amusement park and designer shopping mall, something for the whole family. With gambling, too—only now it was called gaming.

The entertainment changed as well. As headliners in the Mirage's main showroom, Wynn installed the glam illusionists Siegfried and Roy. The two had met in the 1960s aboard a German cruise line, where Siegfried Fischbacher was working as a steward and doing magic shows for the passengers, and Roy Horn, another ship employee, convinced him to incorporate a pet cheetah (which Roy had smuggled on board) into the show. The two developed a unique magic act that they were soon performing in nightclubs across Europe. Eventually they moved to Las Vegas, where they appeared in the *Lido de Paris* and other production shows, before headlining their own show, *Beyond Belief*, for seven years at the Frontier Hotel. For the Mirage, they enlisted directors John Napier and John Caird—the Royal Shakespeare Company team responsible for *Nicholas Nickleby* and *Les Misérables*—to fashion a $28 million, effects-laden extravaganza, featuring a menagerie of white tigers, elephants, and other jungle animals, that set a new standard for Vegas spectacle.

Then came Cirque du Soleil, the new age Canadian circus troupe, founded in 1984 by a couple of street performers in Montreal, which opened its first Vegas show, *Mystére*, on Christmas Day 1993, in a specially designed, fifteen-hundred-seat theater at the Treasure Island resort. The Cirque shows, with their mix of aerial acrobatics, circus stunts, clowns, puppetry, music, and special effects, were an entirely new kind of spectacle for Las Vegas: hugely expensive to stage, but capable of running forever. A half dozen more Cirque shows would soon be fixtures on the Strip—the water-themed *O*, the erotic *Zumanity*, tributes to the Beatles and Michael Jackson—reinventing the city's family-friendly entertainment for the new millennium.

The new Vegas was an astonishing success. Twenty-eight million people visited Las Vegas in 1994, more than double the number just ten years earlier. The critics who once scorned Vegas as the bad-taste capital of America suddenly saw the town in a new light. The over-the-top

stage spectacles and theme-park hotels were now viewed as an authentic, and somehow lovable, expression of all-American kitsch. "How can
a large-spirited American not love Las Vegas, or at least smile at the
notion of it?" wrote Kurt Andersen in a 1994 *Time* cover story, which
celebrated all the ways in which the Vegas esthetic had transformed
American culture, from postmodern architecture to Michael Jackson
concerts. Even Wayne Newton was now corny enough to be hip.

The Cirque du Soleil spectacles, along with other production
shows, magic acts, and performance troupes like Blue Man Group, all
but pushed out the traditional Vegas headliners. But in the early 2000s
came the stirrings of a revival. Colonel Tom Parker himself—who settled in Las Vegas after Elvis's death and became a consultant to the
Hilton—heard a young Canadian singer named Céline Dion perform
Elvis's "Can't Help Falling in Love" on a 1994 Disney TV special and
urged her manager-husband, René Angélil, to bring her to Las Vegas.
He demurred, saying she wasn't ready. But nine years later, in 2003,
Caesars Palace signed Dion to a blockbuster three-year contract—five
shows a week, forty weeks a year, in the hotel's new $95 million, four-
thousand-seat Colosseum theater.

Dion's high-tech show (created by former Cirque du Soleil director
Franco Dragone) featured more than fifty dancers, a huge LED screen
displaying vistas ranging from ancient Rome to New York's Times
Square, shooting stars, meteor showers, and a tree blooming onstage—
along with Céline's rafter-raising soprano, belting out everything from
"I've Got the World on a String" to her signature hit, "My Heart Will
Go On." Her show was a huge success, and the inspiration for a new
wave of Vegas "residencies," from Elton John to Jennifer Lopez, Mariah
Carey, and Lady Gaga—all pop stars with big followings, at least one
foot in the rock world, and a flair for spectacle. Just like Elvis. Said Dion
in a 2007 Vegas tribute, "Elvis *was* Las Vegas. If it wasn't for him, so

many performers like myself would probably never have had the chance to do what we do in this town."

Their shows were more extravagantly staged than anything Elvis Presley could have imagined. But they all owed a debt to Elvis's comeback show in 1969. He taught Las Vegas to think big.

On August 16, 1977, the day Elvis Presley died, the Hilton Hotel lowered its flag to half-staff. Barron Hilton, in a perfunctory statement, called Elvis "more than just a great talent, he was a good friend to all of us at the Las Vegas Hilton." Elvis's doctor, Elias Ghanem, expressed shock at his death; he had given Elvis a physical exam only recently, he told reporters, and "why, he was in perfect health." That night, shortly after midnight, a weeks-long drought in Las Vegas ended when an inch and a half of rain poured down in just three hours. Could even the heavens be weeping?

The first formal tribute to Elvis in Las Vegas came a year later, in September 1978, when Colonel Parker and Elvis's father, Vernon, coproduced the Always Elvis Festival at the Hilton Hotel. It featured an audiovisual tribute to Elvis's career, a display of his costumes and other personal effects, and the unveiling of a bronze statue of Elvis, given a place of honor outside the hotel's rechristened Elvis Presley Showroom. Las Vegas had found its most enduring icon, and the Elvis industry was underway.

Elvis impersonators had been around since before the King's death. Elvis himself reportedly went to see singer Brendan Bowyer, who did an impersonation of him as part of the Royal Showband's act in the Stardust Hotel's lounge. The spangled jumpsuits, curled-lip sneer, and jet-black, aging-greaser hairdo made Elvis easy to imitate, or at least approximate, and soon Elvis impersonators were as ubiquitous in Las Vegas as quarter slot machines. They starred in tribute shows, entertained in hotel lounges, competed in Elvis Tribute Artist contests, appeared at conventions, rode in parades, and played in celebrity golf tournaments. The winner of the 2016 Las Vegas Marathon was a man in an Elvis costume.

At least three museums or exhibitions of Elvis memorabilia have opened and closed in Las Vegas in the years since his death. (The Elvis estate in Memphis owns most of Elvis's costumes and personal effects, but there's still plenty of freelance memorabilia to go around.) Visitors to the Westgate Hotel—the former Hilton—can tour the thirtieth-floor suite where Elvis once stayed, since redecorated and divided into luxury suites for paying customers. A troupe of skydiving Elvis impersonators, dubbed the Flying Elvises, were the comedic highlight of the 1992 movie (and later Broadway musical) *Honeymoon in Vegas*. Fans of the King congregate every July for the annual Las Vegas Elvis Festival, one of several such fan gatherings around the country that keep his legacy alive among the faithful. The street leading from the Strip to the Westgate Hotel has been renamed Elvis Presley Boulevard.

One Elvis impersonator, Jesse Garron (real name Jesse Grice, before he adopted the name of Elvis's twin brother, misspelled), was given a key to the city by former mayor Oscar Goodman; now Jesse calls himself the Official Elvis of Vegas, appears as Elvis in various shows and events, and gives tours of the Strip in his 1955 pink Cadillac. Donny Edwards, who played the King for years at the now-defunct Elvis-A-Rama Museum, has toured with former Elvis backup musicians D. J. Fontana and the Sweet Inspirations and stars in an Elvis tribute show at the South Point Hotel and Casino. Vegas has a "Big Elvis"—aka Pete Vallee, a four-hundred-pounder who sits in a chair while delivering Elvis songs on weekday afternoons in

Harrah's piano bar. And there's "Little Elvis," a pint-size Greek im-
migrant named Dimos Greko, who dons a red-and-black jumpsuit
and hires himself out for weddings and parties.

Quickie weddings have been a major Vegas attraction since the city's
earliest days. But it took the Gretna Green Wedding Chapel (opened in
1947 and supposedly visited by Elvis in 1967, just before his wedding
to Priscilla) to come up with the bright idea, just after Elvis died, of
changing its name to the Graceland Wedding Chapel and making Elvis
part of the ceremony. Now it conducts more than four thousand Elvis
weddings or renewals of vows a year and is one of several chapels lined
up along Las Vegas Boulevard, between the Strip hotels and downtown, that will furnish an Elvis impersonator to walk the bride down
the aisle, serenade the happy couple with Elvis songs, and maybe even
conduct the ceremony.

Ron Decar spent twenty years singing on the Strip in such shows
as the *Folies Bergere* and *Moulin Rouge* before donning a studded black
jumpsuit, sunglasses, and jet-black wig as the resident Elvis (and owner)
of the Viva Las Vegas Wedding Chapel. "Elvis changed the whole idea
of what you could do with a Vegas show," said Decar. "People expect to
see him here." For each couple, he'll sing two or three Elvis songs (usually "Love Me Tender" and "Can't Help Falling in Love"—and he pays
royalties), administer the vows (he's licensed as a minister), and close
out the ceremony in the proper campy spirit: "Do you promise to adopt
each other's hound dog? Not to wear your blue suede shoes in the rain?
To always be each other's teddy bear? And to give each other a hunka-
hunka burnin' love?" Then he escorts the couple down the aisle, out the
door, and into the bright Vegas sunlight, where their names, at least for
a few minutes, are emblazoned in neon lights on Las Vegas Boulevard.

The couples at the Viva Las Vegas chapel were streaming in like
patients in a busy doctor's waiting room on the hot August afternoon

I visited. Benito and Miriam Villanueva, a young couple from Madrid, Spain, were inspired to tie the knot there by a Spanish TV reality-show couple, Alaska and Mario, whose Vegas wedding was televised on their popular show a few years ago. David and Denise Law, a middle-aged couple from Minnesota, stopped in to renew their vows on their twenty-fifth anniversary. Steven and Karen Coling came all the way from Brisbane, Australia, so that Elvis could help them celebrate thirty-four years of marriage. "Just a bit of fun," Steven explained—but also a tribute to his mother, who died a few months earlier. "My mum was the world's number one Elvis fan. Her one and only trip outside of Australia was to Graceland."

There have been signs in recent years that Vegas' long infatuation with Elvis may have peaked. A Cirque du Soleil tribute show, *Viva Elvis*, produced in collaboration with the Elvis estate, opened at the Aria Hotel in 2008, but closed after two years of lackluster ticket sales. An Elvis exhibit and tribute show at the Westgate Hotel opened to much fanfare in 2015 (also in conjunction with the Presley estate), but shut down abruptly after just a few months, when the third-party producer pulled out because of disappointing business, prompting a lawsuit.

Yet Elvis remains an unavoidable presence in Las Vegas, everywhere from souvenir shops to the nostalgic tribute shows that populate the smaller venues on the Strip, helping visitors fill the downtime in between the slot machines and Cirque du Soleil.

I went to see one of the Elvis tribute shows, *All Shook Up*, and brought along Pat Gill, one of my favorite sources for this book. Pat grew up in South Africa, began performing at the Moulin Rouge in Paris at age fifteen, and came to Vegas in 1967, a striking five-foot-eight-inch blonde, for a role in the *Casino de Paris*. She was lead dancer in the topless lounge show *Vive Les Girls* in 1969, when Elvis Presley came to see the show, went backstage to meet her, and invited her to his opening night at the International Hotel. Pat, an Elvis fan ever since she saw him in *G.I. Blues* as a teenager, sat at one of the VIP tables and went backstage after the show for some photos with Elvis. The two generated some gossip and continued to see each other for years afterward, whenever Elvis came to town. Pat always insisted they were "just friends," but she was smitten. "I adored him," said Pat. "He was charming, kind, generous—a true Southern gentleman."

Pat was almost surely the only person in the audience of eighty or so in the tiny V Theater on that Tuesday evening who actually knew Elvis Presley. The show itself was passably entertaining. Star Travis Allen, re-creating an Elvis Vegas concert, didn't so much do an impression of Elvis as simply wear his clothes (gold jacket in the first half, white jumpsuit in the second) and sing his songs. "Elvis never did moves like that," Pat said, turning to me early in the show. She was right: Allen's swivel-kneed, moonwalking gyrations were more Michael Jackson than Elvis Presley. When he sang "Return to Sender," both Pat and I noted that Elvis never performed that song in concert. Allen closed, predictably enough, with "Viva Las Vegas," and here we disagreed. There's no record that Elvis ever performed the song in Las Vegas. But Pat claims she saw him do it.

Pat spent twenty years as a Vegas dancer, working with some of the top choreographers in town. When her performing days were over, she remained in Vegas and worked as a photographer and blackjack dealer, before retiring. At seventy-two, she's had her health issues. She survived a bout with cancer many years ago (Liza Minnelli and Joan Rivers helped pay for her therapy), and when I saw her, she was still moving slowly after knee-replacement surgery. She never married and lives alone in a two-bedroom condo a few blocks off the Strip. She goes to church three times a week. Most of her friends have left Vegas or died.

She gets depressed, but stopped taking her antidepressants because she couldn't handle the side effects. She complains that Las Vegas is a bad place to grow old.

But like many of the people I interviewed for this book, she embodies the vibrant, hard-headed, irrepressible spirit of Las Vegas. She is smart, talkative, unsentimental, not so much nostalgic for the old days as simply appreciative of the privilege she had to be part of one of the great eras of American entertainment. "I was blessed," she says. She was friends with Sammy Davis Jr., who helped her get a green card so that she could remain in the country after her work visa expired. She played a Bond girl in *Diamonds Are Forever*, starring Sean Connery, which was shot in Las Vegas. (Her one line was cut, but she still gets residuals.) Cary Grant once threw her a twenty-first birthday party. And she fell for Elvis Presley.

So did Las Vegas.

ACKNOWLEDGMENTS

If you grew up in the Midwest during the 1960s, the summertime family car trip to California was an eagerly awaited coming-of-age ritual. My own family—two parents, four kids, and one Chevrolet station wagon—headed west from Kansas City in the summer of 1964. In between the Grand Canyon and Disneyland, we stopped for two nights in Las Vegas. We stayed at the Gold Key Motel—no fancy Strip resort for these frugal Midwest travelers—and saw two shows: Johnny Carson at the Sahara Hotel (his very first Vegas engagement) and the Kingston Trio (my sister's favorite) at the Riviera. I remember few details about our stay, aside from going backstage to get Johnny's autograph (I still have it, on an old Sahara Hotel postcard). But the impossibly glamorous atmosphere—the glittering showrooms, the cacophonous casinos that we were not allowed to enter, the neon fabulousness of the hotels lining the Strip—made a lasting impression on me. So I want to thank, first of all, my parents—who returned to Vegas many more times, usually without the kids—for giving me one indelible glimpse of Las Vegas in the golden age.

It was Jonathan Karp, Simon & Schuster's publisher, who came up with the idea, when I proposed a book about Las Vegas' 1960s heyday, that I frame it around Elvis Presley's big comeback show there in 1969. And it was my old friend Steve Dougherty who helped me realize what a great idea this was. Steve is a lover and chronicler of rock 'n' roll of all kinds and eras, but he always loved Elvis best. I once asked why. Because, he said, when he first heard Elvis as a grade-schooler in the 1950s, the music made him happier than he ever felt in his life. Not a bad recommendation for any artist.

In reconstructing Elvis's great comeback show in Vegas, I am grateful to the people who shared their firsthand memories, including Ronnie Tutt, Bobby Morris, Sammy Shore, Terry Blackwood, as well as (via email) Jerry Scheff and (after much cajoling) James Burton. Jerry Schilling was especially generous with his time and insights into Elvis and his Vegas years. Peter Guralnick, whose definitive two-volume biography of Elvis was such an important resource for me, was gracious in counseling another writer just venturing into territory that he has so expertly plowed. David Beckwith, Kevin Kern, and Gary Hahn, of the Presley estate, were helpful when they could be—and honest when they couldn't. And Jeroen Vanderschoot, of ElvisMatters Belgium, made sure I stuck to the rules.

While Elvis's life and career are well-trod ground, Vegas' golden age of entertainment is, in many ways, almost virgin territory for a historian. There are few books or authoritative records to draw on, and a dwindling number of people with firsthand accounts of that era. I am grateful to Lisa Gioia-Acres, Lynn Zook, and Peggy King (widow of the late Vegas lounge singer Sonny King), who were so helpful at the outset in giving me ideas and connecting me with sources. Mike Weath-erford, longtime observer of the Vegas entertainment scene for the *Las Vegas Review-Journal*, was also helpful to a Vegas newbie, as were several other Vegas scholars and historians, among them Michael Green, Karan Feder, Deirdre Clemente, Larry Gragg, and Claytee White.

I am indebted to all of the people quoted in the book who ran-sacked their memories of both Elvis and Vegas. But I owe particular thanks to Corinne Entratter Sidney, whose trust I won early on and who rewarded me with hours of memories, stories, and insights into the world of her late husband, former Sands Hotel chief Jack Entratter. Among the many others who were so welcoming to an outsider diving into the world of classic Vegas entertainment, I am especially grate-ful to Maria Pogee, Pat Gill, Vera Goulet, Marty Beck, Kathy McKee, Sonny Charles, Ruth Gillis, Claire Plummer, Jerry Jackson, and Nelson Sardelli. And also Shecky Greene, who gave me two of the most enter-taining lunches I can remember.

Su-Kim Chung was an invaluable guide through the Special Col-lections at the University of Nevada, Las Vegas. Crystal Van Dee helped me sort through the Mark Tan Collection at the Nevada State Museum. Kelli Luchs and Jim Rose at the Las Vegas Convention and Visitors Authority were a most accommodating resource for photos and video of Vegas' golden age.

Jeff Abraham, who always seems to know more about my book top-ics than I do, was his usual font of ideas, connections, and tidbits of in-formation. Joanne Kaufman, Arthur Hochstein, Steve Koepp, Barbara Graustark, Richard Gurman, Harvey Myman, Steve Oney, Kathleen Brady, and Peter Newman were among the many friends and colleagues who followed my progress on the book and provided counsel, support, and in some cases specific help. And Kristiina Laakso was an enthusi-astic cheerleader and sympathetic sounding board all the way through.

My editor at Simon & Schuster, Priscilla Painton, was once again a dream to work with: encouraging but tough, and such a good friend that I knew our clashes would always end happily. Her assistant, Megan Hogan, and the rest of the Simon & Schuster team made the process as orderly and painless as possible. And my deepest thanks, as always, to my agent, Kris Dahl, who has been so supportive for so long, whose words are always comforting, and whose advice is never wrong.

Finally, a remembrance of two people who couldn't be around to see this book. Richard Corliss, my longtime colleague at *Time* magazine, was a great fan of both Elvis and Vegas, and I regret that he didn't get a chance to read this book—or, even better, to write it. He was a passionate devotee of popular culture, who not only showed me what great critical writing is, but taught me to never be embarrassed about what you love.

And, of course, my thoughts are always with my late wife, Charla Krupp. She has been gone for more years than I want to admit, and this is the first book I have written entirely without her input. But her great, generous, uplifting spirit continues to hearten and inspire me. I hope she would have liked this.

LIVE FROM VEGAS
A Selected List of Recordings

ELVIS

Elvis in Person at the International Hotel (1969, RCA)

Elvis Presley on Stage (1970, RCA)

Elvis Aron Presley (four-disc box set, with excerpts from 1956 Vegas engagement and later performances, released 1980, RCA)

Elvis: Live in Las Vegas (four-disc compilation, released 2015, RCA)

Elvis: Viva Las Vegas (compilation, released 2007, Sony BMG Europe)

Elvis: The Return to Vegas (recorded 1969, released 2014, Follow That Dream/Sony). This August 3 performance, the earliest known recording of Elvis's '69 Vegas show, is one of the several live Vegas recordings from Follow That Dream, Sony's Elvis collectors label.

Elvis: That's the Way It Is (1970 documentary; special edition two-disc DVD, 2007, Warner Bros.)

SINATRA AND THE RAT PACK

The Rat Pack Live at the Sands (recorded 1963, released 2001, Capitol)

Sinatra at the Sands (1966, Reprise)

Sinatra: Vegas (four-disc compilation, released 2014, Reprise)

Live at the Sands: Dean Martin (recorded 1964, released 2001, Bianco Records)

Live from Las Vegas: Dean Martin (recorded 1967, released 2005, Capitol)

Sammy Davis Jr./That's All! (two-disc LP, 1966, Reprise)

CLASSIC VEGAS

Tony Bennett: Live at the Sahara (recorded 1964, released 2011, Columbia/
   Legacy)

Nat King Cole at the Sands (1960, Capitol)

Bobby Darin: Live from Las Vegas (recorded 1963, released 2005, Capitol)

No Cover, No Minimum: Billy Eckstine (1960, Roulette, reissued 1992, Blue
   Note)

Tom Jones Live in Las Vegas (1969, Decca, Parrot)

Wayne Newton Live at the Frontier (1969 LP, MGM)

Louis Prima and Keely Smith: Live from Las Vegas (released 2005, Capitol)

Don Rickles: Hello, Dummy! (recorded 1968, released 1995, Warner Bros.)

Nancy Wilson: Live from Las Vegas (released 2005, Capitol)

NOTES

Quotations, excerpts, and descriptions of performances are taken either from audio recordings or from reviews and contemporaneous accounts in *Variety* and other sources.

ONE: VEGAS MEETS ELVIS

1   *In a town addicted to building:* The history of the Last Frontier and New Frontier hotels is drawn mainly from Stefan Al, *The Strip: Las Vegas and the Architecture of the American Dream* (MIT Press, 2017), 18–22, 44, and Eugene Moehring, *Resort City in the Sunbelt*, 2nd ed. (University of Nevada Press, 2000), 46–47.

2   *"with sides running to such length":* Variety, April 20, 1955.

2   *Mario Lanza . . . was booked:* Variety, April 7, 1955.

2   *"Seldom in the history":* Ralph Pearl, *Las Vegas Is My Beat,* rev. ed. (Citadel Press, 1978), 86.

3   *But first, Elvis played Vegas:* The details of Elvis's 1956 engagement at the New Frontier are taken primarily from Peter Guralnick, *Last Train to Memphis: The Rise of Elvis Presley* (Back Bay Books, 1994), 270–75, and

Paul Lichter, *Elvis in Vegas* (Overlook Duckworth, 2011), 13–34, as well as contemporaneous accounts as cited below.

4 *"No check is any good"*: "The Man Who Sold Parsley," *Time*, May 16, 1960.

4 *"easily the talking point of this show"*: *Variety*, May 2, 1956.

4 *"What is all this yelling"*: Guralnick, *Last Train to Memphis*, 271.

4 *"Elvis Presley, coming in on a wing"*: *Variety*, May 2, 1956.

4 *"like a jug of corn liquor"*: "Hillbilly on a Pedestal," *Newsweek*, May 14, 1956.

4 *"For the first time in months"*: Guralnick, *Last Train to Memphis*, 271.

5 *"They weren't my kind"*: Ibid.

5 *"He came out in a dirty"*: Shecky Greene, interview with author.

6 *"The carnage was terrific"*: Lichter, *Elvis in Vegas*, 17.

6 *"This cat, Presley"*: Ibid., 24.

7 *"He recognized me"*: Ibid., 32.

7 *One day he ran into Bing Crosby*: Greene, interview with author.

8 *"Man, I really like Vegas"*: Guralnick, *Last Train to Memphis*, 274.

9 *"supernatural, his own resurrection"*: David Dalton, "Elvis Lights Up Las Vegas," *Rolling Stone*, February 21, 1970.

12 *"Buddy Greco, if you're hearing this"*: Lezlie Anders (Greco's widow), interview with author.

12 *"The town was so much fun"*: Norm Johnson, interview with author.

12 *"You told 'em what you wanted"*: Pete Barbutti, interview with author.

12 *"Vegas was kind of an adult"*: Paul Anka, *My Way: An Autobiography* (St. Martin's Press, 2013), 1–2.

13 *"It's syrup city"*: Ron Rosenbaum, "Do You Know Vegas?," *Esquire*, August 1982.

13 *"yukking across the stage"*: Hunter Thompson, *Fear and Loathing in Las Vegas* (Vintage Books, 1971), 44.

14 *"his act was not working"*: John Gregory Dunne, *Vegas: A Memoir of a Dark Season* (Random House, 1974), 43.

14 *"Dante did not write"*: Nick Tosches, "The Holy City," in *Literary Las Vegas: The Best Writing about America's Most Fabulous City*, ed. Mike Tronnes (Henry Holt, 1995), xvi.

14 *"The biggest no-talent dork"*: Richard Meltzer, "Who'll Stop the Wayne?," in *Literary Las Vegas*, 271.

15 *"You gotta do a lot of up things"*: Vic Damone, interview with author.

16 *"There was no experimenting"*: Dennis Klein, interview with author.

18 *"For many, Vegas Elvis"*: Dylan Jones, *Elvis Has Left the Building* (Overlook Duckworth, 2014), 87.

TWO: HOW VEGAS HAPPENED

20 *The Las Vegas Valley*: In recounting the early history and development of Las Vegas, I have relied mainly on Moehring, *Resort City*; Al, *Strip*; Don Knepp, *Las Vegas: The Entertainment Capital* (Lane Publishing, 1987); Sally Denton and Roger Morris, *The Money and the Power: The Making of Las Vegas and Its Hold on America* (Vintage Books, 2001); and Larry Gragg, *Bright Light City: Las Vegas in Popular Culture* (University Press of Kansas, 2013).

25 *"The town has been converted"*: Mike Weatherford, *Cult Vegas* (Huntington Press, 2001), 3.

25 *"The third day all the stars"*: Rose Marie, interview in *The Real Las Vegas*, History Channel documentary (A&E Networks, 1996).

26 *"The fun of Las Vegas"*: Mel Tormé interview, Mark Tan Collection, Nevada State Museum, Las Vegas.

26 *"one of the greatest handshakers"*: Pearl, *Las Vegas Is My Beat*, 93.

27 *"probably the turning point"*: Richard English, "The Million Dollar Talent War," *Saturday Evening Post*, October 24, 1953.

27 *"nobody gets killed in Vegas"*: Susan Berman, *Lady Las Vegas* (TV Books, 1996), 79.

27 *In fact, Kefauver's investigation*: Denton and Morris, *Money and the Power*, 116.

28 *"a hunk of promotion"*: *Variety*, December 24, 1952.

28 *"Jack Entratter is responsible"*: Sands Hotel publicity material, Sands Collection, University Libraries Special Collections, University of Nevada, Las Vegas.

28 *the Sahara had to be more creative*: Stan Irwin interview in Mark Tan Collection, and Bill Miller profile in *Las Vegas Review-Journal*, February 7, 1999.

29 *"It's worth any price"*: *Variety*, February 24, 1954.

29 *She caused quite a stir*: Steven Bach, *Marlene Dietrich: Life and Legend* (University of Minnesota Press, 2013), 368–69.

29 *"Las Vegas, as now constituted"*: *Variety*, February 11, 1953.

30 *Concerns about the escalating salaries:* Variety, May 17, 1950, and November 19 and August 20, 1952.

30 *"Failure of the entertainment industry":* Variety, December 24, 1952.

30 *"We put him with a musical":* George Schlatter, interview with author.

31 *"The artistry of her delivery":* Joel Lobenthal, *Tallulah!: The Life and Times of a Leading Lady* (Aurum Press, 2005), 435.

31 *"Why do we do it?":* "Las Vegas: It Just Couldn't Happen," *Time*, November 23, 1953.

31 *He had urged Dietrich:* Bach, *Marlene Dietrich*, 368.

31 *"This is a fabulous, extraordinary madhouse":* Noël Coward diaries, in *Literary Las Vegas*, 211.

33 *"Jake Kosloff wanted them to stop":* Schlatter, interview with author.

33 *"the Andrews Sisters doing":* "Natural Seven Muzak," *Time*, August 11, 1961.

33 *"Frank Ross stirred the pot":* Lorraine Hunt-Bono, interview with author.

34 *"Mary Kaye was incredible":* Pete Barbutti, interview with author.

34 *"You could shout out requests":* Weatherford, *Cult Vegas*, 46.

34 *"The lounges were freedom":* Ibid.

34 *The group was started:* Description of the Treniers' act in Weatherford, *Cult Vegas*, 56–60, and Skip Trenier and Sonny Charles, interviews with author.

35 *"It was like a three-ring circus":* Trenier, interview with author.

35 *"Everybody loved the Treniers":* Joe Darro, interview with author.

35 *Black entertainers like the Treniers:* The account of the racial history of Las Vegas is drawn largely from Moehring, *Resort City*, 173–202, and Claytee D. White, interview with author.

35 *"The other acts could move around":* Sammy Davis Jr., Jane Boyar, and Burt Boyar, *Yes I Can: The Story of Sammy Davis, Jr.* (Farrar and Rinehart, 1965), 123.

35 *"There was a color line":* Stan Irwin interview, Mark Tan Collection.

36 *When Harry Belafonte made his:* Belafonte describes the incident in his memoir, *My Song* (Knopf, 2011), 105–9.

36 *The racial barriers were challenged:* The Moulin Rouge's short life is recounted in Janis L. McKay, *Played Out on the Strip: The Rise and Fall of Las Vegas Casino Bands* (University of Nevada Press, 2016), 35–36, as well as in Moehring, *Resort City*, 182–84.

37 *"We were the only ones"*: Interview with Anna Bailey, Las Vegas Women's Oral History Project, University of Nevada, Las Vegas, 1997.

37 *Wardell Gray, the highly regarded*: *Variety*, June 1, 1955.

37 *"tyranny of names"*: *Variety*, January 8, 1958.

38 *The French music-hall revue*: The Folies' history is recounted in George Perry, *Bluebell: The Authorized Biography of Margaret Kelly* (Pavilion, 1986), 47–52; Paul Lewis, "For Folies-Bergère: 100 Naughty Years," *New York Times*, July 8, 1987; and *Encyclopaedia Britannica* article, https://www.britannica.com/topic/Folies-Bergere.

38 *the Folies had a popular*: The Lido's history, in both Paris and Las Vegas, is covered fully in Perry, *Bluebell*, 165–90.

40 *"From the ceiling descend"*: Weatherford, *Cult Vegas*, 222–23.

40 *a new edition of* Minsky's Follies: *Variety*, January 23, 1957.

40 *"Even with bare-breasted beauts"*: *Variety*, July 9, 1958.

40 *"the most spectacular I've ever seen"*: Hedda Hopper, *Los Angeles Times*, August 13, 1958.

41 *"Bare chests are the coming thing"*: *Variety*, August 6, 1958.

41 *"It is time that the people"*: *Variety*, August 13, 1958.

41 *A split emerged*: *Variety*, August 6, 1958.

41 *"The spread of nude shows"*: *Las Vegas Review-Journal*, September 7, 1957.

42 *"Nudes are bad for this town"*: *Variety*, August 6, 1958.

42 *"Please accept my reassurance"*: *Variety*, August 20, 1958.

42 *"We certainly do not mean"*: *Variety*, August 13, 1958.

43 *"The Lou Walters show"*: *Los Angeles Times*, December 30, 1959.

44 *"Nothing kills laughs"*: *Variety*, August 10, 1960.

44 *Louis Prima was born*: Details of Prima's life and career come from Tom Clavin, *That Old Black Magic: Louis Prima, Keely Smith, and the Golden Age of Las Vegas* (Chicago Review Press, 2010).

45 *"absolutely the hottest combo"*: Clavin, *Black Magic*, 84.

46 *"The sound, the feel"*: Bobby Morris, interview with author.

46 *"wild, relentless, driving beat"*: Clavin, *Black Magic*, 85.

46 *"It was havoc"*: Morris, interview with author.

47 *"He was born Wladziu"*: The account of Liberace's life and career is drawn largely from Darden Asbury Pyron, *Liberace: An American Boy* (University of Chicago Press, 2000).

48 *"I longed to please"*: Ibid., 81.

48 *"Go ahead and laugh"*: Variety, April 27, 1955.

49 *"Finally it was impossible"*: Richard Corliss, "That Old Feeling: The Show at the Casino," Time.com, http://content.time.com/time/arts/article/0,8599,546855,00.html.

49 *"They relaxed and enjoyed"*: Pyron, *Liberace*, 81.

50 *"He admires you so much"*: Ibid., 265.

50 *he was wearing a new outfit*: Guralnick, *Last Train to Memphis*, 399.

50 *"He never forgot"*: Jerry Schilling, interview with author.

50 *"When one twin died"*: Guralnick, *Last Train to Memphis*, 13.

51 *It's not clear whether*: There's some evidence that Elvis may have been aware of the connection, since his friend Lamar Fike mentions it in Alanna Nash, *Elvis Aaron Presley: Revelations from the Memphis Mafia* (HarperCollins, 1995), 541.

51 *"When you grew up"*: Schilling, interview with author.

51 *"I didn't date her"*: George Klein, *Elvis: My Best Man* (Three Rivers Press, 2010), 100.

52 *"This desert never-never land"*: Variety, January 27, 1960.

THREE: THE COOL GUYS

53 *"You're the big man"*: Corinne Entratter Sidney, interview with author.

54 *"I used to call him crudely"*: Ibid.

54 *"He had a physical presence"*: Kevin Thomas, interview with author.

54 *He was born Nathan Entratter*: Biographical material in Sands Collection, UNLV Libraries, and Entratter Sidney, interview with author.

55 *"Jack Entratter was the Genghis Khan"*: Jerry Lewis, interview with author.

56 *"I cater to the overprivileged"*: Entratter Sidney, interview with author.

56 *95 million seconds*: Statistics cited in a Sands press release, Sands Collection, UNLV Libraries.

57 *Sinatra demurred*: According to Nathan "Sonny" Golden, Sinatra's business manager, in the liner notes for *Sinatra: Vegas*, CD box set (Reprise Records, 2014), 14.

57 *"As he meanders"*: Variety, October 21, 1953.

58 *"Ooooh, Frankie"*: Weatherford, *Cult Vegas*, 13.

58 *"arrogant, ill-tempered"*: Ibid.

58 *"The new Sinatra was not"*: John Lahr, *Sinatra: The Artist and the Man* (Phoenix Mass Market, 1999), 53.

59 *"I've been trying for more than a year"*: Kitty Kelley, *His Way: The Unauthorized Biography of Frank Sinatra* (Bantam, 1986), 219.

59 *"The thing that amazed me"*: Hunt-Bono, interview with author.

59 *"Frank was the king"*: Damone, interview with author.

60 *"He was the number one guy"*: Paul Anka, interview with author.

61 *"He'd always be there"*: Weatherford, *Cult Vegas*, 15.

61 *"Frank enjoyed a good time"*: Angie Dickinson in liner notes, *Sinatra: Vegas*, 36.

62 *"You look like a goddamn"*: The quote, along with a full account of the Rat Pack's origins, in Shawn Levy, *Rat Pack Confidential* (Broadway Books, 2001), 30.

62 *"a comedy routine"*: James Kaplan, *Sinatra: The Chairman* (Doubleday, 2015), 229.

63 *"The dago's lousy"*: Nick Tosches, *Dino: Living High in the Dirty Business of Dreams* (Delta, 1999), 269.

64 *"Sinatra was enthralled by Dean"*: Ibid., 260.

65 *"Talent is not an excuse"*: Kaplan, *Sinatra*, 241–42.

65 *"That was it for Sammy"*: Ibid., 242.

66 *"a public and aggressive indifference"*: Paul O'Neill, "The 'Clan' Is the Most," *Life*, December 22, 1958.

66 *It was Lawford*: Levy, *Rat Pack*, 105–6.

67 *"Producer Jack Entratter comes up"*: *Las Vegas Review-Journal*, January 8, 1960.

67 *"Which star shines"*: Advertisements in *Las Vegas Review-Journal*, circa January 20, 1960.

68 *"Mr. Entratter, sir"*: Les Devor, *Las Vegas Review-Journal*, January 21, 1960.

68 *"I flew to Las Vegas"*: Hedda Hopper, *Los Angeles Times*, January 23, 1960.

68 *"an entertainment ball which"*: John L. Scott, *Los Angeles Times*, January 22, 1960.

68 *had to turn away eighteen thousand*: Levy, *Rat Pack*, 108.

68 *The myth of the Rat Pack*: Quotes and descriptions of the Rat Pack show are taken from film footage supplied by the Las Vegas Convention and Visitors Authority and by Nora Garibotti (Joey Bishop's friend), as well as from contemporaneous reviews and articles.

69   *"Joey was a ballsy guy"*: Michael Seth Starr, *Mouse in the Rat Pack: The Joey Bishop Story* (Taylor Trade Publishing, 2002), 59.

70   *Bishop, who wrote the line:* J. Randy Taraborrelli, *Sinatra: Behind the Legend*, excerpted in *The Sammy Davis Jr. Reader*, ed. Gerald Early (Farrar, Straus and Giroux, 2001), 185.

70   *"I hated the idea"*: Greene, interview with author.

71   *"They were doing our act"*: Lewis, interview with author.

71   *"For the first time on such"*: Levy, *Rat Pack*, 321.

73   *"There was an electricity"*: Bob Newhart, interview with author.

73   *"There is no Clan"*: Levy, *Rat Pack*, 185.

73   *"I am a member of the Clan"*: Ibid., 186.

74   *"If Frank went to a tailor"*: Entratter Sidney, interview with author.

74   *"I noticed that no matter who"*: Mia Farrow, *What Falls Away* (Nan A. Talese, 1997), 104.

74   *"With Frank it was like walking"*: Entratter Sidney, interview with author.

74   *"But when he was an asshole"*: Lisa Medford, interview with author.

75   *"Sinatra really had Jack"*: Eydie Gormé interview, Mark Tan Collection.

75   *his demands got so out of hand:* The incident described by Entratter Sidney, interview with author.

75   *"Dean Martin is worth his weight"*: *Variety*, July 20, 1960.

75   *"He was nice to everyone"*: Deana Martin, *Memories Are Made of This: Dean Martin through His Daughter's Eyes* (Three Rivers Press, 2004), 79.

75   *"The important thing to say"*: Tosches, *Dino*, 256.

76   *"Sammy always had to be"*: Vera Goulet, interview with author.

76   *"Is Sammy Ashamed?"*: Davis, Boyar, and Boyar, *Yes I Can*, 249.

76   *"Over the years I watched Sammy"*: Wil Haygood, *In Black and White: The Life of Sammy Davis, Jr.* (Knopf, 2003), 181.

77   *"Make yourself comfortable"*: The quote, along with other details of Rickles's relationship with Sinatra, is in *Rickles' Book: A Memoir* (Simon & Schuster, 2008), 64.

77   *"trying to figure out"*: George Jacobs, *Mr. S: The Last Word on Frank Sinatra* (Pan Books, 2004), 125.

77   *"If I want a nigger"*: Ibid., 124.

78   *"the most brutal, ugly, degenerate"*: Kaplan, *Sinatra*, 175.

78   *"I admire the man"*: Guralnick, *Last Train to Memphis*, 437.

79 *"After all, the kid's been away"*: Peter Guralnick, *Careless Love: The Unmaking of Elvis Presley* (Back Bay Books, 1999), 62.

80 *the show drew a phenomenal*: Ibid., 63.

80 *"People call me the king"*: Deana Martin, interview with author.

81 *"It was a party like"*: Guralnick, *Careless Love*, 116.

81 *dubbed them the "Memphis mafia"*: Ibid., 76–77.

82 *"As kids we looked at them"*: Anka, *My Way*, 64.

82 *"They took over"*: Kaplan, *Sinatra*, 396.

82 *"a disgusting display of ego"*: Levy, *Rat Pack*, 187.

82 *"Frank and his henchmen"*: Ibid.

83 *Sinatra noticed the growing chill*: The souring of relations with the Kennedys recounted in Kaplan, *Sinatra*, 435–39.

83 *"Frank was livid"*: James Spada, *Peter Lawford: The Man Who Kept the Secrets* (Bantam, 1991), 293–94.

83 *"the most violent rampage"*: Jacobs, *Mr. S*, 165.

84 *Joey was cast in the third*: Levy, *Rat Pack*, 257–58.

86 *"I'm never coming to see you again"*: Kaplan, *Sinatra*, 537.

86 *"a rotten, horrible, mean"*: Ibid., 542.

86 *"Aren't you people"*: Ibid., 543.

87 *"That little son of a bitch"*: Ibid., 546.

87 *"It just wasn't possible to invite him"*: Levy, *Rat Pack*, 260.

87 *Sinatra's annus horribilis*: A full account of the kidnapping is in Kaplan, *Sinatra*, 552–67.

88 *Bishop resented the joke*: Starr, *Mouse in the Rat Pack*, 115.

89 *"one of those miraculous moments"*: Will Friedwald, *Sinatra! The Song Is You: A Singer's Art*, rev. ed. (Chicago Review Press, 2018), 454.

90 *"Mount Rushmore of men"*: James Wolcott, "When They Were Kings," *Vanity Fair*, reprinted in *Sammy Davis Jr. Reader*, 192–93.

90 *"Their desert hijinks"*: Bill Zehme, *The Way You Wear Your Hat: Frank Sinatra and the Lost Art of Livin'* (Harper, 1997), 60.

FOUR: THE ENTERTAINMENT CAPITAL

92 *TWA inaugurated nonstop flights*: *Variety*, June 22, 1960.

93 *34 percent of US households*: "Television Facts and Statistics," http://www.tvhistory.tv/facts-stats.htm.

93 *the Sands in 1955 became the first*: Moehring, *Resort City*, 182.

93 *"We left the showroom"*: Ruth Gillis, interview with author.

94 *That benighted era ended*: Moehring, *Resort City*, 184–85.

95 *"is now virtually unknown"*: *Variety*, October 11, 1961.

95 *The Sands' Entratter even bragged*: Sands publicity material, Sands Collection, UNLV Libraries.

95 *"Everybody had two salaries"*: Schlatter, interview with author.

96 *"There was a pecking order"*: Newhart, interview with author.

96 *"You really found out who"*: Anka, interview with author.

96 *"There isn't any deal"*: Tony Bennett interview, Mark Tan Collection.

97 *He grew up in Brooklyn*: The account of Damone's life and career is drawn from his memoir, *Vic Damone: Singing Was the Easy Part* (St. Martin's Press, 2009), and Damone, interview with author.

98 *"The cocktail lounges no longer"*: *Variety*, August 4, 1965.

98 *"He could sing 'My Way' "*: Klein, interview with author.

99 *the model, reputedly, for Jerry*: Anders, interview with author.

99 *She walked out of an engagement*: Gerald Clarke, *Get Happy: The Life of Judy Garland* (Random House, 2000), 438–40.

99 *she was so shaky that spotters*: According to Nelson Sardelli, her opening act.

99 *"There are times when her voice"*: *Variety*, December 8, 1965.

100 *"Ladies and gentlemen, I need help"*: Clarke, *Get Happy*, 599.

100 *"curiously unsettling experience"*: *Variety*, December 6, 1967.

100 *Debbie surprised him*: The incident is told from both perspectives in Debbie Reynolds, *Debbie: My Life* (Pocket Books, 1988), 175, and Eddie Fisher, *Been There, Done That: An Autobiography* (St. Martin's Press, 1999), 101–2.

101 *When Eddie discovered he had no cash*: Fisher, *Been There*, 158–59.

101 *"They started that Cleopatra"*: *Variety*, July 18, 1962.

101 *"Instead of warming up"*: Randall Riese, *Her Name Is Barbra: An Intimate Portrait of the Real Barbra Streisand* (Birch Lane Press, 1993), 141.

102 *Milton Prell once offered*: Phil Solomon, who said he personally witnessed the offer, column in *Fabulous Las Vegas*, August 2, 1969.

103 *"He loved Las Vegas"*: Guralnick, *Careless Love*, 118–19.

103 *"so heavily that you couldn't tell"*: Priscilla Beaulieu Presley, *Elvis and Me* (Berkley Books, 1986), 88.

104 *Sammy Davis Jr. was even signed*: Entratter Sidney, interview with author.

105 *"I knew what was going to happen"*: Ann-Margret, *Ann-Margret: My Story* (G. P. Putnam's Sons, 1994), 109.

105 *"She comes around here mostly"*: Presley, *Elvis and Me*, 168.

105 *Colonel Parker was not happy*: Guralnick, *Careless Love*, 151–54.

105 *"About as pleasant"*: Howard Thompson, *New York Times*, May 21, 1964.

107 *Stan Irwin . . . booked them*: The Beatles' visit recounted in Weatherford, *Cult Vegas*, 41–43, and Irwin interview, Mark Tan Collection.

108 *The imported sets and costumes*: Maynard Sloate, producer of the *Folies Bergere*, interview with author.

108 *He was born Arlyle Arden Peterson*: Arden's life and career recounted in *Las Vegas Review-Journal*, February 7, 1999, and Donn Arden Papers, Special Collections, UNLV Libraries.

109 *"It's not entertainment"*: *Variety*, March 14, 1962.

109 *"Competition among big shows"*: *Los Angeles Times*, May 24, 1965.

110 *"From the rousing opening"*: Hank Greenspun, *Las Vegas Sun*, September 30, 1967.

110 *called Pzazz '68 the best Vegas show*: Charles Champlin, *Los Angeles Times*, February 7, 1968.

110 *"There's a certain way"*: Jefferson Graham, *Vegas: Live and in Person* (Abbeville Press, 1989), 168.

110 *"He would scream and holler"*: Sonia Kara, interview with author.

111 *"Ron was slim, sinewy"*: Ron Walker, RecordCourier.com, May 18, 2012.

111 *"When you were a Ron Lewis dancer"*: Sal Angelica, interview with author.

112 *"People from New York"*: Jerry Jackson, interview with author.

112 *"I came to Las Vegas"*: Angelica, interview with author.

113 *Carol Burnett . . . set an advance-sale record*: Carol Burnett, interview with author.

113 *Carson . . . broke the hotel's attendance*: *Variety*, July 22, 1964.

114 *"The audiences in Vegas demanded"*: Klein, interview with author.

115 *found that he had to cut them down*: Newhart, interview with author.

115 *"possibly will zoom over"*: *Variety*, October 9, 1963.

115 *"temperamental without hope"*: Sloate, interview with author.

115 *"It was an achievement"*: Woody Allen, interview with author.

116 *"I felt guilty"*: Ibid.

116 *But he had to see Don Rickles*: Irwin interview, Mark Tan Collection.

117 *"He's doing me!"*: Klipf Nesteroff, *The Comedians: Drunks, Thieves,*

Scoundrels, and the History of American Comedy (Grove Press, 2015), 153.

118 "When he worked clean": Sandy Hackett, interview with author.

118 "Hackett has a definite mission": Variety, January 1, 1969.

118 "Buddy had the ability": Greene, interview with author.

118 "I want to get the audience": Nesteroff, Comedians, 144.

119 Hackett, unhappy to hear that Totie: Barbutti, interview with author.

119 "He was like the devil": Nesteroff, Comedians, 145.

120 "His act had no beginning": Barbutti, interview with author.

120 "When you saw a Shecky Greene show": Klein, interview with author.

120 "I don't feel bad": Line recounted by Greene, interview with author.

121 "Are you proud of Sammy Davis?": Line recounted by Klein, interview with author.

121 Greene could be a terror: Greene's misbehavior is described by many, including Weatherford, Cult Vegas, 98–99.

121 Milton Berle tried to calm: Milton Berle interview, Mark Tan Collection.

121 "I never worked like Rickles . . . I couldn't be Shecky . . . Vegas was very, very good": Greene, interview with author.

122 "A lot of entertainers": Rich Little, interview with author.

122 "I make approximately the same": Quoted in Variety, June 20, 1964.

122 "There was one rule": Henry Bushkin, Johnny Carson (Houghton Mifflin Harcourt, 2013), 185.

122 "Nowhere was Johnny more pampered": Ibid., 176.

122 "The women, who didn't seem": Farrow, What Falls Away, 102.

123 "The one thing you learned": Newhart, interview with author.

123 "I loved being around": Anka, My Way, 170.

123 "They would bring their girlfriends": Lainie Kazan, interview with author.

124 "Because I sing": Nelson Sardelli, interview with author.

124 Shecky Greene liked to tell: Greene, interview with author.

124 "one of the five most powerful": Denton and Morris, Money and the Power, 287.

124 Vic Damone's relationship: Described by Damone in Vic Damone, 23–41, and interview with author.

124 "I became very friendly": Damone, interview with author.

125 "The work was steady": Frank Leone, interview with author.

126 "All the top guys were here": Barbutti, interview with author.

126 *fourteen hundred working musicians:* The membership of the Las Vegas Musicians Union in 1969, in McKay, *Played Out*, 79.

126 *"It was musical heaven":* Mark Massagli, interview with author.

127 *they arrived in Las Vegas:* Marie Pogee, interview with author.

127 *"For a dancer, Las Vegas":* Ibid.

128 *"You had to learn how":* Kara, interview with author.

128 *"Vegas was a great place":* Claire Fitzpatrick Plummer, interview with author.

128 *"typical mob types":* Kathy McKee, interview with author.

129 *"I don't think I would have":* Ibid.

129 *"You had no choice":* Medford, interview with author.

129 *"They'd give us a hundred dollars":* Plummer, interview with author.

129 *"It didn't have to go any further":* Ibid.

130 *Elvis was dismayed:* Recounted by Marty Lacker in Nash, *Elvis Aaron Presley*, 379.

130 *"Each show opened":* Joe Esposito, *Good Rockin' Tonight: Twenty Years on the Road and on the Town with Elvis* (Simon & Schuster, 1994), 92–93.

130 *"he saw a lot of singer Phyllis McGuire":* The fling with McGuire is recounted by Marty Lacker in Nash, *Elvis Aaron Presley*, 324–25.

131 *Elvis got a new hairdresser:* For details of Elvis's relationship with Larry Geller, I relied on Guralnick, *Careless Love*, as well as Larry Geller, *If I Can Dream: Elvis's Own Story* (Simon & Schuster, 1989), and an interview with Geller.

131 *"We were having fun":* Guralnick, *Careless Love*, 176.

131 *"The face of Stalin":* Ibid., 195.

132 *"Remember, you're Elvis Presley":* Geller, *If I Can Dream*, 115.

132 *News of the impending wedding:* Details of the wedding plans, ceremony, and aftermath are taken primarily from Guralnick, *Careless Love*, and Presley, *Elvis and Me*.

133 *"I was simply amazed":* Guralnick, *Careless Love*, 263.

133 *"Well, I guess it was about time":* Ibid., 264.

134 *"Elvis and I followed":* Presley, *Elvis and Me*, 237.

FIVE: CHANGES (ELVIS RISING)

136 *Howard Hughes's stealth arrival:* For the story of Hughes and his Vegas years, I relied on Donald L. Bartlett and James B. Steele, *Howard Hughes:*

His Life and Madness (W. W. Norton, 2004); Peter Harry Brown and Pat E. Broeske, *Howard Hughes: The Untold Story* (De Capo Press, 2004); and Michael Drosnin, *Citizen Hughes: The Power, the Money and the Madness* (Holt, 1985); as well as the various Las Vegas histories cited below.

137 *"greeted with messianic enthusiasm"*: Denton and Morris, *Money and the Power*, 272.

137 *"This is the best way"*: *Variety*, August 5, 1967.

138 *"Did you hear that Hughes"*: *Variety*, October 4, 1967.

138 *"a resort so carefully planned"*: Geoff Schumacher, *Sun, Sin & Suburbia: The History of Modern Las Vegas*, rev. ed. (University of Nevada Press, 2015), 116.

138 *"as trustworthy and respectable"*: Drosnin, *Citizen Hughes*, 108.

138 *"The increased governmental scrutiny"*: *Variety*, March 29, 1967.

139 *"Dalitz and other members"*: Denton and Morris, *Money and the Power*, 284.

140 *"When the bean counters"*: Hunt-Bono, interview with author.

140 *"It was the new bureaucratic regime"*: Anka, *My Way*, 165.

140 *"Howard Hughes maintained"*: Goulet, interview with author.

140 *"Mr. Hughes is very happy"*: Newhart, interview with author.

141 *"He had the shows piped up"*: Little, interview with author.

141 *"I can summarize my attitude"*: Schumacher, *Sun, Sin*, 120.

141 *"In a community of brigand"*: *Variety*, February 5, 1969.

141 *"When the so-called gangsters"*: Florence Henderson interview, Mark Tan Collection.

141 *"Hughes had all these little"*: Gormé interview, Mark Tan Collection.

143 *"Yeah, I sure got married"*: Kaplan, *Sinatra*, 693.

143 *"During this period Sinatra"*: Anka, *My Way*, 173.

143 *"I don't think he actually shot"*: Jackie Mason, email with author.

144 *Sinatra's infamous blowup*: The incident is thoroughly covered in Kaplan, *Sinatra*, 725–30.

145 *"He was already out of the cart"*: Farrow, *What Falls Away*, 110–11.

145 *"He threatened to kill anyone"*: Kaplan, *Sinatra*, 729.

145 *"Singer Tony Bennett left"*: McKay, *Played Out*, 73.

145 *"Frank picked a fight"*: Entratter Sidney, interview with author.

146 *Caesars Palace was the brainchild*: The most complete account of the hotel's birth is in Al, *Strip*, 90–96.

147 *Sinatra got a record $100,000:* The escalating salaries for Sinatra, Martin, and other Vegas stars reported in *Variety*, December 25, 1968.

148 *"A virtuoso display of Sinatra":* Champlin, *Los Angeles Times*, November 28, 1968.

148 *It was inspired by a conversation:* Anka, *My Way*, 208–10.

149 *She would sing her* American Bandstand: Connie Francis, interview with author.

150 *"My manager's vision":* Brenda Lee, interview with author.

150 *"It's too early to know":* Variety, December 13, 1961.

150 *"A lot of us had a good run":* Anka, *My Way*, 98.

150 *"If the rock 'n' roll craze":* Quoted in *Variety*, September 9. 1964.

150 *"They're going to leave":* Quoted in Kaplan, *Sinatra*, 596.

151 *"At least they're white":* Jacobs, *Mr. S*, 216.

151 *"To be honest, I'd describe":* Guralnick, *Careless Love*, 211.

152 *"If it hadn't been for him":* Ibid., 212.

152 *"There's four of them":* Geller, *If I Can Dream*, 124.

152 *"The hotels didn't want them":* Marty Beck, interview with author.

152 *"Only a handful of new acts":* Variety, January 31, 1968.

152 *"At that time Vegas":* Trini Lopez, interview with author.

153 *"We were not an R and B act":* Mary Wilson, interview with author.

153 *"Las Vegas, the bastion":* Billboard, August 26, 1967.

153 *"get out or get groovy":* Weatherford, *Cult Vegas*, 71.

153 *"I wore the bells":* Ibid., 75.

153 *"George Burns has a gold mine":* Variety, December 28, 1960.

153 *"I wanted to bring a Broadway":* David Winters, interview with author.

154 *"It's not often that a different":* Variety, July 19, 1967.

154 *"possibly the highest decibel":* Variety, August 7, 1968.

154 *"sleeper of the year":* Variety, April 10, 1968.

154 *"The lewd stuff will come":* Variety, July 26, 1967.

155 *"We were such an oddity":* Sonny Charles, interview with author.

155 *"He'd come from San Francisco":* Ibid.

156 *"Self-assured, almost cocky":* Quoted in David Evanier, *Roman Candle: The Life of Bobby Darin* (Rodale Press, 2004), 64.

157 *"Bobby sat on a stool":* Ibid., 207.

157 *"Go back and put on":* Michael Starr, *Bobby Darin: A Life* (Taylor Trade Publishing, 2004), 184.

157 *"The young comedian scored"*: *Variety*, August 24, 1966.

158 *"I imagined what I looked like"*: Richard Pryor, *Pryor Convictions: And Other Life Sentences* (Pantheon Books, 1995), 94.

158 *Pryor singing new lyrics*: Beck, interview with author.

158 *George Carlin was another*: Richard Zoglin, *Comedy at the Edge: How Stand-Up in the 1970s Changed America* (Bloomsbury, 2008), 29.

159 *Carson Wayne Newton was born*: The account of Newton's life, career, and Vegas act is taken primarily from "Whatever Happened to Baby Wayne?," *Time*, June 29, 1970; "The Most Successful Performer in Vegas History? Not Frank, Not Elvis—It's Wayne Newton," *People*, April 30, 1979; Ron Rosenbaum, "Do You Know Vegas?," *Esquire*, August 1982; and Newton's own memoir, *Wayne Newton: Once Before I Go* (William Morrow, 1989).

160 *"When he sings 'Dreams'"*: "Whatever Happened," *Time*.

161 *"The Flamingo is charged"*: *Variety*, January 10, 1968.

161 *"Many nights there would come a knock"*: Newton, *Once Before I Go*, 83.

161 *"Everyone leaves The Show"*: Rosenbaum, "Do You Know Vegas?"

162 *"Get that fag"*: Newton, *Once Before I Go*, 99.

162 *"The one show I found"*: McKay, *Played Out*, 133.

162 *"It got to the point"*: Newton, *Once Before I Go*, 162.

163 *"Vegas is unto itself"*: Irwin interview, Mark Tan Collection.

163 *"I'm trying to get across"*: "Ladies' Man," *Time*, July 11, 1969.

163 *"There was a strong sense"*: Tom Jones, *Over the Top and Back: The Autobiography* (Blue Rider Press, 2015), 269.

164 *"Entratter could no more relate"*: Beck, interview with author.

164 *"different both in sound and delivery"*: *Variety*, March 27, 1968.

164 *"The tall, ruggedly handsome"*: John L. Scott, *Los Angeles Times*, March 28, 1968.

164 *"That album is steaming"*: Jones, *Over the Top*, 270.

165 *Tom was flattered*: Ibid., 190.

165 *"What Elvis got from Tom"*: Ken Sharp, *Elvis: Vegas '69* (JetFighter, 2009), 25.

166 *"The Colonel behind the scenes"*: Schilling, interview with author.

166 *The Colonel's original idea*: Guralnick provides a comprehensive account of the NBC comeback special in *Careless Love*, 293–317.

168 *"There is something magical"*: Quoted in Lichter, *Elvis in Vegas*, 68.

168   *"It was like nothing"*: Guralnick, *Careless Love*, 323.

168   *"He could have done it"*: Nash, *Elvis Aaron Presley*, 448.

168   *"I want to tour again"*: Guralnick, *Careless Love*, 317.

169   *"He knew where every goddamn penny"*: Norm Johnson, interview with author.

169   *Miller . . . was a crafty booker*: *Las Vegas Review-Journal*, February 7, 1999.

170   *"The Colonel was in the front seat"*: Weatherford, *Cult Vegas*, 126.

170   *Elvis went into a Memphis studio*: Guralnick, as usual, provides the best account in *Careless Love*, 326–38.

171   *Davis had initially called it*: Mac Davis, interview with author.

172   *"Now you go tell everybody"*: Ibid.

172   *"Elvis was really trying"*: Ibid.

SIX: COMEBACK (ELVIS REBORN)

174   *"You have to remember"*: Richard Goldstein, interview with author.

175   *the worst temper*: Schilling, interview with author.

175   *"I liked him a lot"*: Davis, interview with author.

176   *"God damn it, I didn't ask"*: Presley, *Elvis and Me*, 83.

176   *Colonel Parker usually bears the brunt*: The Colonel's complicated relationship with Elvis is fully chronicled in Guralnick, *Careless Love*; Colonel Parker's passport problems are recounted in Alanna Nash, *The Colonel: The Extraordinary Story of Colonel Tom Parker and Elvis Presley* (Aurum Press, 2002).

176   *"The Colonel did not make"*: Loanne Miller Parker, interview with author.

177   *"The Colonel was forced to speak"*: Esposito, *Good Rockin'*, 144.

177   *"for the time that goes into it"*: *New York Times*, December 4, 1968.

178   *"Teenagers seem to be tiring"*: "Return of the Big Beat," *Time*, August 15, 1969.

178   *But Elvis had a dream . . . he actually hung up on the Colonel*: Ronnie Tutt, interview with author.

179   *"get used to the crowds again"*: Peter Guralnick and Ernst Jorgensen, *Elvis Day by Day: The Definitive Record of His Life and Music* (Ballantine Books, 1999), 257.

179   *"Not many people told"*: Schilling, interview with author.

180   *"management wanted new personnel"*: Sharp, *Elvis: Vegas '69*, 36.

180   *"Elvis wanted me to find"*: Ibid., 37.

181   *"I didn't like Elvis Presley's music"*: Jerry Scheff, *Way Down: Playing Bass with Elvis, Dylan, the Doors, and More* (Backbeat Books, 2012), 13.

181   *"When Elvis started singing"*: Ibid., 14.

181   They had crossed paths: Tutt, interview with author.

182   *"We had this great eye communication"*: Ibid.

182   *"at least one guy onstage"*: Schilling, interview with author.

182   *"I wanted voices"*: Sharp, *Elvis: Vegas '69*, 37.

183   *"I think Elvis was more influenced"*: Terry Blackwood, interview with author.

183   Morris was originally hired: Morris, interview with author.

184   *"Most of us in the band"*: Tutt, interview with author.

184   *"For the first time, Elvis"*: Schilling, interview with author.

185   *"I asked if Elvis wanted"*: Tutt, interview with author.

185   *"Elvis always wanted to know"*: James Burton, interview with author.

185   *"When we started working"*: Scheff, *Way Down*, 18.

185   *"fun but pressurized"*: Sharp, *Elvis: Vegas '69*, 46.

186   *"He was so gorgeous"*: Ibid., 42–43.

186   *"Very seldom would he say"*: Blackwood, interview with author.

186   *"Elvis was in a great mood"*: Scheff, *Way Down*, 19.

186   Elvis snapped at her: Presley, *Elvis and Me*, 271.

187   *"This town has never seen"*: Sharp, *Elvis: Vegas '69*, 55.

187   *"Colonel did not ask how"*: Miller Parker, interview with author.

187   *"schlocky as all hell"*: Nash, *Colonel*, 252.

187   *"If you don't do any business"*: Esposito, *Good Rockin'*, 142.

187   *"They didn't know whether Elvis"*: Miller Parker, interview with author.

188   *"the cafe box-office surprise"*: *Variety*, July 16, 1969.

188   *"We got calls from all over the world"*: Sharp, *Elvis: Vegas '69*, 67.

188   *"The Colonel's philosophy was"*: Jim McKusick, interview with author.

188   *"The way Colonel Parker did promotion"*: Ron Garrett, interview with author.

189   Parker visited him backstage: Sammy Shore, interview with author.

190   The International's opening the following night: *Variety*, July 9, 1969.

190   the press-shy Kerkorian slipped: Miller Parker, interview with author.

191   *"She's a sweet girl"*: Morris, interview with author.

191   *"The jokes she cracked"*: James Spada, *Streisand: Her Life* (Crown, 1995), 239.

191   *"seemed ill at ease"*: *Variety*, July 9, 1969.

191 *"Even allowing for the opening"*: Champlin, *Los Angeles Times*, July 4, 1969.

192 *"I felt hostility"*: Spada, *Streisand*, 239.

192 *"scintillating display of her gifts"*: Champlin, *Los Angeles Times*, August 5, 1969.

192 *"She sucks"*: Lamar Fike in Nash, *Elvis Aaron Presley*, 473.

193 *"It looked like a political convention"*: Sharp, *Elvis: Vegas '69*, 62.

193 *so big that they had to be put up*: Ibid., 61.

193 *"dressed in black pants"*: Ibid., 72.

193 *"We went in there in '69"*: Nash, *Elvis Aaron Presley*, 468.

194 *"I can remember Elvis sitting"*: Scheff, *Way Down*, 24.

194 *"He was pacing back and forth"*: Guralnick, *Careless Love*, 348.

194 *"If you get lost"*: Sharp, *Elvis: Vegas '69*, 79.

194 *Elvis had someone fetch*: Ibid., 78.

194 *"He was scared to death"*: Interview with Burton for *Elvis Unlimited*, http://www.james-burton.net/1999-interview/.

195 *"The audience was very good to us"*: Sharp, *Elvis: Vegas '69*, 86.

195 *"The microphone was dead"*: Shore, interview with author.

196 *"God among the lobsters"*: Scheff, *Way Down*, 24–25.

196 *"I saw in his face"*: Sammy Shore, *The Warm-Up* (William Morrow, 1984), 34.

196 *Larry Geller claimed that Elvis*: Geller, interview with author.

196 *Priscilla said it was because*: Presley, *Elvis and Me*, 135.

197 *"Elvis comes onstage"*: Margot Hentoff, "Absolutely Free," *Harper's*, November 1969.

197 *"They wouldn't shut up"*: Sharp, *Elvis: Vegas '69*, 91.

198 *"I think he did them because"*: Tutt, interview with author.

199 *"He was like a wild man"*: Guralnick, *Careless Love*, 351–52.

200 *"Elvis surprised us"*: Sharp, *Elvis: Vegas '69*, 113.

200 *"one of the rare occasions"*: Ibid., 158.

200 *"Good God"*: Ibid., 140.

200 *When he emerged, the two embraced*: The Colonel's reaction is described by many, including Jerry Schilling and Priscilla Presley in interviews with the author.

200 *Pat Boone . . . brought along*: Sharp, *Elvis: Vegas '69*, 142.

200 *"Ain't you in show business?"*: Ibid.

201 *Bobby Vinton . . . came by with his agent*: Ibid.

201   *"It was absolutely spectacular"*: Blackwood, interview with author.

201   *"Musically and energy level"*: Morris, interview with author.

201   *"I got it"*: Presley, interview with author.

201   *"I never saw anything like it"*: Davis, interview with author.

201   *"I saw the Beatles"*: Sharp, *Elvis: Vegas '69*, 126.

202   *"I thought he was fantastic"*: Steve Binder, interview with author.

202   *"We had to finish up"; "before I loosened up"; "put down the deposit"*: Press conference transcript, Sharp, *Elvis: Vegas '69*, 149–51.

203   *"the glamorous rock and roll movie hero"*: Gragg, *Bright Light City*, 147.

203   *"It was not the Elvis"*: *Billboard*, August 9, 1969.

203   *"very much in command"*: *Variety*, August 6, 1969.

203   *"With his stature"*: Mike Jahn, *New York Times*, August 18, 1969.

204   *"Presley came on"*: Ellen Willis, *New Yorker*, August 30, 1969.

204   *"felt like getting hit in the face"*: Richard Goldstein, *New York Times*, August 10, 1969.

204   *"Elvis was supernatural"*: Dalton, "Elvis Lights Up Las Vegas."

204   *"What did he do?"*: Sharp, *Elvis: Vegas '69*, 169.

205   *"The first night I thought"*: Larry Muhoberac interview, Elvis Australia, May 30, 2015, https://www.elvis.com.au/presley/interview-with-larry -muhoberac.shtml.

205   *"If he felt a certain audience"*: Morris, interview with author.

205   *"He might do the first three songs"*: Burton, interview with author.

206   *"In Vegas Elvis discovered"*: Jones, *Elvis Has Left the Building*, 170.

207   *"Elvis came in with no music"*: Leone, interview with author.

208   *"He was so undisciplined"*: Guralnick, *Careless Love*, 385.

209   *"The pressure is getting"*: Guralnick and Jorgensen, *Elvis Day by Day*, 262.

210   *"I'd go stark raving mad"*: Nash, *Elvis Aaron Presley*, 469.

210   *"Do you realize what kind of hell"*: Ibid., 470.

210   *"He was like a newborn"*: Schilling, interview with author.

210   *"It gave me a new life"*: Guralnick, *Careless Love*, 368.

211   *"I had never even been to Vegas"*: Blackwood, interview with author.

211   *"I wish I could go to church"*: Pat Boone, interview with author.

211   *Even Sammy Shore*: Shore, interview with author.

211   *breakfast that usually included*: The menu according to Sonny West, *Elvis: Still Taking Care of Business* (Triumph Books, 2007), 238.

212   *"He was very nice"*: Little, interview with author.

212   "*The reception Elvis is getting*": Guralnick, *Careless Love*, 355.

212   "*I never heard a better rhythm*": Ibid., 357.

212   "*I wasn't a fan*": Kazan, interview with author.

213   "*They have an expression*": Sharp, *Elvis: Vegas '69*, 113, 116.

213   "*I went in expecting*": Ibid., 94.

213   *Vic Damone . . . thought Elvis was drinking*: Damone, interview with author.

213   "*Elvis at least knew how to do it*": Jones, *Over the Top*, 273.

214   *During the engagement he met*: Joyce Bova recounts the affair in *Don't Ask Forever: My Love Affair with Elvis* (Zebra, 1994).

214   "*Oh, man, it was like going*": Tony Brown, interview with author.

215   "*The guards had me*"; "*He was very, very nice*"; "*But that was probably the best*": Terry Mike Jeffrey, interview with author.

216   *According to the deal*: The agreement between Parker and Shoofey is described in Guralnick, *Careless Love*, 354–55, and (more critically) in Nash, *Colonel*, 254–56.

217   "*The Colonel was one of the best customers*": Nash, *Colonel*, 256.

217   *refusing to allow him even to be photographed*: Ibid., 193.

217   "*We didn't decide to come back*": Sharp, *Elvis: Vegas '69*, 168.

218   *Davis was so nervous*: Davis, interview with author.

218   *Chips Moman . . . thought it ruined*: Guralnick, *Careless Love*, 358.

218   "*That's what a bad marriage*": Ibid., 362.

219   "*The International came along*": Sharp, *Elvis: Vegas '69*, 173.

220   "*It is something of a test*": *Variety*, December 24, 1969.

220   "*Like the Temptation*": Dalton, "Elvis Lights Up Las Vegas."

221   "*Before Elvis went back*": Schilling, interview with author.

221   "*I think Elvis made it OK*": Brown, interview with author.

221   "*I always hated the place*": Jerry Scheff, email to author.

221   "*It was a great place*": Burton, interview with author.

221   "*Elvis was uncultured*": Entratter Sidney, interview with author.

222   "*Elvis looked at me*": Sardelli, interview with author.

222   *Trini Lopez was a little insulted*: Lopez, interview with author.

223   "*OK, I don't know who he is*": Sharp, *Elvis: Vegas '69*, 183.

223   "*Elvis didn't go in saying*": Schilling, interview with author.

SEVEN: AFTERMATH (ELVIS FOREVER)

226 *Elvis said he wanted to try doing:* Interview with Glen D. Hardin, Elvis Australia, https://www.elvis.com.au/presley/interview-glendhardin.shtml.

226 *packed with 1,780 people:* Robert Hilburn, *Los Angeles Times,* February 2, 1970.

227 *"It was a flawless demonstration":* Ibid.

227 *the hotel let him go:* Morris, interview with author.

227 *"Joe was the first one":* Leone, interview with author.

228 *"original Renaldis from Italy":* Weatherford, *Cult Vegas,* 132.

228 *But when news of the planned telecast leaked:* Guralnick, *Careless Love,* 375.

229 *"Nobody could close a song":* Davis, interview with author.

229 *"You don't have to ask":* "Elvis Presley: The Originals," http://davidneale.eu/elvis/originals/list9.html#S1502.

231 *"When he captured Vegas":* Schilling, interview with author.

232 *"Those shows in Vegas in August":* Nash, *Elvis Aaron Presley,* 514.

232 *"As performances go, Elvis Presley's":* McKay, *Played Out,* 100.

233 *They would trade practical jokes:* Marty Allen, *Hello Dere!: An Illustrated Biography* (self-published, 2014), 151–54.

233 *Vikki Carr . . . came to see his show:* Vikki Carr, interview with author.

234 *"one of the most ill-prepared":* Guralnick. *Careless Love,* 504.

235 *"It was like watching a different person":* Ibid., 544.

235 *Barbra Streisand visited Elvis backstage:* Ibid., 563–65.

236 *"After sitting through Elvis Presley's":* Ibid., 617.

236 *did 636 shows:* For years the number usually given was 837. But in 2015 a new, more authorative count by a Graceland archivist put the actual total at 636.

236 *"the end of Vegas":* Judith Miller (Bill Miller's daughter), interview with author.

238 *His former wife . . . always had suspicions:* Entratter Sidney, interview with author.

238 *"uncool polyester dump":* Kurt Andersen, "Las Vegas U.S.A.," *Time,* January 10, 1994.

239 *"blight to spirit and soul":* Neal Karlen, *New York Times,* April 25, 1993.

239 *"Gradually between 1968 and 1975":* Weatherford, *Cult Vegas,* 6.

239 *"Why in hell are you playing":* Davis, interview with author.

239 *"There are a lot of performers":* Petula Clark interview, Mark Tan Collection.

239   *"Genuine Pa Kettles"*: Molly Ivins, *New York Times*, November 25, 1979.

240   *Wayne claimed he saw Elvis's ghost*: Newton, *Once Before I Go*, 157.

241   *"It's what God would've done"*: Al, *Strip*, 137.

242   *The two had met in the 1960s*: The act's history described by Siegfried Fischbacher, interview with author, and on the performers' website, http://siegfriedandroy.com.

242   *Twenty-eight million people visited*: Statistics from Las Vegas Convention and Visitors Authority.

243   *"How can a large-spirited American"*: Andersen, "Las Vegas U.S.A."

243   *Colonel Tom Parker himself*: Josh Tyrangiel, "Diva Las Vegas," *Time*, March 17, 2003.

243   *"If it wasn't for him"*: Celine Dion in *Elvis: Viva Las Vegas*, ABC News documentary, 2007.

244   *"more than just a great talent"*: *Las Vegas Sun*, August 17, 1977.

244   *"why, he was in perfect"*: Ibid.

244   *The first formal tribute*: *Variety*, September 13, 1978.

244   *Elvis himself reportedly went to see*: "Elvis' Star Continues to Shine in Las Vegas," https://www.vegas.com/elvis/.

246   *it took the Gretna Green Wedding Chapel*: Graceland Wedding Chapel website, https://www.gracelandchapel.com/our-history.html.

INSERT PHOTOGRAPH CREDITS

1, 7, 16, 26, and 29: Las Vegas News Bureau

2: Michael Ochs Archives/Getty Images

3, 11, and 12: Las Vegas News Bureau; Elvis Presley™ © 2019 ABG EPE IP LLC

4, 10, 13, and 19: Photofest

5 and 20: Bettmann/Getty Images

6: Hulton Archive/Getty Images

8: Everett Collection

9: Getty Images

14: Archive Photos/Getty Images

15: Mondadori Portfolio via Getty Images

17: Allan Grant/The LIFE Picture Collection/Getty Images

18: Las Vegas News Bureau Archives via Getty Images

21: Joe Buck, Las Vegas News Bureau; Elvis Presley™ © 2019 ABG EPE IP LLC

22: Frank Edwards/Fotos International/Getty Images

23: Fotos International/Getty Images

24: Terry Todd, Las Vegas News Bureau; Elvis Presley™ © 2019 ABG EPE IP

INDEX

ABOUT THE AUTHOR

RICHARD ZOGLIN is a longtime writer, editor, and critic for *Time* magazine. He is the author of *Hope: Entertainer of the Century*, *Comedy at the Edge: How Stand-Up in the 1970s Changed America*, and *Elvis in Vegas*. A native of Kansas City, Zoglin currently lives in New York City.